D1733505

Huntington Library Publications

Charles F. Lummis

Charles F. Lummis
Editor of the Southwest

BY EDWIN R. BINGHAM

THE HUNTINGTON LIBRARY
SAN MARINO, CALIFORNIA 1955

Henry E. Huntington Library and Art Gallery
1151 Oxford Road, San Marino, California 91108
www.huntington.org

Book design by Joseph Simon
Cover design by Doug Davis
Photographs courtesy of the Autry National Center/Southwest
Museum, Los Angeles

Library of Congress Catalog Card No. 55012204

Bingham, Edwin R.
Charles F. Lummis : editor of the Southwest / by Edwin R.
Bingham.
    218 p. 23 cm.
Includes index.
1. Lummis, Charles Fletcher, 1859–1928. 2. Out West magazine
(Los Angeles, Calif.) 3. Editors—United States—Biography.
4. Southwestern States—Biography.
I. Title.
PN4874.L84 B5

ISBN-10: 0-87328-221-3
ISBN-13: 978-0-87328-221-5

To John W. Caughey—a calmer crusader

CONTENTS

LIST OF ILLUSTRATIONS

PREFACE

THIS IS A STUDY of a man and his magazine. It is not biography, nor is it the history of a western monthly, although it contains elements of both. It might be considered a chapter in the history of personal journalism, for Charles F. Lummis and *Out West* can claim a position on the far western flank of that company of American editors inextricably linked with their media — men like Horace Greeley of the New York *Tribune*, Hezekiah Niles of the *Weekly Register*, and E. L. Godkin of the *Nation*. Viewed from another aspect, the study is in large part regional history with a social and cultural emphasis, for much of the narrative is concerned with demonstrating the dedication of Lummis' magazine to southern California and the Southwest and revealing it as a reliable reflector of the regional scene. Is there too much Lummis in the story? Perhaps, but *Out West* was so clear a transmitter of its editor's ideas, so consistent an expositor of his enthusiasms, so faithful an extension of his personality that surely the reader deserves to know Lummis the man as well as Lummis the editor. Frequently the focus is on the magazine, at times to the virtual exclusion of Lummis as in the account of the monthly's founding or in the chapter devoted to lesser contributors. There is then a shifting focus, alternating between the man and the magazine and often merging the two. Through this approach the writer seeks to achieve integration of the two major elements in the story — Lummis and *Out West*.

The suggestion that Charles Lummis and his western monthly were worth investigation came from Professor John W. Caughey of the University of California, Los Angeles. His guidance, encouragement, and understanding while the study was in progress have produced a debt that can be gratefully acknowledged but scarcely repaid.

Turbesé Lummis Fiske made available her father's journals and was a most gracious hostess on the occasion of several visits to her home. Mrs. Alice Van Boven kindly furnished an *Out West* subscription list. The staff of the Southwest Museum was generous in permitting access to correspondence, photographs, manuscripts, and pamphlets in their extensive Lummis collection. Special thanks are due Director Frederick Webb Hodge as a helpful informant; Mrs. Ella L. Robinson, librarian; and Mr. M. R. Harrington for furnishing the photographs to illustrate the narrative. I am very grateful to the Board of Trustees and to the staff of the Henry E. Huntington Library for assistance and support in the preparation of this book. In particular, I wish to thank Director John E. Pomfret and Dr. Robert G. Cleland of the Research Staff for constructive criticism of organization and form; to acknowledge permission to use the C. D. Willard papers upon which the second chapter largely rests; and to express appreciation to Miss Eleanor Towles for her meticulous reading of the manuscript. To my wife, Virginia, I can only borrow a Spanish phrase Lummis used: *Dios te pague! Yo no tengo diñero.*

Finally, I am obliged to the publishers for permission to quote from the following books and periodical: Mary Austin, *Earth Horizon: Autobiography* (Boston: Houghton Mifflin, 1932); May Davison Rhodes, *Hired Man on Horseback: My Story of Eugene Manlove Rhodes* (Boston: Houghton Mifflin, 1938); Farnsworth Crowder, "El Alisal," *Westways* (December, 1947).

EDWIN R. BINGHAM

Pasadena, California
August, 1955

Charles F. Lummis
Editor of the Southwest

Chapter **1** THE MAN

I N THE LAST DECADE of the nineteenth century, in the southern corner of the Far West there grew up an intimate relationship between a man and a magazine that sharply contradicted the national trend away from personal journalism. The man was Charles F. Lummis, newspaperman, author, and western enthusiast. The magazine was the *Land of Sunshine* or *Out West* as it was called after December, 1901. This southern California literary monthly lived as a name in western journalism for more than forty years but only under editor Lummis could it claim genuine prominence and influence. For ten years, between the ages of thirty-six and forty-six, Lummis' absorbing passion was this magazine. Into it he poured unflagging enthusiasm and prodigious labor. In a very real sense the magazine epitomized the man, and it is impossible to read it without forming pronounced and often detailed impressions of its editor. However, Lummis came to the magazine a mature individual possessed of training, experience, and temperament which particularly qualified him to direct the fortunes of the regional monthly and which helped to determine the course the journal followed.

Lummis was a Yankee by birth and upbringing, and patriotic and religious influences were evident in his family tradition. William Lummis, great-great-grandfather to Charles, served under Washington, and Henry Lummis, Charles's father, claimed descent on the maternal side from John Paul Jones. Henry Lummis' father, Reverend William Lummis, was an itinerant Methodist preacher.[1]

Charles's mother, Harriet Waterman Fowler, daughter of Judge Oscar F. and Louise Waterman Fowler of Bristol, New Hampshire, died of tuberculosis before her son was three, leaving

[1] *Zion's Herald*, LXXXIII (1906), Apr. 19, 486, in Charles F. Lummis collection, Southwest Museum Library, Los Angeles. Hereafter cited as Lummis collection.

Charles and a baby daughter.[2] The father, Henry Lummis, lived to be seventy-eight, dividing his adult years between teaching and preaching. He was graduated from Wesleyan University, Middletown, Connecticut, in the class of 1855, and he received his M.A. degree from the same institution. Early positions included a teaching stint at the Methodist seminary at Newbury, Vermont, and the principalship of the high school at Lynn, Massachusetts. He was married in Bristol, May 5, 1858, to Harriet W. Fowler, who had been his pupil at Newbury as well as a member of the teaching staff in the Lynn high school. Five more years as head administrator of New Hampshire Conference Seminary and Female College and another five as professor in Lassell Seminary at Auburndale, Massachusetts, were followed by nearly fifteen years in the Methodist itineracy under the New England Conference. Finally, in 1885, Henry Lummis accepted a professorship of Latin and Greek at Lawrence College, Appleton, Wisconsin. At the time of his death Henry Lummis was senior professor at Lawrence.[3]

Charles Fletcher Lummis was born March 1, 1859, in Lynn, Massachusetts.[4] After his mother's death he lived with her family in Bristol until school age and then, because he balked at formal instruction, his father undertook his son's education, much of which was administered in the cloistered atmosphere of a female seminary.[5] Young Lummis was instructed in Latin, Greek, and Hebrew, and he was required to read at sight the Latin Vulgate Bible at family prayers every morning. So thorough was his grounding in the classics that by the time he entered Harvard at eighteen, he had already read in Latin and Greek nearly everything on the college's elective list.[6] Feeling that, because of his proficiency in Latin, French would be too easy, Lummis decided

[2]Turbesé Lummis Fiske, "Charles F. Lummis, a Brief Biography," MS in Lummis collection.

[3]Charles F. Lummis, "A Successful Life," Out West, XXII (1905), May, 318-21.

[4]Ibid., 321. The most convenient biographical sketch is that by John C. Parish in Dict. Amer. Biog. A more detailed treatment appears in a typescript biography of her father prepared by Turbesé Lummis Fiske in 1936. It forms a part of the Lummis collection.

[5]"Personal History" on file in the History Department, Los Angeles Public Library.

[6]Fiske, op. cit., p. 1.

to enter in German. His only preparation was to master a 3,600-word vocabulary which, when combined with his thorough knowledge of Latin, Greek, and Hebrew grammar, enabled him to pass the entrance examination with something to spare.[7]

In some respects Charles's Harvard career appears to have been a reaction against both the background of rigid discipline in the classics provided by his father, and the sheltered surroundings in which his pre-college training was administered. He placed heavy emphasis on athletics, specializing in boxing, wrestling, running, and walking, and he developed an intense pride in his body and its proper conditioning. This type of activity, begun even before he was of college age, was a major factor in Lummis' development from a sickly, consumptive child to a competent athlete by the time he was twenty.[8] In the light of his previous academic training, many of the prescribed college courses failed to interest Charles and he sampled instead whatever caught his attention, even though a program loaded with electives was relatively unrewarding in terms of graduation credits. Poetry and poker also figured prominently in young Lummis' program, the former consisting largely of translating German, Greek, and French verse into English.[9]

One story of Lummis at Harvard, whether apocryphal or not, has an authentic ring in view of Lummis' subsequent development. Some upperclassmen posted an ultimatum on a bulletin board which read: "If Freshman Lummis doesn't get his hair cut, '80 will do it for him." Within half an hour a reply appeared beside the original notice: "Lummis, '81, will be glad to meet the tonsorially inclined of the class of '80, individually or collectively, at any time, at 16 Holyoke."[10] As the story has it, this sort of defiance saved Lummis his hair and gained him the notice of sophomore Theodore Roosevelt.[11]

At Harvard Lummis regarded Roosevelt as a "dig" and their interests were too divergent to promote close friendship. In

[7]Ibid., 2.
[8]"Chas. F. Lummis," California Writers Club Quarterly *Bulletin*, III (1915), June, 1.
[9]Fiske, p. 2.
[10]Ibid., 3.
[11]Ibid.

later years, however, he developed an admiration for Roosevelt which amounted to hero worship. A more intimate college friendship was formed with Boies Penrose, future United States senator from Pennsylvania. He and Lummis were partners in a number of typical undergraduate escapades.

During the summer of 1878, in the White Mountains of New Hampshire, Lummis prepared a small volume of poetry which he called *Birch Bark Verses*. Printed on thin sheets of birch-bark on a small hand press and bound into booklets about three by three-and-a-half inches, the little twelve-page volume sold over 14,000 copies in three years and helped put its author and publisher through college.[12] Lummis ambitiously forwarded a copy to the well-known critic Andrew Lang who not only gave the young poet a public notice, but sent him a personal word of encouragement as well.[13]

In 1880, his junior year, Charles Lummis secretly married a young medical student named Dorothea Rhodes. Before this, during the same summer in which the birchbark poems were composed, and while working in a resort hotel in the White Mountains, Charles had formed a romantic attachment which resulted in the birth of a daughter. There is insufficient evidence to establish the exact circumstances, but, according to a news story which broke when the daughter, Bertha, joined her father's household some twenty-four years after her birth, Lummis had been unaware of her existence until she had written him shortly before her arrival.[14] On the other hand, in her autobiography, Mary Austin implied that the secret marriage to Dorothea was contracted as a means of extricating Lummis from an involved and uncomfortable situation.[15] Whatever the facts, he was probably under severe emotional strain for some time, which may have contributed to an attack of "brain fever" forcing his withdrawal from Harvard three days before commencement.[16]

---

[12]"The Strange Romance of a New Hampshire Schoolma'm," Sunday Magazine Section, Boston *Herald*, Jan. 28, 1906, in Lummis collection.

[13]Ibid.   [14]Ibid.

[15]*Earth Horizon: Autobiography* (Boston, 1932), p. 294.

[16]"Brain fever" in the days of Lummis' youth was a loose term which today would probably be diagnosed as meningitis or encephalitis.

Looking back on the Harvard experience twenty-five years later, Lummis wrote: "I should have gotten more instruction out of it if I had been looking harder *for* instruction. My chief thankfulness about the whole matter is that four years of Harvard didn't make a fool of me."[17]

Evidence bearing on the events during the three years following Lummis' illness is scanty. He and Dorothea moved west for his health's sake and Charles accepted a position as supervisor of his father-in-law's 7,000-acre farm in the Scioto Valley of Ohio. He was not content with farming, however, and in 1882 he turned to what was for him the more congenial and stimulating activity of running the Scioto *Gazette,* the oldest newspaper west of the Alleghenies. For two years Lummis edited the *Gazette* and dabbled in politics, becoming president of the Young Men's Republican Club.[18] Much of the work connected with the newspaper the editor did himself, thus securing a broad and valuable apprenticeship in journalism. When not working on the paper Lummis roamed the Scioto Valley hunting, fishing, and searching for Indian relics. The latter hobby nourished a growing appetite for archaeology which became a major facet of his interest in California and the Southwest.

Sometime in 1884, Lummis decided to leave Ohio for California and to make the trip on foot. According to his own testimony his motives were: a romantic impulse momentarily to slip the fetters of society; a sense of shame stemming from his unfamiliarity with his own country; and a determination to escape malaria which plagued the residents of Chillicothe, Ohio.[19] His wife seems to have raised no objection to his plan. Moreover, a job with the Los Angeles *Times* awaited him. The offer had grown out of correspondence with the paper's publisher, Harrison Gray Otis, and the position was contingent on the fulfillment of an agreement whereby Lummis would send the *Times* weekly dispatches of his experiences en route.[20]

[17]Fiske, p. 4.

[18]Ibid.

[19]Charles F. Lummis, *A Tramp Across the Continent* (New York, 1892), pp. 2-3.

[20]Los Angeles *Times* (n.d.), in Lummis collection. Lummis also sent dispatches to the Chillicothe *Leader.* See scrapbook in Lummis collection.

When he began his trek from Cincinnati on September 12, 1884, Lummis was twenty-five. He wore a knickerbocker suit, flannel shirt, low-cut shoes, and a canvas coat with capacious pockets stuffed with an assortment of odds and ends including writing materials, fishing tackle, matches, tobacco, and a small revolver. A hunting knife swung from his belt and he was well ballasted with $300 in $2.50 gold pieces buttoned into a money pouch next to his skin. A small valise and a roomy knapsack he expressed ahead from town to town.[21] Evenings, generally by the light of a campfire, the hiker wrote up the day's experiences and each week he mailed a dispatch signed "Lum" to the Los Angeles *Times*.

In his travels Lummis crossed seven states and two territories, consuming approximately 112 days in actual walking time. He walked from thirty to forty miles each day. His longest continuous hike was from Ellsworth to Ellis, Kansas — 79 miles in 21 hours. Major stops were made in St. Louis, Denver, Santa Fe, Albuquerque, and San Mateo, New Mexico. At midnight, February 1, 1885, Lummis, his left arm in an improvised sling, tramped into Los Angeles, having covered 3,507 miles in 143 days, at a total expense of less than $175.[22] Next day he found himself city editor of the Los Angeles *Times*.[23] Thus the coming of Charles F. Lummis to southern California was prophetic of his subsequent career — dramatic, unorthodox, strenuous.

Lummis' cross-country experiences are related dramatically in his book *A Tramp Across the Continent*. He tells of an attempt on his life by two convicts in Colorado. He describes an encounter with a wildcat in a deserted cabin in the Rockies. He recalls the anguish of a fifty-two-mile walk to Winslow, Arizona, with a broken arm, set by buckling one end of his canteen strap around a tree, wrapping the other end about the wrist of the fractured left arm and throwing himself violently backward. Most of his adventures more than hold their own in

---

[21]Lummis, pp. 4-5.

[22]Chillicothe *Leader*, Feb. 28, 1895, clipping in Lummis collection.

[23]"Letters and Diary of Charles Fletcher Lummis to Maurice N. Newmark, 1911-1917," (3 vols., W. P. A. Library Project, No. 12287, Oct. 7, 1943, special collection, Los Angeles Public Library), I, preface. Hereafter cited as Letters and Diary of Lummis to Newmark.

the telling. A case in point is Lummis' account of the death of Shadow, a young greyhound adopted in Colorado. The dog served as Lummis' constant companion for some 1,500 miles only to go mad on the Arizona desert. Lummis writes:

My foot caught Shadow glancingly on the chest and he went rolling down the thirty-foot embankment. But he was upon his feet in an instant and sprang wolfishly toward me. . . . Just as he was within four feet I wrested the Colt loose, "threw it down" with the swift instinctive aim of long practice, and pulled the trigger even as the muzzle fell. The wild tongue of flame burned his very face, and he dropped. But in an instant he was up again and fled shrieking across the barren plain. The heavy ball had creased his skull and lodged in his flank. I knew the horrors of a gunshot wound; my poor chum should never go to die by inches the hideous death of the desert. A great wave of love swept through me and drowned my horror. I had tried to kill him to save myself, now I must kill him to save him from the most inconceivable of agonies. My trembling nerves froze to steel; I must not miss! I would not! I dropped on one knee, caught his course, calculated his speed, and the spiteful crack of the six-shooter smote again upon the torpid air. He was a full hundred and fifty yards away, flying like the wind, when the merciful lead outstripped and caught him and threw him in a wild somersault of his own momentum. He never kicked or moved, but lay there in a limp, black tangle, motionless forever.[24]

Passages of this sort not only impair the reliability of *A Tramp Across the Continent* as a factual account, but they also reveal the extravagant flair for the romantic and dramatic in the author's nature.

Lummis regarded his cross-country trek as the most effective physical conditioning he ever underwent. More important, his contact with the Southwest, as he labeled the region encompassing New Mexico, Arizona, southern California, and adjoining areas, played havoc with his New England-nurtured sense of Anglo-Saxon superiority. The simplicity and charm of the country's inhabitants, Indian and Mexican alike, roused his liking and respect; the region's romantic history fascinated him; its dramatic combination of "sun, silence and adobe" fired his imagination. In fact, the Southwest had made an impact on Lummis in many respects as potent as a religious conversion,

[24]Lummis, pp. 105-106.

with the result that he became a self-appointed and zealous missionary in its name.

In 1886 Lummis received his second taste of the Southwest when the *Times* sent him to Arizona Territory to cover the Apache disturbances and to report the facts concerning General George H. Crook's conduct of the campaign. Lummis' stay was short but he was there long enough to encounter some of the unsavory aspects of the government's Indian policy and to become convinced of Crook's integrity. Upon his arrival at Fort Bowie, March 31, 1886, the outbreak was ostensibly ended, and a truce with the leading insurgents was in force. Two days later, however, Nachez, Geronimo, and about thirty others, drunk on whisky sold them by a white trader, broke parole and took to the trail. During part of the campaign that followed Lummis routed dispatches back to his newspaper defending Crook and doing what he could to expose the sordid scramble among unscrupulous traders for government contracts which he felt was largely responsible for prolonging the Apache outbreaks.[25]

Shortly after General Nelson A. Miles had replaced Crook, but before the capture of Geronimo, the correspondent was called back to the *Times* to assist in the paper's reorganization. Some fourteen years later Lummis was still regretting that he had been unable to accept a place offered him by Captain Henry Lawton in the last expedition against Geronimo. At the time neither Lummis nor Harrison Gray Otis was aware that Lawton had intended to make Lummis his chief of scouts.[26]

His three months on the Arizona frontier exerted some lasting influences on the young correspondent. He formed a lifelong friendship with Leonard Wood, then contract assistant post surgeon.[27] He came to know something of the Indians themselves and he developed a respect and admiration for the Apache warrior which is expressed in his narrative poem about Geron-

[25]Fiske, p. 12.

[26]Charles F. Lummis, "In the Lion's Den," *The Land of Sunshine*, XII (1900), Mar., 253-54.

[27]Charles F. Lummis, *A Bronco Pegasus* (New York, 1928), pp. 35-50. Leonard Wood was later military governor of Cuba and governor general of the Philippines.

imo, "Man-Who-Yawns." Further, this period of reporting on the Apache trouble helped prepare Lummis for subsequent crusades on behalf of the Indians of California and the Southwest.

When "Lum" returned to the *Times* in mid-1886, the real estate boom of the eighties was under way and as population climbed, the newspaper's circulation and importance mounted with it. The city editor immersed himself in a struggle his paper was waging against the saloon and gambling element in Los Angeles which flourished with the aid of a corrupt police system. For the next two years Lummis was reckless in the expenditure of his time and energy on the newspaper. He rarely got more than four hours' sleep out of twenty-four; more often it was two. Added to this, the evidence, although sketchy, points toward immoderate use of tobacco and alcohol.[28]

Despite warning symptoms of numbness in hands and feet, Lummis refused to slacken his pace. Inordinately proud of his physique, he was convinced that his body was equal to any demand he might make upon it. At last, in 1888, toward the end of his third year with the *Times*, months of excess culminated in a paralytic stroke which deprived him of the use of his left arm and rendered most of his left side helpless. After being confined to bed for three months, on February 5, 1888, Lummis left for New Mexico hoping to regain his health.[29]

The struggle to overcome paralysis, related fully in *My Friend Will* (1911), consumed more than three years. Much of that time Lummis spent at San Mateo, New Mexico, in the hacienda or on the range of Amado Chaves, son of Colonel Manuel Chaves, Indian campaigner and Civil War veteran. Refusing to go to bed, the invalid began a strenuous program of riding horseback, hunting, fishing, and exploring, calculated to get his mind off himself. It was slow going at first, and he had to teach himself to handle a rifle like a revolver and to roll a cigarette with one hand. In a journal entry in 1927 Lummis recalled: "Thirty-eight years ago in San Rafael, New Mexico,

[28]Charles F. Lummis to Dr. Norman Bridge, Mar. 8, 1923, in Lummis collection; Lummis to Edgar L. Hewett, Apr. 21, 1919, in Edgar L. Hewett, "Lummis the Inimitable," *Papers of the School of American Research*, Archaeological Institute of America (Santa Fe, New Mexico, 1944).

[29]Letters and Diary of Lummis to Newmark, 1911-1927, II, entry of Feb. 5, 1927.

the paralyzed, one-armed hunter bagged 11 mallards — that kind of medicine helped me to the cure."[30] Evenings he spent with the Chaves family playing Spanish games and learning Spanish songs.

After a time Lummis left San Mateo and the Chaves home to live in the Indian pueblo of Isleta. He spent his time studying the Tiguas, learning their folk songs and stories, and exploring and photographing the area. Eventually he was adopted by the Tiguas. It was during this period that Lummis, at some personal risk, photographed the bizarre spectacle of the secret "Penitente" ceremonies consisting in part of a procession of self-flagellating "brothers," and culminating in a crucifixion which, if not fatal, was exceedingly painful to the volunteer victim.[31]

The invalid's recovery was not a steady process. In fact, Lummis sustained two more paralytic attacks in New Mexico, the last of which left him unable to speak or walk. According to Lummis, a letter from his wife Dorothea precipitated the third shock.[32] Presumably she asked for her freedom, although the record is not explicit on this point. He was taken to a Catholic hospital in Santa Fe where: "Lying helpless and speechless in the spotless bed in the Sisters Hospital, I wrote on my scratch pad 46 paragraphs or jokes which sold to *Life* and *Time* and *Judge* and *Puck*, I guess all of them at four bits each. In fact the funniest things I ever wrote were during those months after the third shock."[33] A clever and amusing parody of Poe called "Cannibalee: A Poe'em of Passion" was another product of the same period.[34]

Lummis took a long stride toward recovery when he had himself hoisted on the back of a horse and found he could ride successfully. Next he moved from the hospital to a small adobe on the property of George W. Lane, secretary of the New Mexico Territory. He formed the habit of riding out to a

[30]Ibid., entry of Mar. 1, 1927.
[31]Lummis, "An American Passion-Play," *Land of Sunshine*, IV (1896), May, 255-65.
[32]Letters and Diary of Lummis to Newmark, II, entry of May 4, 1927.
[33]Ibid., entry of Mar. 1, 1927.
[34]Ibid., entry of July 7, 1927.

stream in the Santa Fe Canyon, falling from his horse, and fishing most of the day from a prone position. One day he caught himself humming a fragment from a Spanish song and soon after he regained his speech. Finally he succeeded in moving the fingers of his left hand and from then on his recovery was rapid.[35]

One day in August, 1888, in the midst of a New Mexico sandstorm, Adolph F. Bandelier walked into Lummis' camp at Los Alamitos. This chance meeting proved to be the beginning of a lifelong friendship between the two men. Bandelier, Lummis' senior by nineteen years, already had a reputation for combining painstaking historical research with archaeological field work of a high order. His original and penetrating works on prehistoric Mexico had earned him the respect of the academic world. In time the younger man took on the role of student-companion to Bandelier, and the two of them covered much of the Southwest on foot, surveying, photographing ruins, and recording archaeological data. After nearly four years of what Lummis termed a "trial period" Bandelier offered to take him on an archaeological expedition.[36] The prospect must have pleased and excited the young man but, although he enthusiastically agreed to go, he made it clear that he did not want to become a scientist in the strict sense of the term. He was convinced that "science" needed an audience. As he explained it to Bandelier:

With your leave, I am going to make it my part of this, to say to the World: Lookee! Don't be scared! All these Greek words are harmless! All these Ologies are only the Story of Man—the story of you and me . . . and carried back five or ten thousand years. And it's fun! If we can give back to that perennial Story the Humanness that belongs to it, a million Americans will understand where one understands now; and where you have now one supporter you will have fifty; and while your epoch-making research now is buried in sacrosanct reports for a few Bostonians, it will become part of the consciousness of America.[37]

[35]Ibid.

[36]Fiske, p. 18.

[37]"The Works of Chas. F. Lummis," Lummis Foundation, Los Angeles, 1928. Booklet in Lummis collection.

Bandelier understood and accepted this point of view, cautioning only that Lummis never sacrifice truth to enthusiasm. With Lummis, then, it was a kind of compulsion to strip history, archaeology, and ethnology of pedantry and pretension and to present them accurately but often in informal and original prose.

In July, 1892, Bandelier and Lummis went to Peru and Bolivia to engage in archaeological and historical investigations under the patronage of Henry Villard, railroad builder and financier.[38] The expedition, originally scheduled to last three years, was cut short in just half that time by Villard's bankruptcy. Nevertheless the experience was a rich one, giving Lummis further training in archaeological field work, furnishing him with numerous photographs as well as Peruvian fabrics, skulls, and other artifacts, and yielding material for one book, *The Gold Fish of Gran Chimu* (1896), and part of another, *The Enchanted Burro* (1897).

Meanwhile a marked change had taken place in Lummis' personal life. During the process of recovery from his third stroke a young woman named Eva Douglas helped care for the paralytic and the two fell in love. Eva had come from Connecticut to visit her sister and she met Lummis through her sister's husband who was a trader among the Indians of Isleta.[39] After the divorce from Dorothea became final, Eva and Charles were married in San Bernardino, California, March 27, 1891.[40] The couple returned to New Mexico and settled down in the pueblo of Isleta where, on June 9, 1892, a daughter, Turbesé (Sunburst), was born.[41]

In the decade of the nineties Charles Lummis emerged as a writer of some prominence. Aside from his edition of birchbark verse, Lummis' first offerings were to the magazines, and

[38]F. W. Hodge, "Biographical Sketch and Bibliography of Adolph Francis Alphonse Bandelier," *New Mexico Historical Review*, VII (1932), Oct., 365. German-born Villard had taken over Ben Holladay's transportation empire in the Pacific Northwest and with the extension of the Northern Pacific to Portland in 1883 Villard gave the Northwest its first transcontinental tie.

[39]Los Angeles *Times*, Oct. 13, 1910, clipping in Lummis collection.

[40]"Personal History," on file in the History Department, Los Angeles Public Library.

[41]Ibid.

in the late eighties and early nineties the by-line "Chas. F. Lummis" was familiar to readers of *Harper's, Youth's Companion, St. Nicholas, Century,* and *Scribner's.* His first book, *A New Mexico David,* was published in 1891. This was followed in the same year by *Pueblo Indian Folk Stories* (known in later editions under the title *The Man Who Married the Moon*), and *A Tramp Across the Continent.* Then, in rapid succession, came *Some Strange Corners of Our Country, The Land of Poco Tiempo,* and *The Spanish Pioneers. The Gold Fish of Gran Chimu, The Enchanted Burro, The King of the Broncos* (1897), and *The Awakening of a Nation: Mexico of Today* (1898) rounded out the second half of a productive decade. Nearly all of these were variations on a single theme—the Southwest, its history, its archaeology, and its people. All attested to Yankee Lummis' capitulation to a new and radically different environment from that which had nurtured him.

A New Mexico David contained simple stories and sketches of the Southwest drawn almost entirely from the author's experience. Intended essentially as a book for boys, it commanded a broader appeal because it dealt with a section of the country unknown to many American readers.

Pueblo Indian Folk Stories was a collection of thirty-two tales made during its author's sojourn among the Tiguas of Isleta. More than one critic likened this collection to Kipling's *Jungle Book* or to the tales of Uncle Remus.[42] Not only were these stories of interest to the folklorist but, when closely analyzed, they had significance in terms of early history and ethnology of the region.

A Tramp Across the Continent was the result of converting into book form the series of newspaper accounts, which had appeared as Lummis walked west. The passage already quoted is representative of the work's style and of the strain that was sometimes put on the reader's credulity.

In *Some Strange Corners of Our Country* Lummis made an evident effort to publicize the Southwest. He concentrated on the dramatic and the unique, offering, among others, sketches

[42]"The Works of Chas. F. Lummis," op. cit.

dealing with the Moqui snake dance, the rites of the "Penitentes," Inscription Rock, and Acoma, the sky city. All in all, the volume served as a compact and valuable handbook on the history, archaeology, and folklore of the Southwest. Enthusiasm and affection for the region were conspicuous in the writing. It was popular enough to warrant an enlarged edition thirty-three years later bearing a new name, *Mesa, Canyon and Pueblo*.

In 1893 *The Land of Poco Tiempo* appeared. According to Frederick W. Hodge, then of the Bureau of Ethnology in Washington, D. C., the book, reflecting as it did the influence of Adolph Bandelier, was sound in its archaeological and historical aspects. Hodge considered it the best work published up to that time on the Southwest from the popular point of view.[43] One reviewer noted an overindulgence in the use of superlatives and an occasional hasty generalization, but in the end found Lummis to be "thoroughly satisfactory."[44] In the foreword of a 1952 edition of Lummis' book, Paul A. F. Walter, New Mexico banker and coeditor of the state's historical review, suggested that those with time to read only one book on the Southwest ought to read *The Land of Poco Tiempo*.[45]

In *The Spanish Pioneers*, one of his better-known works, Lummis sought to combat the popular conception of cruelty fastened on the *Conquistadores* by Anglo-Saxon writers, particularly William H. Prescott. The book went into some fifteen editions as well as translation into Spanish, and it earned its author a decoration from the king of Spain in 1915 for his interpretation of the Spanish conquest.[46] Prior to the publication of Lummis' work, histories and textbooks had not sufficiently emphasized the importance of Spanish pioneering in the New World. However, in his efforts to administer a necessary corrective, Lummis was inclined to overrate the character and motives of the Spanish leaders. Nonetheless the book has

[43]*American Anthropologist*, VII (1894), Jan., 120-121.

[44]*Nation*, LVIII (1894), Feb. 15, 127.

[45]Joseph Henry Jackson, "Bookman's Notebook," Los Angeles *Times*, Aug. 18, 1952.

[46]Letters and Diary of Lummis to Newmark, I, entry of July 31, 1926.

generally fared well at the hands of historians and has frequently found a place on required or recommended reading lists in university courses in Latin-American history. Reviewing the work in the *Hispanic American Historical Review*, Fanny R. Bandelier noted with approval Lummis' statement that the legislation of Spain in behalf of the Indians was more humane than that of Great Britain, the colonies, or the United States. Lummis, she believed, deserved recognition for his attempt to appraise the Spanish conquest on the basis of the facts.[47]

Lummis produced four more books before the turn of the century. *The Gold Fish of Gran Chimu* was a work of fiction with a flimsy plot revolving around attempts to frustrate archaeological investigations in Peru. Lummis and Bandelier appear, thinly disguised, as two of the central characters. A noteworthy feature of the work, anticipating Ernest Hemingway, was the author's experiment with literal translation of the Spanish idiom. Reviewers differed as to the advisability of utilizing such a technique as well as to the degree of success the author achieved.[48]

The King of the Broncos, a series of New Mexico vignettes, included an autobiographical piece called "My Friend Will" which related the author's hard-won victory over paralysis. Later, due probably to its inspirational value, this sketch, along with the editorial comment upon the death of his son Amado which appeared first in the *Land of Sunshine*, was published separately. *The Enchanted Burro*, a work in the same vein as *The King of the Broncos* but with a broader locale, followed shortly.

Finally, in 1898, Harper's published *The Awakening of a Nation*. Here Lummis called attention to the tremendous material progress made by Mexico under the administration of Porfirio Diaz. The author's didactic intent was evident in his characterization of the book as "not a description of Mexico, but a fingerboard along the path to comprehension."[49] Crowded with passages

[47]Vol. II (1919), Aug., 461-62.

[48]*Nation*, May 21, 1896; San Francisco *Argonaut*, Apr. 27, 1896, clipping in Lummis collection.

[49]Preface, p. ii.

bespeaking an appreciative judgment of the Spaniard in Mexico, the book's publication during a period of strong anti-Spanish sentiment was unlikely to promote sales.

After 1898 the flow of books virtually ceased, to be renewed only late in Lummis' life. However, the separate edition of *My Friend Will* was published in 1911, and *The Memorial of Fray Alonso de Benavides, 1630,* translated by Mrs. Edward Ayer, and edited and annotated by F. W. Hodge and Lummis, was issued in a limited edition in 1916.

By and large, Lummis' writings of the nineties met with a favorable reception. Most reviewers concentrated on the content, commenting upon the knowledge and experience which informed the writing, and welcoming the treatment of a unique and little-known part of North America. References to literary merit, or its lack, were relatively infrequent and when they occurred were generally limited to a passing remark on the informality of the author's style or to comment on his addiction to the use of superlatives.[50] A striking exception to this general practice was the treatment accorded Lummis by reviewers in English periodicals. One excerpt from a review of *The Land of Poco Tiempo* taken from the *Spectator* will illustrate the point:

Owing to the popularity of many American authors and certain American magazines, we have become acquainted with a language which is not our own, tho it is said to be the best kind of English. Greater familiarity has not endeared it to our minds. It is, we regret to say, the language of Mr. Lummis. Sometimes it is picturesque, and forgiveness is easy. More often it is the reverse. The author describes in one place the heroism of a woman who, single-handed beat back a band of Apache murderers, her companion being killed. "Later in the day was found the body of the dead American, and beside it the four empty shot-gun cartridges used by gritty Belle Davis, of Tombstone, in her fight for life." *Gritty*—is that an epithet to be applied to a heroine? It literally sets one's teeth on edge. Not even the author's constant deviations from the strict rules of grammar are so annoying as his misuse of familiar words, or his use of words which are so far from being familiar as to be unknown to the ordinary dictionary. What is "the roily pulse of the river"? And what kind of an ass is a "devoluted

[50]Cf., Baltimore *Sun*, Nov. 13, 1893; Cincinnati *Times-Star*, Feb. 1, 1894; *Nation*, May 21, 1896; and *Ideas* (Boston), Dec. 4, 1897. From clippings in Lummis collection.

donkey"? His painful efforts to find striking phrases or words are so evident as to give the ordinary reader a sense of physical discomfort. Every now and again he lights by accident, perhaps, upon some really happy expression; but as a rule, the finery of his language is of the shoddiest kind. It is strange that a man who has written some really fine descriptive passages should be capable of such rubbish as "where you naked babes sport dimpled in a dimpling pool, stark warriors wallowed in a grimmer bath, and gasped from dying lips, undying hate." Nevertheless he has succeeded on the whole in giving a very effective account of an extremely interesting subject.[51]

Although well aware of the opportunity to capitalize on the literary potential awaiting release in his adopted territory, in its exploitation Lummis was undoubtedly motivated by a genuine desire to reveal and interpret the Southwest to the rest of the country. Thus the primary significance of these early books lay in the fact that they stimulated interest in southwestern subjects and fostered the growth of tolerance and appreciation in connection with the region's Indian, Spanish, and Mexican cultures. Despite their obvious deficiencies as works of literature there is no gainsaying that they entitle Lummis to a secure place as a pioneer interpreter of the Southwest.

Late in 1893 Lummis returned from Peru to make his home in Los Angeles. Not long afterward Charles Dwight Willard offered him the editorship of the *Land of Sunshine*. Entry after entry in Lummis' journal during the last half of the nineties testified that the magazine claimed most of its editor's time.[52] He solicited contributions and then selected and edited them; he read proof; he took photographs; he made posters; he wrote aggressive and individualistic editorials; he conducted a monthly section of book notes; he organized a league of western writers; he translated and edited Spanish documents for publication in his journal; and he contributed at least one feature article to almost every issue. Lummis insisted that he worked harder than any eastern magazine editor and that during his first five years

[51]*Spectator*, Dec. 30, 1893, clipping in Lummis collection.
[52]Charles F. Lummis Journal, "The Week as Was," Dec. 27–Jan. 2, 1894-1895; Jan. 17–24, 1895; Jan. 3–16, 1896; Jan. 3–16, 1898; Jan. 17–24, 1899; Feb. 1–17, 1900; in possession of his daughter, Mrs. Turbesé Lummis Fiske, La Jolla, California. Hereafter cited as Lummis Journal.

in the editor's chair he was compelled to refuse to undertake an average of five books a year and uncounted articles.[53] Even with generous allowance for exaggeration it is clear that most of Lummis' literary output went into his magazine.

Important as the *Land of Sunshine* loomed in his years of editorial control, there were other aspects to the editor's life. He took an interest in civic affairs, serving on a planning committee of the Los Angeles fiesta of 1895 and conceiving historic themes for a number of the floats.[54] In November of the same year Lummis founded the Landmarks Club for the preservation of the missions and other historic relics of southern California's past.[55] Another civic obligation fulfilled by the editor involved the chairmanship of the city commission on Los Angeles street names. The last session of the commission in February, 1897, nearly resulted in violence when the picturesque Major Horace Bell, one-time filibusterer with William Walker in Nicaragua, threatened to kill someone should the commission change Georgia Bell Street, named after his wife. Bell was told he might have it Georgia or Bell street as he preferred but not both. After considerable bluster the Major departed without consenting to a change of any sort. Nevertheless the commission decided in favor of Georgia, the name the street bears today.[56]

About the time of the establishment of the Landmarks Club Lummis began preparations for the erection of a personal landmark — a house on the west bank of the Arroyo Seco, constructed largely of river-bed boulders and adobe, and set in a grove of some thirty sycamores which gave the site the name El Alisal. Although the three-acre location was purchased in September, 1895, actual construction was not begun until 1898. The house which arose from the river bed was built by Lummis with the help of Pueblo Indian boys who joined the editor's household from time to time. Including the patio, the structure covered a ninety-foot square. Architecturally it defies precise

[53]Lummis, "In the Lion's Den," *Land of Sunshine*, XII (1900), Feb., 190.
[54]Lummis Journal, Jan. 25–31, 1895.
[55]Ibid., Nov. 15–21, 1895.
[56]Ibid., Feb. 15–28, 1897.

classification, exhibiting Mexican, Peruvian, Spanish, and Indian influences. The fifty- by seventy-five-foot patio with its four-trunked sycamore, christened El Alcalde Mayor, formed the heart of the house, for every interior room opened onto it. The house was single storied except for two upstairs rooms that Lummis reserved for himself. A double front door, six feet wide and seven feet high, formed the main entrance. Each of its two leaves weighed close to one thousand pounds. After the death of Amado, the eldest son, in 1900, this door was never opened while Lummis lived. Access to the house was through an entrance off the patio leading into a sixteen-foot square living room. Most remarkable of the rooms was the museum. Its walls were old rose in hue, the floor, strewn with Indian rugs, was of gray cement, and the ceiling was beamed by ten-inch logs stripped of bark by an adze and charred to achieve the appearance of age. Paintings by William Keith, Charles Nahl, Thomas Hill, and other western artists crowded the walls. The pane of one large window consisted of photograph negatives of southwestern scenes taken by the builder. A number of the rooms had fireplaces, each of which bore an inscription over its mantel. In the living room this legend appeared: "Gather about me! Who can weld iron — or friends — without me?" In his wife's room the lines were: "Love and a Fire they're easy lit; but to keep either — wood to it!" The inscription in the guest bedroom read: "A casual savage cracked two stones together — a spark — and Man was armed against the Weather."[57]

Few days went by without some work being done on El Alisal. As the house took form beneath his hands, Lummis established a pattern of old California hospitality. Dinners at the Lummis home became famous in part for the food, but in greater measure for the company. These gatherings frequently included figures such as John Burroughs, Mary Garden, Helena Modjeska, Edwin Markham, Joaquin Miller, and Mary Austin, and they assumed the flavor of a European salon. A custom developed whereby when some distinguished person visited the city he was summoned to appear at El Alisal for arraignment

[57]*A Bronco Pegasus*, pp. 125-26.

before El Alcalde Mayor, the sprawling sycamore, on some such charge as "not knowing a good old California time when they see it."[58] Lummis termed the affairs "noises" and he was a dynamic and entertaining, if often domineering, host.

The building process continued over a stretch of nearly fifteen years and resulted in fourteen rooms. The house assumed the function of a gymnasium, for Lummis relied largely upon the labor expended in its construction to maintain the physical fitness of which he was so proud. El Alisal gave tangible and appropriate expression to its builder's philosophy that: "A man's home should be a part of himself. It should be enduring and fit to endure. Life and death will hallow it; it mellows with the generations — if it outlasts them. It should be good architecture, honest construction, comfortable, convenient . . . something at least of the owner's individuality should inform it. Some activity of his head, heart and hands should make it really his."[59] Also, the planning and building of his own home undoubtedly ful- filled Lummis' frequently expressed and deep-seated desire to create with his hands. "Any fool can write a book and most of them do," he was fond of remarking, "but it takes brains to build a house."[60] At any rate, Lummis raised an enduring personal mon- ument which was far from being the least of his achievements.

From the time of his first contact with the Pueblos of New Mexico on his way to California in 1885, Lummis had been a friend of the Indians of the Southwest. Therefore it was not sur- prising that he should come to the aid of a group of some three hundred southern California Indians threatened with eviction from their traditional home at Warner's Ranch in San Diego County. In connection with his crusade on their behalf he founded a national society known as the Sequoya League through which Lummis hoped to "make better Indians by treat- ing them better."[61]

[58]Lummis, California Writers Club Quarterly *Bulletin*, III (1915), June, 3.

[59]Walter Phillips Terry, "A Man Worth Knowing," *Mosher's Magazine*, XVII (1901), Jan., 217.

[60]Farnsworth Crowder, "El Alisal," *Westways*, XXXIX (1947), Dec., 3.

[61]*Out West*, XVI (1902), Feb., 177. The activities of the League receive extended treatment in a later chapter.

During the years of magazine editing, housebuilding, and crusading for the preservation of landmarks and Indian rights, Lummis and his wife were acquiring a family. Two years after the birth of Turbesé, a son arrived who was named Amado Bandelier after Amado Chaves and Adolph Bandelier, the two firmest friends Lummis made in New Mexico. This was the boy who died at the age of six on Christmas Day, 1900.[62] Two more sons were born to the Lummises: Jordan, named for David Starr Jordan, president of Stanford University, and Keith, namesake of William Keith, the California landscape artist.[63] A further addition appeared unexpectedly in 1906, when Bertha, the offspring born out of wedlock in 1879, came to live at El Alisal.[64]

Almost from the outset of his association with Los Angeles, Don Carlos, as Lummis came to be called locally, evinced a keen interest in the Los Angeles Public Library. It received reasonably frequent editorial mention in his magazine, and more than once he recommended to the library board the acquisition of items calculated to enhance the institution's value to scholars. Then, on June 21, 1905, the public library board elected Lummis city librarian.[65] Such action aroused considerable opposition, particularly on the part of the city's females who resented male encroachment in a sphere they regarded as peculiarly their own. Nevertheless Lummis served Los Angeles as librarian for nearly six years, during which time the library replaced the magazine as his major activity. Under Lummis a number of neglected aspects of the library received attention. Upon assumption of his duties the new librarian praised the clerical efficiency displayed in the organization of the library, but he pointed out that in addition to serving as a circulation bureau the library should provide scholars with research tools and business men with up-to-the-minute data. Accordingly, one of Lummis' first steps was to build up the reference department

[62]"Personal History," on file in the History Department, Los Angeles Public Library.
[63]Ibid.
[64]"The Strange Romance of a New Hampshire Schoolma'm," op. cit.
[65]Della Haverland, "Charles Fletcher Lummis," *Pacific Bindery* (1935), pp. 8-11.

to the point where it was the finest in the Far West.[66] As might be expected, Lummis emphasized regional history and through relatively heavy accessions the library laid the foundation for a splendid collection of source and secondary materials on western history.

The tolerance behind his policy of book selection was displayed when Lummis announced that "personal creed, politics or literary taste of a manager of books should not be allowed to play Czar to the users of books."[67] Thus he promptly replaced works which he felt had been unjustly outlawed, including studies on Mormonism and Christian Science, and the writings of Rider Haggard. The reforms and innovations extended into the administrative phases of the library. Lummis organized a representative body known as the library senate, composed of the librarian, the heads of departments, permanent assistants, and three delegates-at-large selected by staff members. He succeeded in securing a raise in every employee's salary. He cut red tape involved in registration by authorizing the immediate issue of borrower's cards to any person in the current city directory or to anyone guaranteed by a person in the directory.[68] More radical innovations, such as the roof-garden reading room, the history-material department which digested and indexed the newspapers, and the evaluation of textbooks which Lummis called "pure food laws applied to scholarship," were abandoned by his successors, but his work in reinforcing the reference and research departments was of lasting value.

Lummis resigned as librarian in 1911 at the age of fifty-one, in part because of opposition to some of his policies, but largely in order to devote more of his time to writing, to supervising the preservation of the missions, and above all to the realization of his most cherished dream — the Southwest Museum.[69]

"I founded the Southwest Society of the Archaeological Institute of America in October, 1903," wrote Lummis to a friend, "for the specific purpose of establishing here a great museum

[66]Ibid.
[67]Ibid.
[68]Los Angeles *Herald*, Jan. 1, 1908.
[69]Los Angeles *Times*, clipping in Lummis collection.

of the Southwest, and then building tributary and regional museums in the small cities of the Southwest not otherwise scientifically provided for."[70] Actually the genesis of the idea for a museum of the Southwest to be established in Los Angeles, the region's hub city, went back at least as far as to an article by Lummis in an early number of the *Land of Sunshine*.[71] In two years Don Carlos had made the Southwest Society the largest of the Institute's twenty-one societies but the movement for a museum made slower progress.[72] Turbesé Lummis Fiske described her father's efforts on behalf of the museum thus:

He went from friend to friend, from stranger to stranger preaching the Southwest Museum. He enlisted the aid of even his small children, to raise the money to purchase the site which stands now as a testimonial to his wisdom and artist vision. Wishing the whole citizenry of Los Angeles to feel that the museum was a personal possession, he solicited small contributions, either of time, heart or money, and at the ground-breaking he had scores of persons distinguished neither for wealth, influence nor great name, but for what to him was just as valuable: a simple neighborly interest and pride in "their" museum.[73]

Maurice M. Newmark, a member of the Southwest Museum board, recalled that when he objected to the large draft Lummis was willing to assume on the property to build the museum, the latter exclaimed violently, "To hell with the money. We will have the building."[74] According to one writer this was not the careless retort of an irresponsible promoter but rather the prophetic expression of a deep conviction that time would see the museum on its hill and with its debts paid.[75] Such an interpretation perhaps is somewhat naïve; nonetheless Lummis' remark was a manifestation of determination which often got results.

In 1907 the Southwest Society incorporated the Southwest

[70]Lummis to Colonel David Collier, Feb. 19, 1925, in Lummis collection.
[71]"The Palmer Collection," Vol. II (1895), Mar., 68.
[72]"The Works of Chas. F. Lummis," op. cit.
[73]Fiske, p. 29.
[74]Ben Field, "Charles Fletcher Lummis," *Overland Monthly*, N. S., LXXXVII (1929), July, 199.
[75]Ibid.

Museum, turning over to the corporation a $50,000 building site of nearly twenty acres, $50,000 in cash for the construction of of the first buildings, and collections valued at more than $300,000.[76] Another $50,000 contributed by Carrie M. Jones at the solicitation of Henry W. O'Melveny, chairman of the site and finance committees, placed the Southwest Museum Foundation in a position to get under way.[77] With Sumner P. Hunt, who already had served the Landmarks Club in supervising the preservation of the missions, as architect, the ground plan and elevation of the museum were begun in May, 1911.[78] At this critical stage Lummis suffered temporary loss of sight, presumably the result of jungle fever contracted in Guatemala during an archaeological expedition from which he had returned early that same year. Lummis had seen and approved the first elevations, but with the onset of blindness he had to feel the plans by tracing them repeatedly with his fingertips. Despite his handicap he was able in rough pencil sketches to indicate crudely the position of doors, windows, wall cases, and the stair well and ironwork galleries of the complicated Caracol Tower.[79] After some fifteen months of total darkness Don Carlos began to recover his sight. By 1913 he was able to undertake the supervision of the museum's construction for which he received one hundred dollars per month.[80] This post he held for three years.

In a letter to Maurice Newmark, Lummis claimed that up until 1915 every officer and member of the Southwest Museum board held his position by virtue of his (Lummis') personal recommendation.[81] After 1916, however, under circumstances which are not entirely clear, the founder of the Southwest Museum found himself, in a sense, barred from the house he had built. Evidently dissension had arisen over matters of policy. Lummis

[76]"Chas. F. Lummis," California Writers Club Quarterly *Bulletin*, III (1915), June, 5.
[77]Lummis, "The Southwest Museum," *Out West*, XXVI (1907), May, 409; Lummis Journal, Jan. 3–16, 1910.
[78]Fiske, p. 30.
[79]Ibid., 32.
[80]Letters and Diary of Lummis to Newmark, I, letter no. 2.
[81]Ibid.

had never intended to stop with the establishment of the Southwest Museum of Los Angeles. Rather he conceived of it as a parent organization to similar institutions on a smaller scale, which he hoped would arise in a number of cities throughout the Southwest for the purpose of preserving regional history and archaeology. The heavy investors in the Southwest Museum Corporation were not in sympathy with Lummis' plans.[82] Perhaps they regarded them as visionary or it may be they objected to the dissipation of funds in scattered localities to build up collections that would not redound directly to the fame of the Los Angeles institution and to the city. Whatever their reasoning, their hold on the purse strings helped their point of view prevail. On March 11, 1915, Lummis resigned as secretary of the Southwest Museum.[83] Although his influence waned rapidly, Lummis continued to fight for his concept. The final blow was dealt, however, in 1918, with the disincorporation of the Institute of the West, the agency Lummis had founded to put into effect his scheme of a network of museums in the Southwest.[84] Restitution of a sort was made in 1923 when Don Carlos received official recognition as founder of the Southwest Museum in a ceremony involving the dedication of the Lummis Caracol Tower.[85]

Although one of Lummis' expressed reasons for resigning from the city librarianship was to enable him to resume writing, no series of books such as followed his literary debut appeared. Nonetheless he continued to wield a prolific pen, turning out reviews, preparing articles for the encyclopedias *Britannica* and *Americana*, and maintaining all the while a voluminous correspondence, part of which consisted of circulating a daily journal among intimate friends which ran from fifty to one hundred thousand words a year.[86] Lummis' chief work involved labor on a concordance-dictionary and encyclopedia of Spanish

[82]Lummis to J. S. Torrance, president of the Southwest Museum Corporation, May 18, 1918, in Lummis collection.

[83]Letters and Diary of Lummis to Newmark, I, letter no. 2.

[84]Lummis to Torrance, May 18, 1918, in Lummis collection.

[85]"The Works of Chas. F. Lummis," op. cit.

[86]Fiske, p. 33.

America from 1492 through 1850. According to Lummis, he was "covering not only the Spanish language as enormously enlarged and enriched in the New World, but every title of the history, biography, geography, ethnography, etc., reduced to a universal index from all the original 'sources.' "[87] This meant a larger work than the *Britannica* and he admitted that he could not hope to finish it alone. He hoped for an endowment that would permit a staff of experts to work in collaboration on the project but none was ever forthcoming.[88]

Early in the twentieth century Lummis began seriously to collect Spanish and Indian folk songs of California and the Southwest. His technique was to search out old-timers and record on phonographic cylinders as many songs as they could remember. Lummis termed it "catching archaeology alive." In 1923 Arthur Farwell transcribed fourteen Spanish American folk songs from recordings made by Lummis.[89]

Mesa, Canyon and Pueblo, perhaps Lummis' most popular book, was published in 1925. In this revision and expansion of *Some Strange Corners of Our Country*, the substitution of photographs, most of them taken by the author, for the sketches of the Southwest which had served to illustrate the earlier work, was a marked improvement. In the judgment of a modern reviewer, *Mesa, Canyon and Pueblo* represented a synthesis of most of Lummis' accumulated knowledge. Despite haphazard organization, the reviewer contended that the book probably contained a greater variety of information on the Southwest, past and present, than any other single work in the field.[90]

In the twenties, age, the rapid pace of his life, and the accumulated effects of past personal tragedy began to tell on Lummis. Paralysis and the death of Amado had taken their toll. In 1910 Charles and Eva had separated, with divorce following shortly and depriving Lummis of the company of his youngest son and

[87]Autobiographical sketch of Lummis furnished Harvard for the 6th report, 25th anniversary of the Class of 1881, in Lummis collection.

[88]Ibid.

[89]Letters and Diary of Lummis to Newmark, I, letter no. 2.

[90]Vernon A. Young, "Paso Por Aqui: Recent Interpretations of the Southwest," *Arizona Quarterly*, III (1947), Summer, 166.

daughter for long periods.[91] About the same time came the temporary blindness as well as recurrent and severe attacks of rheumatism. Ever since his experience with paralysis Lummis had made it a rule never to put in a work day of more than twenty hours, but too frequently he stopped just short of the line. In 1922 his health gave way and his weight sank from a normal 135 to 90 pounds.[92] Although a vacation at Camulos Ranch put back most of the pounds, Don Carlos continued to suffer intermittently from angina pectoris, rheumatism, and failing eyesight caused by the development of cataract.[93]

On November 9, 1927, the following entry appeared in Lummis' diary:

Well I have my Ticket and Destination but not Train-time as yet. I never was late for a train but once in my life—but I think perhaps I will miss a few on *this* Road—entirely without prejudice, but with the feeling that I know of a lot more things that I want to do at this end of the line than at the other. . . . Seriously, I have taken my sentence without a pang. I have had my Share—and reasonably I have Done My Part. And now we will see how much more I can do while I stay.[94]

Lummis had an advanced cancer of the brain. He set himself three tasks to complete before he died: the preparation of a new edition of *The Spanish Pioneers*, the compilation of a book of informal historical essays on the early Spanish American epoch, and a collection of his verse.

The man's race against the final ravages of cancer was a dramatic climax to a dramatic life. Through the help of a devoted friend, the services of an efficient stenographer, the co-operation of an understanding publisher, and the exercise of a disciplined will, Lummis lived long enough to hold *A Bronco Pegasus*, the volume of verse, and the revised edition of *The Spanish Pioneers* in his hands. Also, he received telegraphic confirmation of the acceptance of his collection of essays which he entitled *Flowers of Our Lost Romance*. The next day, November 25, 1928, Charles F. Lummis was dead.

[91]Los Angeles *Times*, Oct. 13, 1910, clipping in Lummis collection.
[92]Letters and Diary of Lummis to Newmark, I, letter, Oct. 16, 1922.
[93]Ibid., Nov. 7, 1922.
[94]Ibid., III.

What manner of man was Lummis? Although not large, his frame was compact and muscular. He normally weighed between 135 and 140 pounds and he stood five feet seven inches. Many described his unconventional garb—the corduroy suit, soft white shirt, red sash, stetson, and moccasins or sandals, or the white, loosely knit underwear which was often all he bothered to wear at home—but few remarked on his features. Photographs of Lummis as a youth reveal a pleasant-appearing young man with a slightly aquiline nose, thick, wavy, brown hair, and a swarthy complexion.[95] His eyes were "blue and kindly,"[96] and most observers commented on his perennial tan. Lummis likened himself to a hickory sapling, doubtless implying toughness and resilience.[97] His walk was confident, cocky, his speech staccato, and his writing often had an abrupt and explosive quality. The over-all impression seems to have been one of intense enthusiasm and energy confined under considerable pressure.

Contemporary personal appraisals of Lummis vary markedly. Maurice Newmark, a close friend, said of him: "On the one hand, he was as keen as a blade, on the other as simple as a sage of old. He loved his friends and hated no one. He had less conceit than any man I ever met..."[98] However, Perry Worden, president of the Southern California Historical Society, wrote of the abnormal development of Lummis' exulting ego, of his intolerable conceit in staking out the entire Southwest for his exclusive literary exploitation, and of his "voluptuous vanity, freakish attire, and often boorish manners."[99] The following fragment from an anonymous verse appearing in a San Francisco paper tends to support Worden's estimate:

[95] *A Bronco Pegasus*, p. 130.

[96] Elizabeth Baker Bohan, "Lummis and His Work," *Sentinel*, Sept. 8, 1895, in Lummis collection.

[97] "In the Lion's Den," *Land of Sunshine*, XII (1900), Mar., 253.

[98] Field, p. 194.

[99] "Agua Mansa," Pasadena *Star-News*, Mar. 31, 1934, in Lummis collection. For a more balanced appraisal of Lummis and an appreciation of his contributions to the Southwest, see the resolutions drawn up by the Southern California Historical Society shortly after his death and signed by Perry Worden. Copy in the Huntington Library.

Façade of El Alisal

Down East—Out West

My name is Lummis, I'm the West!
For culture I don't give a hang;
I hate the puny East, although
I can't conceal my Yankee twang.
My trousers they are corduroy,
Ditto my jacket and my vest;
For I'm the wild and woolly boy,
My name is Lummis; I'm the West!
Who first beheld the Indian race?
Columbus, say you? 'Tisn't true.
I was the first to see his face;
I've had him copyrighted too.
I am the mountains and the sea,
I am the salty plain between;
You've seen the orange crop; That's Me,
I did it with my magazine.[100]

In her autobiographical *Earth Horizon*, Mary Austin, writing in the third person, made a shrewd appraisal of Lummis: "She thought him romantic and felt that he placed too heavy an emphasis upon the lesser achievements; on working too many hours a day; on sleeping too little; on drinking too much; on his wife's translations of Spanish manuscripts."[101]

On the other hand, Edgar L. Hewett, director of the School of American Research, characterized Lummis as "many-lived, myriad-minded, and golden-hearted."[102]

Inevitably a number of anecdotes have collected about a figure as colorful as Don Carlos. One, Lummis related about himself. He tells of conducting an excursion party near Acoma, New Mexico, in June, 1898. The group entered an old Indian church and one member of the party, a Protestant minister, neglected to remove his hat. "I reminded him it was a church," recalls Lummis. "He sneered that it was only an Indian and Catholic church.

---

[100]George Wharton James, "Founding of the Overland Monthly and History of the Out West Magazine," *Overland Monthly*, LXXXI (1923), May, 10-11.

[101]P. 294.

[102]Hewett, p. 1.

I pulled my six-gun and told him unless he took his hat off I would shoot it off. I didn't have to shoot."[103]

Elbert Hubbard once addressed a letter to Lummis which read, in part: "My Dear Carlos: I do not find your name on my list of Immortals [those who, upon payment of $100 would receive Hubbard's publications for life]. Is this an oversight?" The letter went back with this scrawled at the bottom: "My dear Elbert — not an oversight but an insight."[104]

Henry Edmond Earle writes of his experience while living in the Lummis house engaged in transcribing and annotating recorded Indian and Spanish folk songs. One evening Lummis was entertaining friends by having Amate, his Mexican troubador, sing some old California folk songs. As a check on the quality and correctness of his performance the conscientious servant kept deferring to Earle. At length Lummis cried out angrily, "You are not singing for Mr. Earle, you are singing for me!"[105]

Lummis held no formal religious creed although he developed strong sympathy and respect for Roman Catholicism. He liked to define God simply as the "best we know."[106] In the opinion of John Steven McGroarty, Lummis had little faith in a life hereafter. "I think his mind was poised to wait and see," wrote McGroarty, "and not to be afraid, no matter which way it might prove out."[107] Lummis himself contended that there were so many things of the world which he could understand and to which he could devote his energy that he did not have to consider problems beyond his comprehension.

Courage and tenacity were dominant Lummis traits. He applied a philosophy to physical ailments which he called "wearing it out." This consisted simply of proceeding as if a physical complaint did not exist until it disappeared. Thus in his

---

[103]Letters and Diary of Lummis to Newmark, II, entry of June 20, 1927.

[104]Hewett, p. 3.

[105]"An Old-Time Collector: Reminiscences of Charles F. Lummis," *California Folklore Quarterly*, I (1942), Apr., 182.

[106]"In the Lion's Den," *Land of Sunshine*, XII (1900), May, 379.

[107]Tribute by John Steven McGroarty, in *El Palacio*, XXV (1928), Nov. to Dec., 340.

tramp across the country, when severe blisters appeared on his feet, he kept walking until the blisters were replaced by calluses. The most spectacular display of courage, of course, occurred during the three-and-a-half-year contest with paralysis. It was shortly after the third shock left Lummis helpless in a hospital bed that he drafted this statement which came to serve as his personal creed: "I am bigger than anything that can happen to me. All these things — sorrow, misfortune and suffering — are outside my door. I'm in the house and I've got the key."[108] There was an element of heroics in the Lummis brand of courage which made him prone to dramatize adversity and to describe its conquest in colorful terms.

Lummis' individuality was frequently commented on by friends and associates. McGroarty claimed that he was lawless or rather that he made his own laws.[109] In Lummis the urge to be distinctive took numerous forms. His costume was perhaps the most obvious. Another was his use of capital letters for emphasis, or his preference for flint and steel to matches. Unusual to the extreme was his habit of coating pie with a layer of mustard before consuming it.[110] It is impossible to say how much of this sort of thing was conscious striving for effect and how much was the expression of a nature resentful of being bound by convention.

Lummis' championship of racial minorities — Negro, Spanish American, Indian, and Jew — bears witness to his substantial tolerance. His relative objectivity in matters of religion and politics has already been indicated. However, when he became embroiled in controversy over a point of historical or scientific accuracy, his broad tolerance sometimes deserted him and he became vindictive and picayune.

From the standpoint of profession or activity Lummis resists

[108]Printed card, in Lummis collection. Lummis' testimony has been followed in recounting his various ailments. There seems to be no way of knowing precisely where organic difficulties left off and psychosomatic illness began. There are those who believe that Lummis' paralysis and blindness alike were largely delusory.

[109]Tribute by John Steven McGroarty, op. cit.

[110]Maurice Salzman, "Charles Fletcher Lummis: The Very Last of the Mohicans," *Progressive Arizona and the Great Southwest*, VIII (1929), Jan., 16.

classification. The tags journalist, historian, promoter, ethnologist, writer, archaeologist, poet, scholar, folklorist—all of these have partial application to Don Carlos, but no one is strictly accurate. Perhaps the most satisfactory all-round term is the label he often gave himself, Americanist. In the disciplines of history, archaeology, and ethnology, Lummis lacked formal training. Nonetheless he claimed to be an authority on the Southwest; and the combination of wide reading, experience with the people, and intimate knowledge of the area, plus the fact that he was early in the field lent validity to his claim.

As a writer Lummis was little better than second-rate. According to a twentieth-century critic, he was never able to purge his style of the "preposterous cadences bequeathed him by the worst fashion of nineteenth century oratorical journalism" which employed a special jargon composed of archaic English constructions, apostrophizing, and poetic diction. He undoubtedly had a genuine flair for apt and picturesque phrasing, as when he dubbed New Mexico the "land of sun, silence, and adobe," or when he described California as "the right hand of the continent." Too often, however, this talent degenerated, producing slogans which were awkward, pretentious, or in poor taste, such as "God made California and He made it on Purpose," or, describing the Grand Canyon as "this masterpiece of His gladdest moment."[111]

In one respect at least Lummis was conventional, and that was in his poetry. As he himself observed, he was simply capable of correct verse and he aimed no higher. Narrative and dialect poems, with an occasional parody, were the verse forms he used most frequently. *A Bronco Pegasus* marshaled the poetic results of various stages in his life and thus was, to a marked degree, autobiographical. Some of the poems are clever, some lyrical; almost all may be classified as facile, serving to do little more than indicate the essential mediocrity of their creator's verse. Perhaps in the informal essay which lent itself readily to his breezy, epigrammatic style, Lummis attained his highest literary mark. The best example of this type of writing is *Flowers of Our Lost Romance*, published posthumously.

[111]Young, p. 167.

As a personality Lummis presents something of an enigma. He displayed noteworthy courage in the face of severe misfortune, yet apparently much of the tragedy in his life stemmed from his inability or refusal to exercise a less spectacular brand of courage, namely, restraint. His penchant for self-dramatization, always evident in his make-up, developed in later years into a consuming egocentricity. He was known for his hospitality, yet there are those to testify that he overstepped the bounds of good taste by monopolizing the center of the stage. Finally, his southwestern costume was doubtless a bid for attention as well as a concession to comfort. Nevertheless Don Carlos had the capacity to draw to himself close and loyal friends; he could be unstinting in praise of someone he admired, and he was capable of generously acknowledging a debt to a friend as when he wrote William Keith: "No man has done me more good and . . . no man has wrought upon me in the line in which, perhaps more than any other, I needed such inspiration. I hope my work is not wholly unspiritual, but it is grubbing; it needs the very uplift you give me — and I and all the work I shall do or have done since I knew your work — am indebted to you. I wish the influence were more visible in the result, but that's as God made me."[112]

However, excluding the controversial and contradictory aspects of his character, by the pragmatic test of accomplishment Charles F. Lummis was incontestably a significant and influential figure. He was the foremost pioneer in the literary discovery of the Southwest. He was, as a subsequent chapter demonstrates, an effective crusader for the rights of Indians and a successful campaigner for the preservation of historic landmarks. He developed a distinctive and representative regional journal. He founded the Southwest Museum. He got things done.

[112]Typescript in Keith Miscellany, Book VIII, p. 1079, Bancroft Library, Berkeley, California.

MAGAZINE PUBLISHING on the Pacific slope reached an early peak in 1868 with the founding of the *Overland Monthly* and with its rapid rise to fame through the literary sparkle provided by editor Bret Harte and contributors Mark Twain and Joaquin Miller. The *Overland* represented the culmination of a journalistic boom made possible by the swarming of the gold seekers to a San Francisco sufficiently isolated from the rest of the nation to blunt competition from the eastern journals.

Inevitably some of the journalistic flurry spread to the southern part of the state; and pioneer newspapers such as the *Star* and the *Southern Californian* in Los Angeles, the *Herald* in San Diego, and the *Gazette* in Santa Barbara were established in the fifties. However, in the more ambitious and more hazardous sphere of magazine publishing, no transfer south occurred. Minor local journals evidently appeared fleetingly in the late seventies and during the eighties, for their names are cited in nineteenth-century city directories and in newspaper annuals, but the first southern California magazine of any consequence was published in Los Angeles in 1877. It was called *Southern California Horticulturist*, a name derived from its founding society. This neatly printed, illustrated monthly of forty-eight double-column pages was devoted to topics relating to farm, orchard, and home. By 1893, its name shortened to *Rural Californian*, the journal claimed a circulation of 5,000.[1]

In 1882 Horace Bell, a sort of poor man's Ambrose Bierce, founded his aggressive weekly *Porcupine*. This outspoken journal accented politics and held no public figure sacred. Five years later, symptomatic of a general decline in the northern magazine field, the once vigorous and independent *Golden Era*

[1]N. W. Ayer and Sons, *American Newspaper Annual* (Philadelphia, 1893), p. 47.

was lured to San Diego by promise of a \$5,000 subsidy,[2] and incidentally proved one exception to the popular boast that "everything grows in southern California."

The southern counties never experienced a rash of magazines comparable to San Francisco's, for by the time southern California achieved a population dense enough to support a magazine, its isolation was gone and with it the cushion against eastern competition. The regional impulse, often a dominant factor in launching pioneer magazines, instead of falling to individual editors and publishers, was appropriated by organized groups and used to stimulate immigration to southern California. Broadly speaking, much of the talent and energy which under different circumstances might have gone into the founding of independent literary journals was diverted into impersonal promotional channels.

First in this field were the railroads whose managers were interested in selling land and building future business, as well as in swelling the immediate proceeds from tourists in the form of passenger fares. The purchased enthusiasm of journalists such as Charles Nordhoff, Jerome Madden, and Ben C. Truman contributed substantially to the extent and intensity of the real estate boom of the eighties. In this same decade publicity agents of the tourist hotels, representatives of immigration societies, and newspapers joined the railroad propagandists in advertising southern California. After the collapse of the boom much of the systematic production and distribution of promotional literature passed into the hands of chambers of commerce and boards of trade. For example, the Los Angeles Chamber of Commerce distributed illustrated pamphlets in batches of fifty and seventy-five thousand cataloguing the virtues of the Southland and appraising commercial and agricultural opportunities.[3] The first object of these later propaganda programs was to attract immigrants who would locate permanently in southern California.

Out of this welter of propaganda-laden literature produced

---

[2]Charles S. Greene, "Magazine Publishing in California," *Publications of the California Library Association*, No. 2 (May, 1898), 8.

[3]Charles Dwight Willard, *History of the Los Angeles Chamber of Commerce* (Los Angeles, 1900), p. 147.

and disseminated by railroads and newspapers, by hotel associations and immigration societies, by boards of trade and enthusiastic residents, there emerged an illustrated monthly magazine called the *Land of Sunshine*.

In some respects conditions in southern California during the early nineties were not particularly propitious for launching a new enterprise — especially in the magazine field where mortality rates were notoriously high. The orange growers suffered a severe slump in the eastern market aggravated by the participation of many dealers in consignment buying. In addition, in June, the month the *Land of Sunshine* first appeared, traffic between Chicago and the West was virtually paralyzed as a result of the railroad strike of 1894.

However, viewed in broader perspective, the times were not so out of joint. The panic of 1893 had left California relatively unscathed. The citrus industry, despite its difficulties, was firmly established and in a year or so the California Fruit Growers Exchange would solve the marketing problem. The potentialities of irrigation were being demonstrated in communities like Ontario and Pomona. The struggle for a free Los Angeles harbor was joined in earnest in the early nineties and midway in the decade the city recorded a greater amount of construction than in any previous year. In short, during the last decade of the century, southern California was experiencing a solid and highly diversified economic expansion with Los Angeles, its hub, about to emerge as a modern city.

The *Land of Sunshine* appeared on Los Angeles newsstands in June, 1894. It was quarto in size, studded with half-tone photoengravings and printed on slick, white paper in broad, double columns. In the upper half of the cover appeared a heavily retouched photograph of a southern California valley with dubbed-in palm trees in the right foreground and snow-crowned peaks as a backdrop. The lower panel carried the table of contents. The magazine sold for ten cents a copy or one dollar by the year. The only clue to proprietorship was the name F. A. Pattee Publishing Company. The masthead declared the magazine to be "an illustrated monthly journal, descriptive of Southern California," but no mention was made of an editor. Actually two other men, Harry Ellington Brook and Charles Dwight Willard, were associated with Pattee in the publishing venture.

Frank A. Pattee, originally a Pennsylvanian, migrated from Kansas, where he was a registered pharmacist, to Los Angeles in November, 1886. Two years later he joined S. W. Lockett in establishing a prescription drugstore.[4] By 1893 Pattee dropped the drug business and became a solicitor for the Los Angeles Chamber of Commerce. In this capacity he may well have met Brook and Willard.

Harry Brook, an Englishman, arrived in Los Angeles about the same time as Pattee. He was employed as an editorial writer on the Los Angeles *Times* and intermittently he served as a pamphleteer for the Los Angeles Chamber of Commerce. One of his efforts in this connection, a thirty-six-page booklet issued in an 1893 edition of 75,000 copies, was called "The Land of Sunshine" and this became the label of the new journal launched the next year.[5]

Charles D. Willard, a University of Michigan graduate, was born in Illinois. He came to Los Angeles in 1888 seeking relief from a lung infection, and took a reporting job, first with the Los Angeles *Times* and later with the *Morning Herald*. Willard had been a more or less regular contributor to the San Francisco *Argonaut* whose editor, Jerome A. Harte, wrote the following estimate of Willard's literary ability:

Among the younger writers who have appeared in the *Argonaut* of late years is Charles Dwight Willard. Much of his work has appeared over various pseudonyms. He is a modest man, and when he wrote something particularly good he immediately became ashamed of it and affixed some pseudonym. His mediocre work, for some strange reason, he always signed with his full name. One of his most striking stories was entitled "The Fall of Ulysses," and related to the phenomenal intelligence of the Indian Elephant. It was copied all over the world. Another, "The Jack Pot," is a pearl among short stories. It is about one thousand words long, and is a symmetrical well-rounded piece of work. It has a beginning, a middle and an end and in it the dramatic unities are unviolated, the reader is kept in suspense, the climax is looked for breathlessly, and when it comes it is entirely

[4] *An Illustrated History of Los Angeles County*, p. 602.
[5] Willard, p. 159.

unsuspected. . . . It is melancholy to be forced to add . . . that Mr. Willard has ceased story writing. He has become secretary of the Los Angeles Chamber of Commerce, and is doubtless prosperous and unhappy.[6]

Willard was hardly prosperous, but he had a small cash reserve and sometime early in 1894 he decided to invest $1,000 in "a little paper I am interested in."[7] This was the *Land of Sunshine*. It is not clear who first conceived the idea of the southern California monthly but, under the original arrangement, it appears that Pattee gave his name to the publishing company and acted as business manager; Brook donated the magazine's name and became a regular contributor; and Willard provided the initial capital and did most of the editing.[8]

Charles Willard's connection with the *Land of Sunshine* remained secret. In a letter to his sister he stated: "I am the capital of a small publishing house — but no one out here knows it except my wife and the other partners. It would hurt me in my position."[9]

An inspection of the first number of the *Land of Sunshine* helps to explain the need for deception. The journal was sharply slanted in favor of the chambers of commerce and boards of trade of the Southland, with marked attention to the Los Angeles body of which Willard was secretary. The first number carried articles by the presidents of the Los Angeles and San Diego chambers of commerce as well as a two-page spread on the Los Angeles organization, complete with portraits of its twenty current directors. Willard's aim evidently was to secure the Chamber's sanction of the magazine without disclosing his relationship and, more important, to persuade the Chamber to buy the *Land of Sunshine* in quantity for distribution in other states as a means of inducing immigration to southern California. Indicative of the success of his scheme is the following letter, boldly reproduced in the July issue of the magazine:

[6]Ella Sterling Cummins (Mighels), *The Story of the Files* (San Francisco, 1893), p. 208.
[7]Willard to father, Dec. 19, 1897, in Charles D. Willard MSS, Huntington Library, San Marino, California.
[8]Willard to father, Oct. 23, 1894, in Willard MSS.
[9]May 5, 1894, in Willard MSS.

8 June, 1894

F. A. Pattee, and Co.
        City
Dear Sir:
    I enclose order for copies of the Land of Sunshine monthly, which I am instructed by the Board of Directors to purchase from you for circulation by the Chamber.
    Your communication to Mr. Freeman dated May 31st was read at the meeting of the Board June 6th, and I take pleasure in telling you that the commendation of your work was emphatic and general on the part of the members present.
    Wishing you success with your undertaking, I am
                                        Very respectfully,
                                        C. D. Willard
                                        Secretary[10]

The extent of this subsidy was not disclosed but it was doubtless a sustaining factor during the early, uncertain months of the journal's existence. The same sort of support but presumably on a much smaller scale was extended by the president of the San Diego Chamber of Commerce.

The *Land of Sunshine* was confronted almost immediately with a crisis in the form of the railroad strike of 1894. In a letter to his father, Willard expressed his apprehension for the magazine's security:

There is no turbulence here and no prospect of any but if it continues much longer—the freight stoppage I mean—it is going to be ominous to business of all kinds. I don't know whether my venture will weather the storm. The Land of Sunshine started off very prosperously with a good outlook and barring that I am very short of money I had very little to find fault with. But now I am all at sea. I don't know where I am coming out.[11]

After about twelve days, however, traffic was resumed and the *Land of Sunshine* suffered nothing more serious than a slight delay in getting the July issue to its eastern readers.

Like most magazines, the *Land of Sunshine* was first of all a business venture run by businessmen in the expectation of making profits. Also it had the broader, though ultimately no

[10]Vol. I, 31.
[11]July 9, 1894, in Willard MSS.

less commercial, objective of attracting "desirable" settlers to the region. The opening number contained the publisher's credo:

It is the belief of the publishers of this periodical that a monthly paper, handsomely illustrated, artistically printed, containing well written matter on Southern California topics, will find a good many readers, both here and in the East, among travelers, health seekers, and intending settlers; and the Land of Sunshine is offered to the public on the basis of this faith.

It is no exaggeration to say that there are several hundred thousand people east of the Rockies who are talking and thinking of California, who hope sometime to come to this State, either to visit or to settle, or who are anxious to learn more about it. . . . The Land of Sunshine will be made to them a reality rather than a dream, through the pages of this journal.[12]

C. R. Pattee, the publisher's father, said it a little differently:

From where the broad Pacific leaves the shore—
Where stand the City of the Angels—comes
A timely messenger to every door,
And cries: "Ho! ye, who long for health and homes,
In some fair clime where every human need
May be supplied,—give ear! and hearing, heed!

Who is this messenger? dost wish to know?
Who thus this welcome message doth proclaim?
Look ye! and see inscribed upon his brow:
THE LAND OF SUNSHINE!—read ye there the *name*,
And bid it welcome; then, without delay,
Come to this land where it doth point the way.[13]

In the July issue a more explicit statement of policy appeared. On the one hand the material and commercial aspects of southern California would be detailed: its commerce, citrus products, and manufactures; while on the other hand increasing space would be consigned to cultural and recreational topics: architecture, history, education, hunting and fishing, and photography. This dichotomy was to characterize the magazine throughout most of its life.

[12]Vol. I (1894), June, 12.
[13]Ibid., 13.

Techniques designed to increase circulation were employed early and continually. Forms were distributed which made it convenient for the magazine's readers to subscribe on behalf of relatives or friends. The first number carried this somewhat ingenuous offer: "If you are bothered with numerous letters of inquiry from the East, send them to us. We will not only answer them, but will induce the writers to subscribe for the Land of Sunshine."[14] Appeals to readers were seldom either subtle or modest and often they were marked by wishful thinking. For example, the September number offered the following "suggestion":

Let us suppose that you who are reading these words are a happy and contented resident of Southern California. You bought this paper at a news-stand from a large pile that were [sic] selling like hot cakes. It occurs to you that it would be a good idea to subscribe for the magazine for a year for several of your old friends in the east. You thereupon draw a check for five dollars and send it to us, and we send your friends each our subscription card.

Doesn't it strike you that it is a bright idea? Your friends have not forgotten you, and it will please them to know that you still remember them.[15]

An early policy adopted to increase circulation and encourage immigration was to supply public libraries of the country with the *Land of Sunshine*. With the November number the publishers inaugurated a positive plan to boost circulation by calling for resident agents. "The publication is now well established," ran the announcement, "and any man or woman with some spare time can make an acceptable addition to their income by securing a local agency. Those only who can present first-class recommendations are requested to write for terms and full particulars to the publishers."[16]

Meanwhile the new monthly's reception had been encouraging. A month after the debut of the journal the publishers announced happily: "Within ten days from the time it appeared the entire edition of 5,000 copies was practically exhausted, and

[14]Ibid.
[15]Ibid., Sept., 78.
[16]Ibid., Nov., 119.

all efforts to push the number were necessarily discontinued."[17]

By October, 1894, increased orders from many of the seventy-nine southern California newsstand dealers who carried the *Land of Sunshine* testified to the new magazine's local success. A Spring Street dealer raised his standing order from 30 to 150 copies per month and proportionate increases were requested by a number of the smaller agencies.[18] Although optimistic reports of sales appearing in the journal itself may properly be viewed with suspicion, remarks in Willard's personal correspondence tend to substantiate the magazine's claims. Thus, late in October, 1894, he wrote: "All the *weekly* and monthly magazines and papers of San Francisco and Los Angeles combined together do not sell as many copies as the Land of Sunshine in Los Angeles. That shows we are taking hold."[19]

Three months later, the two leading newsstands of the city certified that their combined sales of the January number of *Harper's, Century, Scribner's, McClure's, Cosmopolitan,* and the *Overland* were 385, as compared with 527 of the January *Land of Sunshine*.[20] With this same January issue, the customary printing of 5,000 per month was sold out within three days and, for the first time, it was necessary to order a second edition, leading the publishers to observe: "the Land of Sunshine honestly believes that it has today a larger genuine subscription list than any other monthly published in California — and that means than any other this side of Kansas City."[21] This was overly sanguine, for at least two other monthlies, the *Overland* in San Francisco and the *Rural Californian* of Los Angeles, topped the *Land of Sunshine* in circulation.[22] Both of these, however, were well-established journals. Actually there was some justification for the new monthly's optimism.

Despite the fact that the *Land of Sunshine* was fashioned

[17]Ibid., July, 44.

[18]Ibid., Nov., 125.

[19]Willard to father, Oct. 23, 1894, in Willard MSS.

[20]*Land of Sunshine*, II (1895), Mar., 71.

[21]Ibid., Feb., 53.

[22]George P. Rowell, *American Newspaper Directory* (New York, 1895), pp. 49, 63.

more for export than for local consumption, its eastern sales campaign progressed slowly. The principal problem, distribution, was solved only when the American News Company finally agreed to handle the *Land of Sunshine* beginning with the May, 1895, number. The delay may have been a matter of cost, for the American News Company had a reputation for charging excessive rates, especially in cases of struggling young periodicals.[23]

Apparently the measures to increase circulation were effective, for at the close of the first twelve-month period the certified list had reached the 8,000 mark.[24]

Despite steady circulation gains, recognition of the new monthly by other periodicals came slowly, especially on the local scene. The Los Angeles *Evening Express* in its annual review number of January 1, 1895, made a comprehensive survey of the year past including a summary of building activity, an appraisal of the new oil industry, a review of Chamber of Commerce activities, and even a note on the furnishings of the Maier and Zobelein brewery, but no mention of the *Land of Sunshine* appears. As late as February, 1895, the *Overland Monthly* claimed to be the only monthly magazine west of the Rockies. There was, however, some compensation in the brief but cordial and uniformly complimentary notices which appeared in journals such as the *Dial, Harper's Monthly,* and *Scribner's.* Finally, in October, 1895, the *Overland* got around to welcoming the *Land of Sunshine* as its southern colleague.[25]

Financial progress kept pace generally with the rise in circulation, but advance was relative. The initial investment had been Willard's $1,000 and at the end of nine months the magazine was earning approximately that sum each month. However, expenses continued to exceed income and, in Willard's words, the journal had already succeeded in accumulating a "very respectable debt."[26] Nevertheless he expected the company's

[23]Frank Luther Mott, *History of American Magazines* (Cambridge, 1938-1939), II, 13.
[24]*Land of Sunshine*, III (1895), Aug., 133.
[25]P. 460.
[26]Willard to father, Feb. 17, 1895, in Willard MSS.

income to double within a year and stoutly declared he would not sell out for twice his original investment. Three months later, at the close of the first year of publication, Willard found it difficult to suppress his elation when he wrote: "It [the magazine] has accomplished far more than I ever hoped for in the same length of time and the outlook is so good that it almost frightens me."[27] The same letter, however, contained a sobering note as he reminded his father that the dry summer season which again confronted the new magazine would tax the company's resources severely.

Scarcely separable from matters of circulation and finance was the question of advertising. The value of advertising as financial reinforcement of American magazines had been clearly established in the early eighties and the *Land of Sunshine* sought such support from the start. Throughout the first year its rates were not made public, perhaps because no consistent policy had been formulated. A year or so later rates were quoted at $13.00 a half-page, $25.60 a full page, and $50.00 for the outside of the back cover. These figures applied to advertisements running for twelve-month periods and the cost varied inversely with the length of the run.[28]

Consistent with the promotional aim of the journal, the bulk of the advertisers were either tourist hotels or real estate and land companies. The Santa Fe Railroad purchased advertising space regularly, as did the local photoengraving companies. Examples of miscellaneous advertisements during this early period included: Mullen and Bluett, clothing; the Los Angeles Business College; H. J. Wollacott Wines; and Sharp and Samson, funeral directors. Most of them were Los Angeles firms, but Pasadena, Pomona, Redlands, Santa Barbara, and San Diego were regularly represented. Late in the year the Palace Hotel in San Francisco purchased half a page. Somehow, for the one month of October, 1894, the London, Chatham and Dover Railroad's advertisement was wedged between that of the Brewster Hotel of San Diego and the Green of Pasadena, demonstrating

27Ibid., May 19, 1895.
28Land of Sunshine Publishing Company, advertising rate card, in folder labeled "Personalia," in Lummis collection.

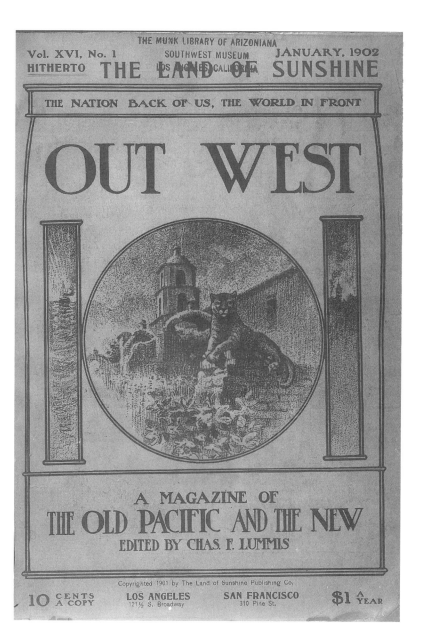

THE MUNK LIBRARY OF ARIZONIANA

Vol. XVI, No. 1   SOUTHWEST MUSEUM   JANUARY, 1902

HITHERTO   THE LAND OF SUNSHINE

LOS ANGELES, CALIFORNIA

THE NATION BACK OF US, THE WORLD IN FRONT

OUT WEST

A MAGAZINE OF

THE OLD PACIFIC AND THE NEW

EDITED BY CHAS. F. LUMMIS

10 CENTS A COPY   LOS ANGELES   SAN FRANCISCO $1 A YEAR
121½ S. Broadway   310 Pine St.

First Cover—Out West

either the broad tolerance of the *Land of Sunshine's* advertising policy or the financial desperation of its owners.

During its first year frank appeals to advertisers appeared in the editorial pages of the *Land of Sunshine* pointing out the advantages of utilizing a publication which appeared with regularity and which was produced in the area in which the advertisers lived. Attention was called to the impracticality of buying space in pamphlets of distant origin, questionable permanence, and dubious circulation.[29] The effectiveness of such direct pleas cannot be determined accurately, but it is true that between its inception and the last issue of its first year the magazine increased its pages of advertising from five and a half to thirteen.

The new monthly's most conspicuous weakness was that it lacked a genuine editor. Ghost-editor Willard was severely handicapped because the Chamber of Commerce held first claim on his time and talent and because he was unable to conduct an editorial policy under his own name. Despite his faith in the ultimate success of the *Land of Sunshine*, he apparently could not make up his mind to cut himself off from the Chamber of Commerce and devote full time to the journal. Finally, after the magazine was six months old, he prevailed upon a friend to assume the editor's chair. The new editor was Charles F. Lummis and the conditions of his acceptance were three: first, he was to exercise absolute control over policy; second, he was to receive $75 per month, $50 in cash and the balance in a lien on the stock; finally, he was to have one-third interest in the business.[30]

Aside from their friendship Willard was influenced in his choice by the fact that Lummis, a former newspaperman and author of half a dozen books, was one of the few residents of the city who could claim any degree of literary distinction. Moreover, the idea of editing a regional and literary magazine was not new to Lummis, for as early as 1891 he and a Los Angeles printer named Ernest Foster had talked of founding a literary monthly, representative of southern California, although nothing had come of the project.[31] Willard evidently was satisfied with the new editor for he wrote in February, 1895:

[29]Vol. I (1894), Nov., 119; II (1895), Apr., 91.
[30]Lummis Journal, Nov. 18, 1894.   [31]Ibid., Nov. 29–Dec. 3, 1889.

Our Land of Sunshine is doing first rate under Lummis' editorship. He is a tireless worker and is throwing his whole soul into the undertaking. He is a scholarly fellow, rather a purist in matters of language —though he tries to write slangy sometimes. He has certain oddities but you soon forget them. He has a severe conscience and a strict sense of duty. Don't you think we were lucky to get him?[32]

Lummis' impact on the *Land of Sunshine* was immediate and obvious. He wrote the leading article in the January number, an appraisal of the ethnological imprint made by the Spaniard in the Western Hemisphere and an elaborate tribute to the physical and moral virtues of the Spanish-American woman. The same number carried Lummis' "The Spanish Lesson," a dialect poem reprinted from *Life*.

In his first editorial Lummis briefly analyzed the characteristics of the incoming population, redefined the magazine's objectives, and enumerated the factors which he was convinced augured success for the new journal. First, he contended that the southern counties were in the main being settled, not by failures or adventurers or runaways, but rather by people of comfortable means, sound education, and good morals. Second, he pointed out that most southern Californians were residents by preference rather than by birth. Third, he claimed the Southland commanded greater interest and curiosity from the rest of the world than any other section in the United States. Lummis' Puritan background would not allow him to deny completely that adversity developed strength, but he did maintain: "A decent comfort in the home need not make one effeminate to battle with the world; nor is man to be undone by choosing Nature where she is mother, not stepmother."[33]

Afraid of seeing the *Land of Sunshine* stigmatized as a boom periodical, Lummis "assumed" that his readers would be prompt to sense the difference "between the hireling 'promoter' and the business enterprise which has sense enough to be honest," and he promised that the journal's treatment of developments in southern California would be "concise, interesting, expert, accurate" so as to merit the trust of its eastern readers.

[32]Willard to father, Feb. 17, 1895, in Willard MSS.
[33]Vol. II (1896), Jan., 21-22.

Lummis concluded his first editorial by suggesting that southern California offered a virgin field in romance, poetry, history, and archaeology as well as furnishing a rich area for geologist, botanist, and conchologist. "No equal area in the United States," he insisted, "has so great a variety of interests for all minds; yet several local magazines live on the far narrower suggestiveness of New England."[34] The new editor was not addicted to understatement and yet there was more than a kernel of truth in most of his assertions.

The most significant result of Lummis' assumption of the editorship was the emergence of an editorial policy which placed increasing emphasis on the cultural and intellectual scene in southern California. Negative indication of the change was revealed in a reduction in the average of promotional articles per issue from ten during the first six months to six during the last half of the year. Increased cultural awareness was reflected positively in an article on Los Angeles churches; in a recapitulation of the plans of a Pasadena society to further the study of local California history; in a paper on California artists by John Gutzon Borglum; in an editorial advocating the establishment of a southern California museum; and in several articles on archaeological topics. Moreover, the journal's literary pretensions were bolstered through the policy, inaugurated by Lummis, of including a short story in each issue. Although he evidenced no intention of deserting the original promotional objective, the new editor was clearly concerned with elevating the journal's tone. Consistent with the shift in emphasis was Lummis' statement that "The Land of Sunshine will be a magazine of Southern California first, last, and all the time, but it will realize that Southern California grows brains as well as oranges."[35]

With the appearance of the May number in 1895 the *Land of Sunshine* was one year old, and, despite the fact that it was still in debt, the magazine's prospects of celebrating a second anniversary appeared to be good. Circulation had mounted steadily. Advertising was on the increase. Recognition and encouragement had come from newspapers and periodicals in

[34]Ibid.
[35]Ibid., I (1895), Mar., 53.

the East. There was no question of competition since no rivals had appeared in its field. The magazine had an editor who knew where he was going and who was working hard to give the magazine stability and significance. Above all, in a southern California on the verge of multiform expansion, there was genuine justification for an instrument to shape its culture, and to preserve its heritage. Perhaps the *Land of Sunshine* would serve.

Chapter **III** THE MAGAZINE

CHARLES F. LUMMIS reigned as sole editor of his magazine from January, 1895, until February, 1903. On the latter date Charles Amadon Moody appeared on the masthead as assistant editor, rising by July, 1905, to the position of joint editor. After Lummis sold his stock in the periodical and removed his name from the cover in November, 1909, the journal deteriorated rapidly in the hands of a succession of editors including C. F. Edholm, George Wharton James, and Lannie Haynes Martin. The magazine ceased to appear with any regularity after June, 1917, and its identity was only partly regained when, in May, 1923, it was consolidated with the *Overland Monthly* in an attempt to revitalize the two well-known western monthlies. In July, 1935, the *Overland Monthly and Out West Magazine* ceased publication, thereby removing from public view a pair of pioneer names in the development of Pacific Coast magazine publishing. Actually, however, as the brief life history above indicates, the effective influence of the *Land of Sunshine* or *Out West* was limited to the period of Lummis' active editorship, for those who followed him could neither maintain his pace nor set a new one of their own.

From the time he assumed the editor's chair in January, 1895, Lummis urged the reduction of the magazine's size from quarto to demi-octavo, a form he deemed more appropriate to a journal with literary and cultural aspirations.[1] The change was accomplished in June, 1895, with Number I of Volume III and was accompanied by a new cover design executed by John Gutzon Borglum which pictured a mountain lion sprawled on a ledge, a golden sun framing his head. Beneath the lion was a graceful

[1]Lummis Journal, Jan. 25-31, 1895.

rose branch symbolic of southern California culture. Attached to the name "Land of Sunshine" was the subtitle "A Southern California Magazine," and in the upper margin of the cover appeared the Spanish proverb: *"Los Paises del Sol dilatan el Alma"* (lands of the sun expand the soul). Other printed information included the month, year, volume, and number, the editor's name, place of publication, and price, ten cents an issue, one dollar a year. This remained the basic cover plan for a number of years although the design became increasingly stylized and the subtitle varied to conform with the journal's steady expansion of scope, progressing to "A Magazine of California and the Southwest," and then becoming "The Magazine of California and the West."

The adoption of the name "Out West" called for radical cover revision. The first design, two perpendicular columns tangent to each side of a circle framing a California mission and a mountain lion in indolent repose on a fragment of wall, lasted only a month. It was replaced by the more classical but less western device of a winged globe with a naked youth astride it in hurdle position and holding a green branch aloft in his right hand. Inscribed on a band around the middle of the globe was the word "Destiny." In the background a city rose silhouetted against a setting sun. The graceful Spanish proverb gave way to the aggressive slogan: "The Nation Back of Us, the World in Front," and the subtitle now read: "A Magazine of the Old Pacific and the New." Only two things reminiscent of the original magazine were retained: the inevitable mountain lion, much smaller but still at ease, and the phrase in the upper margin "Formerly the Land of Sunshine," which assumed the permanency of a trade-mark. J. D. Gleason, a local artist, was responsible for the new design.

Over the next three years the cover scheme varied somewhat in color and form but the classical theme persisted and Gleason was retained as artist. Finally, in January, 1905, the advertising firm of J. C. Hewitt worked out a cover which the magazine adopted. "Out West" appeared in large letters on a bronze strip. Against a bronze, plaque-like background appeared a sleepy looking mountain lion encircled by a wreath. Slogan and sub-title were unchanged, and this cover was still in use at the time Lummis left the magazine.

The only change in the magazine's dimensions, after the reduction from quarto, occurred when it assumed the name "Out West." At that time the journal was enlarged from demi-octavo to medium octavo. The magazine grew too in number of pages and the gain per volume was steady through the year 1903, climbing from approximately 260 to 800 pages and then leveling off at from 550 to 580 pages per volume through 1907. Peak years from the standpoint of number of pages were 1902 and 1903.

The make-up of the journal of course varied with the contents but a general plan prevailed throughout most of the magazine's life. As a rule, the early pages contained feature articles, poetry, and stories; then came the editorial section, the book notes, and the pages devoted to the various agencies for which the periodical served as official organ; the back pages were usually given over to regional write-ups of an openly promotional nature. Advertisements appeared both before and after the reading matter with much the heavier padding of this sort in the back. An "index," really nothing more than a consolidation of tables of contents, was published at the end of each six-month volume.

Lavish use of illustrations, most of them half-tone photo-engravings, demanded paper of high quality. For the most part a heavy, white, slick stock supplied by Blake, Moffitt and Towne was used. After January, 1896, the magazine began to use cheaper, rougher stock for the unillustrated editorial, book review, and organization sections. As the number of stories and the amount of documentary material increased, they too were printed on the more porous paper. Typographically the magazine held to a high standard and rarely was legibility impaired by worn or imperfect type.

In the hands of editor Lummis the magazine's original policy of developing simultaneously the commercial and cultural assets of southern California underwent marked extension and refinement. Evolution in purpose and scope is not only apparent in changes in the journal's subtitle and in its contents, but it can also be traced in the editor's own words, for Lummis on numerous occasions took stock of past performance, detailed current objectives, and forecast future policy.

Early in his period of editorial control Lummis made it clear that practical considerations as well as sentiment conditioned the dedication of his journal to a locality. He believed that the general trend toward specialization was invading the field of magazine publishing and that the best guarantee of success, especially in the case of a newcomer, was to specialize, whether geographically or topically, thereby avoiding the severe competition responsible for the high mortality rate among magazines. Having justified regional concentration on a business basis, Lummis went on to gloat over the inexhaustible possibilities for historical, literary, and descriptive exploitation of the region he had chosen.

The editor was determined to give his magazine distinction, authority, and interest. Distinction he felt would result naturally from an honest and comprehensive portrayal of California and the "Southwestern Wonderland." Authority and interest he sought to achieve by striking a judicious balance between material which reflected his special training and subject matter of general appeal. As he expressed it in a letter to a contributor: "This little magazine tries to be 'popular' enough to live and substantial enough to *deserve* to live — not always an easy adjustment. . . . We believe it a magazine's duty to teach as well as tickle; and we believe the ordinary 'intelligent reader's' soul is worth saving."[2]

In carrying out his design to make the journal instructive as well as entertaining Lummis published translations of basic Spanish documents relating to far western history. Many of these appeared in English for the first time and some perhaps for the only time in the pages of the *Land of Sunshine*. The documentary section included such items as: a summary of the

[2]Lummis to W. J. McGee, Bureau of American Ethnology, Washington, D. C., Oct. 26, 1897, in J. Manuel Espinosa, "Some Charles F. Lummis Letters, 1897-1903," *New Mexico Quarterly Review*, XI (1941), May, 149.

history of California from 1768 to 1793 by Viceroy Revilla Gigedo,[3] an account of the history of New Mexico between 1538 and 1626 by the Franciscan missionary Geronimo de Zarate de Salmeron,[4] the diary of Junipero Serra kept during the march from Loreto to San Diego in the spring of 1769,[5] and the memorial on New Mexico of Alonso de Benavides, 1630.[6]

Lummis' conception of what constituted sound magazine policy did not go unquestioned. In October, 1899, the editor of *Capital*, a Los Angeles financial monthly, impelled by a rumor to the effect that the *Land of Sunshine* was a financial failure, set out to examine what he believed to be the cause of the magazine's alleged downfall. His diagnosis was that the *Land of Sunshine* was too faithful and too frequent a reflector of its editor's rather narrow and, to the average reader, somewhat peculiar interests. "If Lummis' admirable articles on Indians, Spanish history and California matter," he wrote, "were distributed among a half dozen eastern magazines, the arrangement would be excellent. But those articles served month after month in the one magazine constitute too much of a good thing, and a good thing too often administered."[7]

Lummis made what was for him a very mild rejoinder when he informed the editor of *Capital* that the *Land of Sunshine* was not a financial failure and that it was minding its own business which was simply to produce a journal fairly representative of western intelligence. In this aim Lummis was confident his magazine was succeeding because: "Every critical publication in the East respects it; every great library preserves and binds it. Our theory is that California would not really prefer a magazine the East would laugh at."[8]

Early in 1898 the scope of the journal was enlarged to include the entire West. However, the editor refused to be held to a

[3]Vol. XI (1899), June to Oct.

[4]Vol. XI (1899), Nov. to Dec.; XII (1900), Jan. to Feb.

[5]*Out West*, XVI-XVII (1902), Mar. to July.

[6]*Land of Sunshine*, XIII (1900), Oct. to Dec.; XIV (1901), Jan. to Mar.

[7]"Under the Library Lamp," *Capital*, XIV (1899), Oct., in clippings relating to Charles F. Lummis, Lummis collection.

[8]Ibid.

precise delimitation of West, resorting to the vague but characteristic definition: "Anything is West which is far enough away from the East to be Out from Under."[9]

Lummis did not always speak for his associates in his magazine. For example, in February, 1900, W. C. Patterson, president of the Land of Sunshine Company, inserted a statement in the publisher's department addressed to the readers of the magazine. In the statement he recognized the right of the editor to his own opinions and conceded Lummis' absolute sincerity, but he felt impelled to declare: "...personally my judgment and honest convictions are not in accord with the sentiments which for many months have appeared in the editorial columns of this journal, touching the acts of the present National Administration in relation to the late Spanish War, the Philippine War, and also upon the bugbear of 'Imperialism.' "

Patterson's statement demonstrated the free hand Lummis enjoyed in editorial matters; it also gave the editor an opportunity to expatiate on the aims and policies of the journal as he saw them. He began by asserting the obligation of every citizen to work for the good of the republic, each in his own way and according to his independent convictions and beliefs. He admitted that the magazine preferred the West because the West epitomized independence of action. He declared emphatically that the journal was not aimed at those who imagined that it "alienates friends for fun or indigestion; that it loves to lose money; that it is a vehicle for vanity or a refuge for failure — or that friends, enemies, 'policy', fear, favor, anonymous letters or signed ones, comfort or convenience or its own 'tired feeling' will be reckoned in whatever it may happen to deem its obligation." He affirmed that while many western periodicals had been born simply because no eastern periodical cared to relieve the promoter's itch for type, the *Land of Sunshine* was based on the faith that the West deserved something better, and that "what is too illiterate for the East is too illiterate for the West...." In concluding, the editor acknowledged the magazine's debt to its readers, many of whom he admitted might care little for

[9]"In the Lion's Den," *Out West*, XVI (1902), Jan., 60.

"orange crops, frontier stories, Indian policies, Western history, climate as a means of grace, or some other things the magazine cares much about," but who did care about Americanism.[10]

The editor's habit of summing up the magazine's progress every six months or so permitted him to reaffirm its objectives at regular intervals. Independence was frequently stressed as when Lummis characterized the *Land of Sunshine* as: "Exclusively Western in text, unswervingly American in spirit, intractably free and direct; 'entertaining if possible, valuable anyhow'; and afraid of nothing on earth but wrong and error and cowardly 'policy'—."[11]

The final and logical extension in the magazine's field came in January, 1902, with the adoption of the name "Out West." Under the new and broader title Lummis envisioned the projection of the journal's mission into the Pacific which he predicted would become the world's greatest highway with the West Coast serving as its American door.[12]

In connection with the change in name and scope the editor assured friends and enemies alike that the *Land of Sunshine* "has not sold out, tired out, gone out, nor changed its mind. It has simply grown up....The men who have made it will continue to make it under the new name; with more power to their elbow; with strong new men enlisted that agree with them; . . . Under the new form it will still be the magazine you have liked (or disliked) 'only more so.'"[13]

The editor went into some detail in explaining the motives behind the scrapping of the old name and the assumption of a new one. He claimed he had intended to change the name from the start, feeling that the title "Land of Sunshine" smacked about equally of Sunday school and immigration bureau, but that he feared to take the critical step of swapping names either early in his editorial career or later during the years of stress. Now, he was sure, was the time and he had looked for a name that was original, dignified, short, characteristic, significant,

[10]"In the Lion's Den," *Land of Sunshine*, XII (1900), Feb., 189-90.
[11]Ibid., XIII (1900), Nov., 367.
[12]Ibid., XV (1901), Oct., 265.
[13]Ibid., Dec., 470.

and a clear improvement on the name it was to supplant. "Out West," the editor felt met these criteria. However, the Springfield *Republican* wrote to Lummis advocating "Pacific Monthly" as being more consistent with the statements of the journal's ambitions and also as offering an interesting comparison and contrast to the *Atlantic Monthly*. Lummis, in a clever and able defense of his choice, asserted that "Pacific Monthly" was the first name he had thought of, years ago, and was the last he would adopt. He declined to challenge comparison and contrast with the *Atlantic Monthly*, for which he confessed he still retained much of his New England awe, pleading that it was not reasonable to compare any other magazine with it, least of all a "little Western magazine which is come to bring not peace but the sword; which stands not for culture in the easy chair but for what culture can be kept in a noble strife; fighting its own way and hewing a thoroughfare for some causes it believes in — not as academic dreams but as vital needs for better individual and national living." His magazine, he went on to say, could scarcely compete with the *Atlantic* in buying the work of famous authors, although he stoutly maintained that in its chosen field "Out West" could be quite as ready as the old, established eastern magazines to select the best of the material offered, to stimulate and encourage burgeoning talent in western literature and scholarship, and to "discourage dishonest work — and draw that definition quite as sharply."[14]

Not yet content to let the matter rest, the editor could not resist informing the *Republican* that on the West Coast the word Pacific was hardly unique. Somewhat facetiously he observed that there were "Pacific bakeries, steamships, hotels, dairies, railroads, saloons, churches, stables, Universities, streets, transfer companies, cigar-stands, corsets — by the ocean." He mentioned "floods of Pacific printing offices, bookstores, almanacs, periodicals; daily, weekly, monthly and occasional Pacifics; Pacifics religious, secular, christian science and osteopathic. There is," he concluded, "at least one Pacific Monthly at the present." On the other hand, the editor was satisfied that "Out West" covered

[14]Ibid., 471-72.

precisely what the magazine was intended to cover, saying in two plain words what it wanted to say and including in seven letters, instead of the old or suggested seventeen, half the continent and all that lay beyond.[15]

Amidst all the discussion of the magazine's intentions to represent the West from a literary and cultural standpoint the early promotional objective was not lost. The magazine devoted a varying but usually substantial fraction of its pages to detailed description of specific southwestern localities — counties, towns, beaches, parks, and the like. Many of these were in fact elaborate advertisements stressing such things as business and home-building opportunities, agricultural assets, and recreational and educational facilities. The preponderance of hotel owners, real estate agencies, and transportation companies among the advertisers gave the monthly a strong promotional flavor. Lummis himself was generous with editorial comment of the "booster" variety.

A survey of the objectives and policies of Lummis' magazine suggests several generalizations. In the first place, a well-defined extension of the journal's ambitions is evident, and this culminated in the determination to represent a somewhat amorphous region labeled the West which by extension embraced as much of the Pacific area as actively concerned the United States. Second, the journal was militant in its espousal of things western. It stood for California and the West against the East, even against the world. And, while in the magazine's ardent advocacy of the region there was much of genuine vigor and pride and independence, at the same time there was more than a hint of overcompensation employed perhaps to cloak a basic sense of inferiority. The editor's awe of the *Atlantic Monthly*, his insistence that much of the West's merit derived from the fact that it was being developed by easterners, and his repeated reliance on testimonials from the *Dial* and the *Nation* as bestowing the definitive accolade on his magazine help to support such an assertion. Third, although an over-all unity of purpose characterized the periodical, a distinct ambivalence in method pre-

[15]Ibid., 473.

vailed from the outset. On the one hand, the magazine sought to impress the East with its cultural competence by such means as the development of a literary school, reproduction of primary sources in western history, and emphasis on scientific and artistic activities in the West; on the other, it attempted to stimulate "desirable" immigration by detailing the practical and material advantages of western living. It need hardly be added that California, and more particularly southern California, came in for the major share of the emphasis under both types of promotion. Finally, the objectives of the journal faithfully reflected the opinions and enthusiasm of its editor, for it was this translation of a personality into type which early established the magazine's reputation for individuality.

The relations of Lummis and his magazine with other periodicals were on the whole routine. He had had, and continued to have, contact with a number of the eastern journals in the capacity of contributor as well as in the role of a fellow editor, and for the most part the contacts were pleasant. Nevertheless Lummis was quick to expose and deride any eastern publication which allowed inaccuracies relating to any phase of the West to be printed. Two journals, the *Nation* and the *Dial*, Lummis almost idolized, and he tossed many an editorial bouquet in their direction.

On the West Coast relations were not always so amicable. This was largely due to Lummis' antipathy toward the *Overland Monthly*, especially during the period of Rounseville Wildman's editorship. Antagonized in the beginning by the *Overland's* persistent claim to be "the only monthly magazine published West of the Rockies," matters were aggravated when Wildman criticized Stephen M. White and southern Californians for their position in the fight for a free Los Angeles harbor. The following comment at the time Wildman left the *Overland* indicates Lummis' feelings toward its editor: "The *Overland* will have to live down its wildman reputation, but there is one consolation. It cannot be worse than it was; therefore it should be better. And we hope it will."[16] Two years later Lummis accused

16"That Which Is Written," *Land of Sunshine*, VII (1897), Sept., 168.

the *Overland* of "stealing" the *Land of Sunshine's* subtitle for the *Overland's* November cover.

Throughout the period of the war with Spain and the United States venture into imperialism in the years immediately following, Lummis was on good terms with the few periodicals that cared to advocate anti-imperialism. Prominent among these was the San Francisco *Argonaut* whose independence Lummis frequently applauded. However, the editor saw fit to criticize the *Argonaut* a number of times for its anti-Catholic bias.[17] Contacts with other journals were sporadic and were occasioned ordinarily by a specific article or a particular stand on a controversial issue.

At the time of the founding of the *Land of Sunshine* the editorial and business offices were housed in three rooms in the Stimson building. The printing and binding were done by Kingsley-Barnes and Neuner Company located at 123 South Broadway. Kingsley and Barnes, printers in Los Angeles since 1889, and Neuner, founder of a bindery in 1887, had joined forces in 1894. Photoengraving work, the third important mechanical aspect of producing the magazine, was farmed out to various local firms. After four years of operation under this scheme the inconvenience of the physical separation of business offices from the mechanical department caused a consolidation of editorial and business offices at 121½ South Broadway. Here the magazine was in congenial surroundings, for within a block were the plants of the *Times, Herald, Express,* and *Cultivator.*[18]

Further improvement and extension of physical facilities occurred late in 1901 when departments concerned with the production of the magazine were rearranged and the plant was equipped to conduct a general publishing business as well. Six job presses and four cylinder presses permitted a wide variety of job printing in substantial quantity. The largest press was an Optimus cylinder installed especially for the rapid and clear printing of the illustrated pages of *Out West.*[19]

The arrangement described above prevailed until April, 1904,

[17]"In the Lion's Den," *Out West,* XIX (1903), Sept., 316-17.
[18]"The New Sunshine Offices," *Land of Sunshine,* XI (1899), Sept., 239.
[19]"Out West Co.," *Out West,* XX (1904), Jan., i-xi.

when the Out West Magazine Company was formed and the offices of publication once again became distinct from the production plant. The new offices of the magazine were installed at 207 New High Street and, although the Out West Company sold its interest in the magazine to the Out West Magazine Company, it continued to do the printing, binding, and engraving for the latter concern.[20] This plan of operation was maintained until after Lummis severed connection with the periodical.

The publishers of the *Land of Sunshine* employed a variety of techniques designed to lengthen the journal's subscription list. The magazine was displayed in the reading rooms of libraries, resorts, and chambers of commerce, and it was distributed for inspection and sale in local and overland passenger trains and on Pacific Coast steamers. News dealers were supplied with the journal through the American News Company of New York, the Western News Company of Chicago, the Colorado News Company of Denver, and the San Francisco News Company. During the first month of 1896 blueprint posters advertising the *Land of Sunshine* were displayed in Los Angeles. According to the editor these were the first magazine posters to appear in the city.[21] About this time a subscription campaign was launched in the territories of Arizona and New Mexico under the direction of G. H. Paine, who had already proved effective in the Los Angeles area. Reports in March that the *Land of Sunshine* already had more subscribers in Arizona than any other monthly were encouraging if vague.[22]

Meanwhile circulation was making steady gains. At the close of 1895 affidavits showed an average monthly increase of 600 over the first year and a half of the magazine's operation. The figure for December, 1895, was 9,000, which the publishers claimed was the largest certified regular circulation of any western monthly.[23] The magazine closed the year 1896 with an

[20]*Out West*, XX (1904), Apr., publisher's page.

[21]Lummis Journal, Jan. 3—16, 1896.

[22]*Land of Sunshine*, IV (1896), Mar., ad section.

[23]Ibid. (1895), Dec., publisher's page. Affidavits attesting to circulation usually referred to the number printed each month rather than indicating the number of bona fide subscribers.

edition of 12,000 which proved too small to meet demands. The minimum mark registered in that year was 8,000.[24]

By May, 1897, the campaign in the Southwest had progressed to New Mexico. Here an arrangement was made with the Democratic Publishing Company of Albuquerque whereby the publishers of the *Land of Sunshine* agreed to fulfill the unexpired portions of subscriptions to the *Southwest Illustrated Magazine* in exchange for the exclusive use of that journal's subscription books containing about five hundred names and addresses of bona fide subscribers.[25]

At home the magazine was offering two six-month scholarships in the Throop Polytechnic Institute of Pasadena amounting to fifty-five dollars each to the boy and girl sending in the largest list of subscribers to the *Land of Sunshine* before September, 1897, a date which was later extended to the end of the year.[26]

The editor liked to emphasize the fact that the secondary circulation of his magazine was larger than most journals due to the widespread interest in California and the West. In June, 1899, he estimated optimistically that the *Land of Sunshine* had approximately 50,000 readers on the basis that it was read by every member of most families and then frequently sent on to relatives and friends in other areas. This talking point was often used in soliciting advertisements. Actual average circulation for the year ending July, 1899, came to 9,147.[27]

Frequently a lengthy, heavily illustrated article on a particular community appeared in the promotional section of the magazine. For example, the *Land of Sunshine* for August to September, 1901, carried a feature article on Alameda. Instead of asking the community to bear the expense of publication, as was regular procedure for most promotional periodicals, the magazine absorbed the costs, asking only that as many of the

---

[24]Ibid., VI (1897), Jan., ad section. These were unsupported statements appearing in the magazine itself. Rowell's *American Newspaper Directory* records average circulation of the *Land of Sunshine* for 1896 as 8,708.

[25]Ibid. (1897), May, publisher's page.

[26]Ibid. (1897), Mar., publisher's page.

[27]*American Newspaper Directory* (1903).

people of Alameda who "appreciate good literary work" become subscribers.[28]

Small but steady gains in circulation were reflected in June, 1902, when the magazine doubled in price, and again the next year when advertising rates rose. By the close of 1903 circulation stood at 10,766,[29] and a year later it was estimated at 15,000.[30] However, after 1903, the newspaper directories were never provided with a satisfactory report of circulation from the publishers of *Out West*, and the symbol consistently accorded the magazine placed its circulation somewhere between 7,500 and 12,500. Apparently 1903 and 1904 were the years of maximum circulation.

Although circulation figures were never startling, the distribution of Lummis' magazine was national, even international, in scope. Examination of the *Out West* mailing list for January, 1907, indicates that the journal claimed subscribers in England, Belgium, Italy, Germany, Japan, France, Sweden, Brazil, New Zealand, Mexico, Greece, Siam, and North China. Next to California, circulation was heaviest in Arizona Territory, followed by New York State, Massachusetts, and New Mexico, in that order.[31]

The *Land of Sunshine* was organized as a corporation on August 8, 1895, with capital stock amounting to $10,000.[32] The company's first officers were: president, W. C. Patterson; vice-president, Charles F. Lummis; secretary, F. A. Pattee; treasurer, H. J. Fleishman. These men, plus Charles Cassat Davis, attorney, constituted the board of directors. Among its stockholders the magazine counted: F. W. Braun, wholesale druggist; S. H. Mott, secretary of the Los Angeles City Water Company; George H. Bonebrake, president of the Los Angeles National Bank; Cyrus M. Davis, president of Kingsley-Barnes and Neuner Company; C. D. Willard, general manager of the *Evening*

[28]Publisher's page.

[29]*American Newspaper Directory* (1907), p. 64.

[30]*American Newspaper Annual* (1905).

[31]Out West Mailing List, Jan., 1907, in possession of Mrs. Alice Van Boven, Redlands, California.

[32]Charles F. Lummis, "In the Lion's Den," *Land of Sunshine*, III (1895), Sept., 189.

Express; Andrew Mullen of Mullen and Bluett Clothing Company; E. E. Bostwick, comptroller of the Banker's Alliance of California; and F. K. Rule, auditor, treasurer, and secretary of the Los Angeles Terminal Railroad Company.[33]

With a good deal more financial backing than when Willard, Pattee, and Brook launched it, the magazine made its bid for financial independence. There were times when the future looked dark. The editor noted in his journal early in March, 1896, that the printer demanded $888 before proceeding with the March number. By March 7, however, the printer was satisfied and work on the magazine was resumed.[34] In May of the following year Willard wrote of the magazine as defunct, blaming "the bank panics, the strike on the railways, the failure of orange crops and the long continued depression" for the collapse of the periodical he had helped to found.[35] Such pessimism however was premature, and some six months later Willard noted that the *Land of Sunshine* had weathered its difficulties and was in excellent condition.[36] Assistance from two sources had prevented the magazine from going under. Some financial aid was forthcoming in December, 1897, in the form of a generous appropriation voted to the magazine by the Los Angeles County supervisors. The money was to pay for sending yearly subscriptions to eastern libraries and the act was hailed by the publishers as "not politics, but the intelligent use of the immigration fund with an idea of accomplishing the most good."[37] In the same month the journal's financial status was improved by the agreement of Captain E. Pryce Mitchell to invest $5,000 in the *Land of Sunshine*.[38] In the first month of the new year, 1898, Lummis announced that the magazine was self-supporting and out of debt.[39] Just a month later, reflecting increased prosperity and growing confidence, the Land of

[33]*Land of Sunshine*, III (1895), Nov., publisher's page.
[34]Lummis Journal, Mar. 1–14, 1896.
[35]Charles D. Willard to father, May 12, 1897, in Willard MSS.
[36]Ibid., Dec. 19, 1897.
[37]*Land of Sunshine*, VIII (1897), Dec., publisher's page.
[38]Lummis Journal, Dec. 6–12, 1897.
[39]"In the Lion's Den," *Land of Sunshine*, VIII (1898), Jan., 84.

Sunshine Company was reorganized and the capital stock increased to $50,000.[40] Under this new organization a syndicate of western writers was formed whose members received stock in the company instead of cash as payment for contributions to the magazine.[41] Thus was the burden of paying contributors at prevailing magazine rates circumvented.

The fortunes of the magazine continued to improve and by October, 1901, the editor was preparing to undertake the general expansion which occurred with the change of name to *Out West*. This step was taken only after Mrs. Phoebe A. Hearst promised to invest $500 a month in the venture for a year.[42] In a conversation with Mrs. Hearst in January, 1902, after the first number of *Out West* had appeared, Lummis admitted it would take $40,000 to "swing Out West," and Mrs. Hearst arranged a loan of $15,000 for 1902, and $25,000 the following year, with interest at seven per cent.[43] On January 19, 1902, the editor signed three notes of $5,000 each on Mrs. Hearst's loan to the magazine.[44] The Out West Company was incorporated in April, 1902, absorbing and succeeding the Land of Sunshine Publishing Company. Under the new organization Cyrus M. Davis became president; M. C. Neuner was secretary; and L. H. Carpenter was made treasurer. Charles F. Lummis remained vice-president and the new board of directors consisted of Davis, Lummis, Neuner, F. A. Pattee, Carpenter, R. W. Rogers, and C. A. Moody. The same month the editor announced that in the three months since the magazine became *Out West* its circulation had increased fifty per cent.[45] Two months later, on the date of publication of the June, 1902, number, the subscription price was raised to two dollars a year and the price of single copies rose to twenty cents. The price boost, it was explained, was simply business, since the publishers preferred not to sell their magazine below cost and they assumed that

[40]Lummis Journal, Feb. 15–28, 1898.
[41]F. W. Hodge, director, Southwest Museum, to writer, July 20, 1949.
[42]Lummis Journal, Oct. 11–17, 1901.
[43]Ibid., Jan. 3–16, 1902.
[44]Ibid., Jan. 17–24, 1902.
[45]"In the Lion's Den," *Out West*, XVI (1902), Apr., 418.

those who cared for the magazine would be willing to pay cost price.[46]

In 1903 the agreement of Mrs. Hearst to lend the magazine $25,000 was not fulfilled. In fact, early in the year, Mrs. Hearst wrote the editor that she could go no further in the financing of *Out West*.[47] After a personal conference with Mrs. Hearst, Lummis managed to negotiate a $10,000 loan, but there is no record of her supplying additional funds to the magazine.[48]

On January 27, 1904, Lummis and his journal withdrew from the Out West Company to form the Out West Magazine Company. The first meeting of the stockholders of the new company was held February 2, at the editor's home, and the following officers were elected: Charles F. Lummis, president; J. C. Perry, secretary and treasurer; and C. A. Moody, vice-president and general manager. In the announcement of the change two things were stressed: first, that the split was genuine and permanent, and second, that the parting of the ways was not caused by personal disagreements but was unanimously agreed upon as a prudent business step expected to redound to the benefit of all concerned.[49]

Despite this expectation of mutual advantage, the financial health of the Out West Magazine Company deteriorated. Less than a year after the break with the Out West Company, Lummis noted in his journal that Charles Amadon Moody, now assistant editor and general manager, was "in absolute despair of the magazine."[50] Five months later the company offered $5,000 of its own first mortgage coupon bonds for sale, the proceeds to be used as working capital. These bonds, issued in denominations of $100 and $1,000, carried interest at the rate of six per cent per annum, constituted a first lien on all the company's property, and were offered at par.[51] Despite this evidence of shaky financial underpinning the firm managed to remain intact for the duration of Lummis' editorship.

[46]*Out West*, XVI (1902), May, ad section.
[47]Lummis Journal, Jan. 3–16, 1903.
[48]Ibid., Feb. 1–17; 15–28, 1903.
[49]*Out West*, XX (1904), Apr., publisher's page.
[50]Feb. 15–28, 1905.
[51]*Out West*, XXIII (1905), July, ad section.

Lummis' venture was never conspicuously profitable, and the magazine's record of uninterrupted publication for some fourteen years was achieved through a combination of subsidies, personal loans, income from advertising and sales, and corporate reorganization.

Advertising provided substantial financial support to Lummis' magazine, and throughout the career of the journal a good deal of emphasis was placed on soliciting advertisements. In the early years testimonials were printed from time to time as evidence that advertising in the *Land of Sunshine* produced results, and some persuasive copy was written recounting the advantages to advertisers offered by a regional magazine. The following is a fair example:

If he [the advertiser] is a hotel manager or real estate dealer, he knows that the most effective medium he can choose is one unequivocally and intelligently devoted to his locality. If a merchant, he realizes that it is a business proposition to help maintain such a publication in its work of bringing permanent customers to his locality, and he certainly proposes to reach its readers already on the ground. Advertising broadly, intelligently and persistently the judicious advertiser reaps broad results. With him it pays not only today but tomorrow as well.[52]

The amount of advertising and the rate of circulation were positively correlated. There was a steady increase from an average of twenty-four pages of advertisements in 1895 to a peak of sixty-three pages in 1903, and then a gradual leveling off at an average of from forty-two to forty-eight pages after the peak year. The relationship between regional and national advertising followed an interesting pattern. In the early years advertising by nationally known firms was negligible. Thus it was a real triumph for Lummis' magazine when, in December, 1898, the Century Company inserted a generous advertisement for which it paid one hundred dollars.[53] By the peak year of 1903, however, the balance between pages of regional and national advertisements was even. The predominant position of the regional advertiser was re-established at a ratio of better than three to one by 1905.

[52]Vol. V (1896), Oct., publisher's page.
[53]Lummis Journal, Dec. 20–26, 1898.

Policy with reference to charges made for advertising is difficult to follow closely because throughout most of the magazine's
life its rates were not made public. However, comparison of a
card quoting advertising rates which prevailed when the magazine was known as the *Land of Sunshine* with the rates published,
for the first time, in the second number of *Out West*, show only
a slight variation and that more in the method of assessment
than in actual cost to advertisers. For three or more insertions
during a year the charge was twenty-five dollars per page. For
less than three annual insertions, thirty dollars per page was
charged. In cases of space less than four inches, the rate was two
dollars and ten cents an inch.[54] Reflecting increased circulation,
the rates went up somewhat in August, 1903. One page inserted
only once came to forty dollars; one page running six months,
thirty-six dollars a month; and one page left in the year around,
thirty-two dollars a month. The cost of small insertions was
computed on the basis of two dollars and sixty-five cents per
inch per issue or at twenty cents per agate line per issue. Preferred positions commanded forty dollars a page and covers
brought fifty dollars. Advertising forms closed from the fifth
to the fifteenth of the month preceding issue, and publication
occurred on the twenty-fifth of each month.[55] After June, 1905,
the magazine reverted to its traditional policy of furnishing
advertising rates only on request.

Although there can be no doubt that editor Lummis was the
dominant force behind the *Land of Sunshine* and *Out West*,
there were other persons who exercised varying degrees of influence on the magazine. Lummis made an early experiment in the
use of editorial assistants with the appointment of Grace Ellery
Channing, formerly of the editorial staff of *Youth's Companion*,
as associate editor in November, 1898.[56] The appointment was
short-lived for after just eleven months of service Mrs. Channing's name disappeared from the cover and with it went the
post of associate editor. A slight decrease in the incidence of

[54]*Out West*, XVIII (1903), Feb., publisher's page.

[55]Ibid., May, publisher's page.

[56]Charles F. Lummis, "In the Lion's Den," *Land of Sunshine*, IX (1898), Nov.,
310. Grace Ellery Channing was the granddaughter of William Ellery Channing, the well-known Unitarian minister.

feminine contributors immediately after her name left the cover would indicate that Mrs. Channing played a part in soliciting and obtaining contributions to the *Land of Sunshine*, but other than that her editorial influence on the magazine is scarcely discernible.

For a year, almost coincident with Grace Ellery Channing's term as associate editor, Margaret Collier Graham, a resident of South Pasadena and a writer of western short stories, conducted a two-page editorial department called "The Angle of Reflection." Here she wrote calm, reflective little essays with a restrained but unmistakable feminist tinge. These bits of gentle yet perceptive comment afford a refreshing counterpoise to the bristling, often extreme utterances of editor Lummis.

William E. Smythe, author of *The Conquest of Arid America*, dabbler in politics, and enthusiastic exponent of western irrigation, was associated with Lummis' magazine for two and a half years as head of an editorial section known as "The 20th Century West." Here, without interference by the editor, Smythe crusaded for reform of California water laws, participation in co-operative buying, and the launching of a program of public works in the sphere of irrigation.

Charles Amadon Moody came to southern California from Connecticut in 1900 largely as a result of reading the *Land of Sunshine*, and he was soon placed in charge of the subscription department by the business manager, Frank A. Pattee.[57] By October, 1901, Moody's initials had begun to appear after some of the book notes in the review section, "That Which Is Written." For a time Lummis and Moody divided the reviewing assignment and then gradually the latter assumed responsibility for the entire task. Moody was also serving an apprenticeship as contributor by writing an occasional biographical sketch, a promotional article, or a descriptive essay. On the magazine's masthead for February, 1903, Moody appeared as assistant editor, and by July, 1905, his name was bracketed with that of Lummis as joint editor. At this time Sharlot M. Hall, a consistent contributor to the journal from Arizona, and author of the dedicatory poem "Out West" for the first issue under that name,

[57]Lummis Journal, Jan. 3–16, 1900.

moved into the assistant editorship, rising to the rank of associate editor a year later. From mid-1905 on, Lummis' editorial influence waned steadily as he became increasingly absorbed in activities outside the magazine, often working as much as fifteen hours daily as head of the public library.[58] Consequently Sharlot Hall and Moody assumed dominant editorial roles although it is significant that they made no striking departure from the editorial pattern laid down by Lummis.

When Lummis assumed editorship of the *Land of Sunshine*, the problem of securing suitable contributions was acute, and for a time the new editor, with some assistance from Charles Dwight Willard, was obliged to write nearly all the copy for the magazine.[59] In issues to which he had contributed a disproportionate amount of the reading matter, Lummis, known locally at least as Don Carlos, resorted to such transparent pseudonyms as C. Arloz or C. R. Lohs. Even had the subterfuge been more subtle, the editor's individualistic style would have given him away.

Procurement of short stories posed the biggest problem, for, although many were submitted, few were worthy of consideration. Willard himself promised to write the story for every other issue but in six months he was compelled to produce four, one of which, "The Century Plant," was "decided on, plotted, written, corrected and entirely prepared for the printer in the short space of two hours —" and, Willard admitted, "was a flat failure — as it ought to be."[60] Willard wrote to his father of the failure to receive a story promised for the May, 1895, issue, making it necessary to work over a piece of seemingly impossible material already on hand. "It had nothing in it that was decent," he complained, "except a good description in clumsy English of a cloudburst on the desert.... I set to work to repair it — but finally flung it all away and wrote a cloudburst story to which the name of R. Harris is attached. Such is editorship in the far west."[61] Further evidence that the primary

[58]Ibid., Jan. 25–31, 1906.
[59]Charles D. Willard to father, May 19, 1895, in Willard MSS.
[60]Ibid.
[61]Ibid.

difficulty in the early years was more a question of quality than of quantity was supplied by the editor's claim that he received approximately 300 offerings a month.[62]

The magazine was limited in its capacity to attract contributors by the insistence of its editor on California or western themes, and by its inability to pay standard magazine rates. Lummis overcame the latter disadvantage to a considerable degree by enthusiastic and effective personal soliciting of material for his journal. As a writer of some reputation himself, his contacts in literary and artistic circles were substantial and he kept them in good repair, undoubtedly with an eye to the welfare of his magazine. For local writers the journal provided a natural and convenient outlet, but this group, although it supplied a number of faithful contributors, was never large.

Late in 1897 Lummis devised a plan designed to recruit contributors and to encourage writers of California and the West to take advantage of the wealth of inspiration resident in their own environment. To this end he organized a syndicate of established writers, most of them westerners, who agreed to use the *Land of Sunshine* as an outlet for writings produced with western themes. Members of this literary combine were to be attached to the magazine in the dual capacity of contributors and stockholders. In lieu of cash payments those who agreed to join the group were to be furnished stock certificates. Although proposed as a business measure, it is probable that few of those who joined expected a return on their stock. No dividends were ever paid on the shares which bore a face value of one hundred dollars, and it is the belief of one of the former members of the league that "the only stock in the magazine ever sold was purchased by those who wished to help the project, rather than in the expectation of receiving a profit on the 'investment.' "[63] Lummis made his chief appeal on grounds of regional allegiance, urging that by concerted action the West could match the East in excellence of its literary product. The plan was shrewdly calculated to obtain work of relatively high caliber over an indefi-

[62]"That Which Is Written," *Land of Sunshine*, VI (1897), May, 259.
[63]F. W. Hodge to writer, July 20, 1949.

nite period of time and at a financial outlay within the resources of the magazine, as well as to contribute substantially to the journal's prestige by providing an impressive array of the names of western writers and artists for the masthead. No conditions were laid down as regards the submission of offerings of any special number or length.

The editor began to work in earnest on the project late in 1897, and he achieved gratifying results. In December letters from George Parker Winship and Frederick Webb Hodge indicated willingness to join the league.[64] In January, 1898, Lummis journeyed to San Francisco to hunt for recruits. By the time he left for home, February 12, 1898, he had bagged artists Maynard Dixon and William Keith; poets Ina Coolbrith and Edwin Markham; historian Theodore H. Hittell; and educator and scientist David Starr Jordan.[65] In the next few months the masthead lengthened to include names such as Ella Higginson, John Vance Cheney, head of the Newberry Library in Chicago, Charles Warren Stoddard, George Hamlin Fitch, Dr. Washington Matthews, Charles and Louise Keeler, Charlotte Perkins Stetson, Joaquin Miller, and Elliot Coues. Frank Norris, Ambrose Bierce, and Jack London were names conspicuous by their absence. Latecomers to the alliance were Eugene Manlove Rhodes, Sharlot M. Hall, and Mary Austin. Thus the magazine drew from two pools of talent: one made up of more or less regular contributors, usually known only locally; the other consisting of relatively renowned authors, poets, authorities in western history and archaeology, and western artists and illustrators.

In output editor Lummis was by far the leading contributor with over two hundred and fifty poems, stories, articles, and essays to his credit exclusive of his editorial writing and his book reviewing. William E. Smythe, a poor second, followed with some forty-eight items, most of them in connection with his department "20th Century West." Third, with forty-two titles, was Sharlot M. Hall of Arizona who specialized in poetry and

[64]Lummis Journal, Dec. 20–26, 1897. George Parker Winship, specialist in the history of the Southwest, was an authority on the Coronado expedition of 1542.

[65]Ibid., Jan. 17–24, 25–31; Feb. 1–7, 8–14, 1898.

articles on Southwest topics. Julia Boynton Green was fourth with twenty-three entries. After these four, single contributors could rarely claim over eighteen items.

The *Land of Sunshine* for February, 1896, is a fair example of the magazine in its early period. The frontispiece was a photograph of a part of the Mission San Juan Capistrano showing a general state of decay over the caption "How Our Landmarks Are Going." The leading article by Charles Dudley Warner, "Race and Climate," was a speculative essay on the effect of the southern California climate upon the Anglo-Saxon inhabitants. Warner predicted that the semitropical environment would mellow and restrain the restless energy of the Yankee without undermining his moral fibre or sapping his vitality. This was followed by the editor's illustrated article on "Brother Burro," in which Lummis acknowledged the key position of the animal in early southwestern transportation, and protested the stigma of stupidity attributed to the burro, claiming that asininity is a purely human trait. An article, somewhat patronizing in tone, by Mrs. J. Torrey Connor, a Los Angeles writer, concentrated on the unique and romantic aspects of life in the city's Chinese quarter. J. W. Wood of Pasadena contributed a poem descriptive of serape weaving. Bearing out the theme suggested by the frontispiece was an article describing the deterioration of southern California missions and referring to the work of the Landmarks Club as outlined on another page. Photographs of Pasadena's Tournament of Roses, New Year's Day, 1896, occupied another page. H. N. Rust of Pasadena submitted an impressively illustrated account of a two-day trip to the petrified forests of Arizona. "The Cloud Play," a short descriptive poem, was contributed by Jeanie Peet of Harold, California. "Architecture for the Southwest," by Arthur Burnett Benton, secretary of the southern California chapter of the American Institute of Architects, pleaded for the exercise of taste in southwestern design. Benton especially commended the use of mission style and adobe-type construction in brick and stucco, and he endorsed the more frequent use of the patio and roof garden. The only short story in the number was "Under the Copper Sky" by Lillian Corbett Barnes. It was a tragic little tale of death by thirst of a prospector's wife on the Mojave Desert. This was followed by a number of recipes for making Mexican candy by Linda Bell Colson of San Diego, and a short note on the "California Road-Runner" by Bertha F. Herrick of Oakland. Regular features included the page on the Landmarks Club, the editorial section "In the Lion's Den," and the book review section "That Which Is Written," in this instance featuring reviews of Owen Wister's collection of short stories, *Red Men and White,* and George Bird Grinnell's *Story of the Indian.* The number closed with a promotional piece by George S. Wright, "San Buenaventura," which described the picturesque features of the town and catalogued some of its material assets. The number was composed of nine articles, two poems, and a short story. It had thirty-three illustrations. Every offering had a California or southwestern setting and every contributor wrote from somewhere in California, except Charles Dudley Warner of Hartford, Connecticut.

By February, 1903, *Out West* was in its prime. The first article in the magazine for that month was chapter nine of "The Right Hand of the Continent," Lummis' informal and personalized history of California. In this chapter the editor measured some of the material resources of the state, natural and developed, against the unprophetic words spoken in the United States Senate relating to the "vast, worthless area" of the West Coast. "Here Was a Woman," by Charles Amadon Moody, assistant editor, was a eulogistic sketch of Jessie Benton Frémont, stressing her influence on her husband and the significance of both of them to the West. This was followed by the reprinting of three poems on John C. Frémont by Joaquin Miller, Lummis, and John Greenleaf Whittier. Eugene Manlove Rhodes of Tularosa, New Mexico, used his short story "Loved I Not Honor More" as a vehicle to express disapproval of Britain's prosecution of the Boer War. More impressive than the rather inconclusive plot is Rhodes's skillful and realistic handling of the western idiom. Hartley Burr Alexander, philosopher and student of the American Indian, in a poem "To a Child's Moccasin," narrated the death of an Indian mother and her child at the Battle of Wounded Knee. The crushing disillusionment of a convent-raised, half-breed girl who came home to a small town in Canada to find her Indian mother dead and her father lost to liquor, formed the tragic theme of a short story by Constance Lindsay Skinner. Another short story by Clarence Alan McGrew related an episode of outlawry in the Fraser River gold fields. A short poem, "To Californiana," by Lorenzo Sosso completed the belletristic offerings of this number.

In the documentary section the voyage of Sir Thomas Cavendish to the California coast in 1587 was reconstructed from contemporary English accounts. The editor tied various quotations together with a running commentary, but the material was not footnoted to give specific sources. Lummis also published an early version of the famous Argonaut song, "The Days of Forty-Nine." In the pages devoted to the Sequoya League the editor made some pointed remarks about government red tape in achieving the removal of the Mission Indians from their home at Warner's Ranch in San Diego County. The editorial section was devoted to a plea that statehood be granted the territories of Arizona and New Mexico. In the book review section Charles A. Moody paid tribute to Frank Norris, expressing deep regret that the author's death prevented the completion of his trilogy on wheat.

In "20th Century West" William E. Smythe led off with an editorial on the "Ethics of Irrigation" in which he made a persuasive plea for the joining of land and water ownership so as to rid California and other arid and semi-arid regions of the water monopolist. Smythe stood for a large program of public irrigation works constructed by state or nation, or by both in co-operation, in order to achieve justice in the use of water. In the same department an essay, "True Source of Water Supply," by Samuel Armor, president of the Santa Ana Valley Irrigation Company, combatted the widely accepted theory that water used for irrigation upon the upper course of a stream very largely returns to the channel and may be used again. Although Smythe did not agree with this thesis, he published the paper gladly, for it was his policy to open the pages of his department to dissent. A little farther along in the magazine the progress of the California Constructive League, a body formed to achieve political action on state economic issues, was noted.

Two promotional articles, one by C. H. Bigelow, "San Dimas,

La Verne and Charter Oak," the other, "Oakland," by Charles J. Woodbury, completed the number for February, 1903.

All six articles were contributed by Californians and were on California topics. All but one of the five poems had California themes and that one had a western locale. The three short stories had western settings, and of the three, two were written by Californians and one by a New Mexican. In the sphere of western history were the lyrics of "The Days of Forty-Nine," and the narrative of the voyage of Cavendish, both edited by Lummis. Illustrations totaled eighty-nine.

Out West had passed its peak by May, 1907, and although Lummis was listed as editor along with Charles A. Moody, the little time he was able to devote to the magazine was largely in the capacity of contributor rather than editor. In this issue Lummis began with an article on the projected Southwest Museum which described the site, defined the project's scope, outlined the ideals and standards which would govern the museum's operation, and detailed its business methods. The three poems appearing in this issue offered an interesting contrast. "Life's Rose," by Alice Rollit Coe, was a delicate love lyric in five stanzas of three rhymed couplets each. Eunice Ward's "The Sunset Gun" was more conventional and tailored to youthful taste, speaking of the calling in of boats, birds, and small children by the sunset gun. The third piece of poetry was Robinson Jeffers' "Death Valley." Like most of this poet's early poems, there was a rhyme scheme, although it was somewhat erratic. The content and mood were definitely Jeffersian for the poem spoke simply and starkly of the ironic exchange of life for gold on the desert. With the aid of an interpreter, Sharlot Hall transcribed the events recorded on a Pima record rod. In "The Raven of Capistrano," Constance Goddard DuBois presented the first installment of a serial woven around the Mission Indians. The only other piece of fiction was an affected, sentimental short story of love on a California ranch. Virginia Garland contributed an effusive nature essay entitled "Maying," followed by "Some Leaves from a California Calendar" in the same vein by Ethel Griffith. Distinctly practical in tone was Richard Von Heine's "Olives and Olive Oil."

An editorial by William E. Smythe calling for responsible municipal and state government for California foreshadowed the Lincoln-Roosevelt League by insisting that the surest way to defeat the Southern Pacific "machine" was to form a non-partisan group within the state. Editor Lummis held forth on graft in San Francisco and the tragic flood of bad or mediocre books. Finally, National City and Covina came in for treatment in the booster section of the journal.

The breakdown of contents for this month yielded six articles, three poems, two stories, two descriptive essays, and thirty-eight illustrations. Only one of the contributors, Constance Goddard DuBois of Connecticut, was a non-westerner, and all contributions but the poem "Life's Rose" claimed a western setting.

This surface analysis of three issues of Lummis' magazine reveals a noteworthy fidelity in subject matter to the expressed objectives and scope of the monthly, and indicates as well that the arrangement of its contents never varied radically.

Chapter **IV** THE LION IN HIS DEN

ITH THE COMING OF Charles F. Lummis, January, 1895, the *Land of Sunshine* gained an editor who had a mind decidedly his own and cared not at all who knew it. For nearly ten years he unburdened himself with vigor, candor, and courage on such disparate topics as anti-imperialism, simplified spelling, statehood for Arizona and New Mexico, minority rights, California's climate, academic freedom, and free silver. During these years his editorial writings reflected a colorful personality, refreshing in its independence and compelling in its expression.

Lummis had barely settled himself in the editor's chair when he shed the routine publisher's page and inaugurated a full-fledged editorial section appearing beneath the cut of a nonchalant mountain lion and labeled "In the Lion's Den." There are two obvious possible sources of the caption: one, the biblical adventure of Daniel; the other, the reference to bearding the lion in his den in Scott's *Marmion*, which probably has a deeper origin in folklore. Of the two, the latter allusion in which the emphasis is on the lion seems the more likely.

That Lummis had lions on his mind is evidenced by an article he wrote just prior to the adoption of the new editorial department called "The California Lion." Here, in a brief but enthusiastic sketch of its range and characteristics, he bestowed high praise upon the cougar, closing with slanderous comment on the bear, registering disgust that such a "grub-digging, berry-picking, bee-robbing, carrion-contented duffer" should have been chosen to represent California over the sleek and graceful mountain lion.[1] At any rate, within the Den, Lummis became the "Lion," and the "Lion" he remained as long as he was associated with the magazine.

[1]*Land of Sunshine*, II (1895), Apr., 81.

At first Lummis confined himself to three pages of editorial comment, and in the early years the Lion's Den was characterized by an epigrammatic tone, with a line or two of bold-face type in the outside margin furnishing a terse and frequently cryptic guide to each paragraph. As the magazine grew older, Lummis expanded his editorial section to average seven pages. His remarks on individual topics lengthened and sometimes he devoted the entire space to a single item. This was apt to happen when he became involved in controversy.

Above the Lion's Den in March, 1901, appeared a slogan which attempted to compress the editor's credo to a phrase: "To love what is true, to hate shams, to fear nothing without, and to think a little." Close to eight hundred pages issued from out the Den, a productive record rendered more impressive by the fact that the editor frequently contributed full-length articles to his and other magazines, wrote copy for several monthly departments, and for six years conducted a book review section in the *Land of Sunshine*.

When the editorial section is viewed in over-all perspective, certain trends emerge. Lummis spilled more ink in the condemnation of imperialism than in the discussion of any other single theme. Scarcely a month passed between 1896 and 1904 in which this issue was not examined. It dominated discussion of national affairs, and comment on the international plane in any other connection was negligible. Throughout the first five years extravagant homage was paid to California, but after 1900 direct booster comment dwindled rapidly into insignificance. This was in line with Lummis' desire to throw off the chamber-of-commerce stigma resident in the magazine's origin. In the Den after 1902, literary comment suffered a decline, largely because the Lion reserved it for another department of his magazine. Late in the period of his editorship the Den was often given over to controversy generated by Lummis' efforts to combat ignorance and error wherever he met them. Appearing with more or less regularity were: comment on local, state, or regional levels; appraisals of individuals; social criticism; and self-comment.

Editor Lummis exercised considerable ingenuity in discovering ways to boost California and the West, but most often he extolled the climate. This lyrical passage is a fair example of the Lion's promotional prose:

If spring is a green awakening, if it is a triumphal entry of birds and flowers, and hope quickened—then we have not one spring but two. With the first impregning rains of what (for want of a fitter word) we call winter, the brown, wild earth conceives her infinite brood of verdure and of flowers. Ten thousand square miles wear such a carpet of bloom as the "fertile" East never saw in its floweriest day. All through the brown summer our lawns, our gardens, our evergreen trees have kept their richness; and now the virgin lands surpass them. November and December are the first California spring.

But with April (or the frayed ends of March) the rose pink of more peach trees than are in all Maryland flushes across a thousand orchards, and a fainter apple-bloom along the foothill ranches; and upon a thousand slopes glows the halo of apricot and almond (a pure glory no Easterner can imagine); and even the dark orange-trees turn on a sudden frosty with their perfumed bloom; and the noble syca-mores prick into leaf, and slender alders are transformed from naked grace to graceful umbrage.

The only reason why an unmoved Easterner might not deem this spring is that (never having seen so fair a spring) he might take it to be heaven. And the reason why this and like matters have place in this den is that the Lion honestly believes that the best Americans should do themselves the kindness to foregather in the only portion of the United States where Gold is not hostile.[2]

Lummis rarely overlooked an opportunity to criticize eastern and midwestern weather. Returning from what he termed a pilgrimage of penance to the East, he claimed over one hundred people were killed by sunstroke in the cities he visited; and in an unflattering description of Chicago in winter he commented pityingly on the number of "red noses, watery eyes and telegraphic teeth."[3]

He chided President Eliot of Harvard for claiming that the New England climate was one of the best in the world for brain-workers. Lummis contended that "the best brain work in New England is that leading its employer to seek a climate where his brain has a better chance to preserve the tenement

[2]"In the Lion's Den," *Land of Sunshine*, VI (1897), May, 256-57.
[3]"In the Lion's Den," *Out West*, XVI (1902), Jan., 65.

in which it works."[4] "Mr. Eliot," observed the Lion, "never quite escapes the Puritan conviction that whom the Lord loveth He giveth pneumonia."

To easterners reluctant to part with their white Christmas Lummis countered: "California is in truth the Christmas country. Why there is enough mistletoe growing upon the sycamores of one of her canyons to make every girl in New England kissable....In California children live and laugh in the very sort of air the Prince of Peace was born into....Fancy the fate of a babe in a manger in Boston on the 25th of December!"[5]

Any attempt to impugn California's fair name drew forth an immediate rumble from the Den. In reply to the Hartford *Courant*, whose editor boasted of Connecticut Octobers and decried the monotony of California's climate, Lummis wrote: "It [Connecticut] is a pleasant place for people who are content to live one month in twelve — it generally has a fair October. ...But it would be just as intelligent to claim that Hartford is the largest city in the world as to claim it has a good climate." As to the horrors of monotonous climate, he asked the *Courant* writer "how the deuce is he going to get along in heaven, unless he can introduce death, dishonesty and toothache, to break the cursed monotony of eternal peace and joy?"[6]

The earthquake and fire in San Francisco were the sole topic of the Den in May, 1906. Lummis' treatment of the disaster is interesting chiefly because, through the exercise of some promotional prestidigitation involving national and international disaster statistics, he nearly succeeded in transforming the story of California's greatest catastrophe into a booster piece.

Although the Lion was certainly not above stretching the truth, his claims for California's climate are generally clever enough to mitigate their overstatement. However, when he deserted climate for history, there were times when his enthusiasm betrayed him into extreme judgments, as in this passage written in connection with the celebration of California's Admission Day:

[4]"In the Lion's Den," *Land of Sunshine*, X (1899), Mar., 207.
[5]Ibid., IX (1898), Dec., 36.
[6]Ibid., VII (1897), Dec., 28.

If the East were as familiar as it might be with its own history, September 9 would be a national holiday, for no other one act of Congress has done so much for the Union as the admission of California to free sisterhood.

In the first place, it saved the Union. There were 15 Free States and 15 Slave States; and California gave the North a majority in the Senate. It was the death knell of slavery. Financially, it set the Union up in business, invented sound money and up to date has produced the greater part of all the nation ever handled. Geographically, it has doubled the nation in area, for it directly caused all the States between the Mississippi and the Pacific. It taught the country big railroad-building, big mining, big steam-boating and the noblest clipper ships in history.[7]

It would be a mistake to assume that Lummis had lost respect for easterners. He was convinced that the high percentage of New England immigrants had much to do with California's progress. He made it clear that his remarks were meant for a limited audience or, as he put it: "All we care for is the respectable minority that know enough to prefer Eden to an icehouse and can afford to swear off freezing."[8]

The editor's promotional writings will scarcely withstand close scrutiny. Repetitious, wordy, fraught with overstatement, and marred by a tendency to distort and misinterpret facts, they have little to recommend them save genuine enthusiasm, a more than occasional cleverly turned phrase, and a brashness which may amuse if it does not irritate.

Since *Out West* was a magazine of locality, editorial remarks on the local, state, and regional scenes appeared with regularity. Reflecting as they did the interests of the editor, the topics discussed generally had a historical, social, or cultural significance and those which received repeated attention sometimes evolved into small-scale crusades.

Lummis carried on a running fight in his columns to prevent the loss or disfigurement of California place names. He complained of a tendency to fuse article and noun in Spanish names such as Elcajon, Eltoro, and Delmar; or to join two words as Dospalos or Lomalinda. Also abbreviations such as Ventura,

[7]Ibid., XIII (1900), Aug., 182.
[8]Ibid., X (1899), Feb., 149.

Fernando, Frisco, and San Berdoo enraged the Lion. He found the Post Office Department and the railroads to be the most flagrant offenders and his campaign focused upon them. He insisted that such matters were not insignificant. "Shallow disrespect for history is never a trifle," he warned.[9] Lummis also argued that La Jolla must be spelled with a "y" and he printed the following jingle in an attempt to correct the pronunciation of Los Angeles:

> The Lady would remind you please,
> Her name is not Lost Angie-Lees.
> Nor Angie anything whatever.
> She hopes her friends will be so clever
> To share her fit historic pride.
> The G shall not be jellified.
> O long, G hard, and rhyme with yes
> And all about Loce Ang—el—ess.[10]

Some positive action was taken by the War and Post Office departments in restoring place names, and the Southern Pacific Railroad circulated a pamphlet pleading for the retention of historic California labels, but Lummis fought a losing fight in instances such as Ventura, La Jolla, and Los Angeles.

When the question of statehood for the territories of New Mexico and Arizona arose in 1903, the Den was turned over to the controversy. Lummis set out to examine and refute the arguments of the opposition led by Senator Albert J. Beveridge of Indiana. The Lion refused to admit that the status of territorial politics had any bearing on the question. The point is, he said, that the territories have a right to the privilege of self-government whether it proves to be good, bad, or indifferent. Indiana, the Lion was sure, would be better governed from Washington too, and, in passing, he wondered if Beveridge, a Republican, was not in favor of compelling more population before admittance because the territories "are not lined up for his Party."[11] By a comparison of populations in Arizona and New Mexico with the figures in other territories just prior to state-

[9]"In the Lion's Den," *Out West*, XX (1904), June, 569.

[10]Ibid., XXVIII (1908), June, 514. The people of Los Angeles were debating the pronunciation of their city's name forty-four years later.

[11]Ibid., XVIII (1903), Feb., 219.

hood, Lummis invalidated Beveridge's insufficient population argument. In meeting the objection to the large Spanish-speaking element in the Southwest, Lummis reminded Beveridge of the senator's championship of an imperialism which favored "gobbling 10 million *other* people who cannot talk English."[12] The editor cited sheep, cattle, mining, and increases in agricultural output through irrigation as furnishing adequate means of financial support for the territories. He agreed that the territories would suffer somewhat by statehood at the outset but he urged, "the way to learn to walk is to Walk," and there Lummis rested his case.[13]

The next month, however, March, 1903, the Lion conceded the defeat of the statehood bill, but he proceeded to score the opposition for ignorance and intolerance. This was followed by a plea for realization that the cause of New Mexico and Arizona was the cause of California and all the West. "If they [the territories]," he wrote, "need Statehood in fulfillment of their American rights, we no less need the strengthening of Western influence in Congress."[14] The editor reminded the nation of advantages it had derived from the West, especially from California, and pointed out that prosperity of the West meant, in an extraordinary degree, prosperity of the nation. "For both," he continued, "we need more weight of the out-door, traveled, untimorous, non-parasitic, tolerant West in Washington."[15]

Continuing the post-mortem on the defeat of the statehood bill, the Lion pointed to the failing of the congressional committee which had investigated the eligibility of the two territories for statehood: "In the first place we decide that strangers are wrong *ex officio;* and when we condescend to make investigation in a senatorial junket with eyebrows and nose up, we do it condescendingly. But no people were ever discovered from above. We know people only by seeing them face to face, level-eyed; and if the congressional committee could have had the good fortune to be so constituted, and so educated, and so

[12]Ibid., 223.
[13]Ibid., 227.
[14]Ibid. (1903), Mar., 370.
[15]Ibid., 372.

piloted, as to meet the people of the Territories on an equality, doubtless a glimmering of this eternal truth would have reached them."[16]

In 1905 the contest was renewed. This time the issue was the plan proposed for joint statehood of Arizona and New Mexico. The editor derided the efforts of Beveridge and others to force New Mexico into unwilling wedlock and he noted the unwieldiness of joint statehood even had resentment not been running high in both territories. The overwhelming opposition of Arizona, expressed by ballot in 1906, convinced Congress of the inadvisability of joint statehood. This time the Lion's side had won.

Paradoxically, in a magazine dedicated to California and the West, its editor devoted more than half his editorial space to commentary on the national and international scene. The explanation lies in Lummis' adamant anti-imperialism.

The Lion began his protest in 1896, not long after the Cuban revolution, and at a time when opposition to war with Spain meant bucking a revived spirit of manifest destiny maintained at a high pitch by the popular press. This protest took a variety of forms. Lummis condemned the peddling of atrocity stories by misinformed and irresponsible correspondents; he fumed at Congress for encouraging the Cuban patriots and accused that body of pressing for war with Spain to put Cleveland "in the hole"; he railed at the rebel government for hiding in New York; he flayed Henry Cabot Lodge and other supporters of Hawaiian annexation; and he damned the warmongering journals like the New York *World* and the *Journal* for their dissemination of "wanton lies."[17] Stubbornly, in the face of nationwide enthusiasm for action, he insisted that the United States would not go to war. In May, 1898, he wrote:

When the real People of the United States want war—when American women begin to rise up all over the land (the truest patriots of us all, and the bravest) to send their sons and brothers and lovers forth with their godspeed; when the decent pulpit cries to the God of Israel to witness the justice of our cause; when the bravest and best of our

[16]Ibid. (1903), Apr., 504.
[17]"In the Lion's Den," *Land of Sunshine*, VIII (1898), Apr., 234.

business men begin to close their business that they may enlist—why, then the Lion will be for war. But he has not seen any of these things yet. All he has discovered is some newspapers and politicians, generous but emotional people willing to have somebody else get out and fight.[18]

When war came the Lion accepted it with good grace but he urged that reason not be discarded:

War it is, and that shuts all doors but one. . . . We should strike as hard, as fast and as honorably as free men can strike; we should work off in brave deeds our old race hatreds and lay them down when the war is done. . . . And last, but not least, we must come out clean as we shall come out victorious. The Lion knows that designing men had much to gain; but he knows that the American people are backing up this war now out of humane and generous beliefs. The world will watch to see if our war is really for humanity, or if it results at last in our financial gain. Let us prove that we can be true to our ideals.[19]

The editor commented briefly on the loss of eleven subscribers on account of the magazine's war views, expressing sorrow that there were so many Americans as that who did not like free thought and free speech.[20]

While the war lasted the Lion applauded bravery on both sides and decried the prevalent anti-Spanish prejudice. Particularly abhorrent to him were those who would scuttle Spanish place names in California. "Of course," he sneered, "these are people too cowardly to go out and fight Spanish soldiers—the Spanish dictionary is a foe more to their liking. . . .They should get out of America altogether; for it was discovered by the Spanish."[21]

In September, 1898, Lummis noted happily the end of the war and remarked with heavy sarcasm, "the army and navy of course did their humble part as instruments, but we have official assurance that God gave us the war. The Spaniards were praying too; but it is notorious that the creator of the Universe understands no language but English."[22]

Noting the proximity of McKinley's ear to the ground, the Lion wrote: "Abraham Lincoln, the greatest president this

[18]Ibid., May, 277.   [19]Ibid., IX (1898), June, 29.   [20]Ibid., 31.
[21]Ibid., Aug., 140.   [22]Ibid., Sept., 198.

country has ever had; the greatest American—conducted an infinitely greater war not by asking the people what they wanted but by asking his conscience and his God what was right. That is the difference between re-election and immortality."[23]

With the signing of the Treaty of Paris in December, 1898, the prospect of annexation of the Philippines became imminent, reducing the appetite of many Americans for imperialism. After the ratification of the treaty in February, 1899, the Lion became increasingly bitter toward President McKinley, as this passage indicates:

In all the providence of God, the first man that ever defined "Benevolent Assimilation" as the driving of seven or eight hundred naked savages into a river and shooting them down there is William McKinley, President of the United States of America, Asia and the Isles of the Sea.

It is hard to realize that the President of one's country (and incidentally of one's party) can be vacillating and weak; that he can deceive himself with specious cant about our national "duty" to break our pledges to God and man and dishonor the memory of our fathers; that he can so pawn his common sense to an epidemic as to wish to sell our national birthright for a mess of Imperial pottage. . . . But those are the things this reluctant beast has had forced down his throat by the President's own hand.[24]

Lummis objected to United States policy in the Philippines on several counts. His basic complaint was that the imposition of government on an unwilling people was both immoral and unconstitutional. Second, his humanitarian instincts were outraged by the methods employed in subduing the natives. Third, he objected on economic grounds, claiming that the cost of garrisoning the islands would exceed what they would bring the United States, and also that the cheap products of Hawaii, Puerto Rico, and the Philippines would compete with California products.[25] Fourth, he claimed that a nation unable to handle its own problems could hardly afford to assume new obligations by the absorption of alien peoples.

The Lion's hatred for imperialism turned him temporarily

[23]Ibid., Oct., 256.   [24]Ibid., X (1899), Mar., 206-208.
[25]Ibid., XII (1900), Feb., 193.

away from the Republican party and in October, 1900, he endorsed Bryan, reasoning that the only way to reform a party was to defeat it temporarily. He repeatedly insisted that the sole issue of the election was republic versus empire, and he campaigned strenuously for the repudiation of empire. After McKinley's victory Lummis combined a partial change of heart with some rapid rationalization, claiming there need be no further fear of free silver and Bryan, and observing that the election did not commit the nation to imperialism since no election can nullify the Decalogue.[26]

With Theodore Roosevelt in the White House and Leonard Wood serving as governor general in Cuba, the cutting edge of Lummis' anti-imperialism was blunted. Both men were Lummis' personal friends and both had his sincere admiration. Thus, when the flag was hauled down in Cuba and when the President promised that the Filipinos should have their independence as soon as they proved themselves fit for it, the Lion subsided perceptibly. However, the United States action in Panama, which Lummis labeled "a Caesarian recognition of a 'Republic' before it was delivered," was more than he could countenance. By such action, he contended, the United States forfeited the power she wielded as spokesman for the equal rights of man. His strenuous effort to reconcile his belief in the President with what had occurred in Panama is worth quoting:

If no one else on earth cares to protest against the forgetting of fair play and against our recognition of a Graft Republic, the Lion is content to be one. And if none of the entitled and habituate can put up a petition in this behalf to whatever God may be, this unaccustomed beast will make some stagger to Pray that either the Man he believes in may See Better, or that the public sentiment he has led so nobly and so far may now take its turn at the noserope and fetch *him* where he Belongs. For he is one who Belongs on the side of the Right.[27]

Although Lummis' stand on the moral issues involved in the Panama affair was sound, he proved a most unreliable prophet when he wrote: "...but if in 20 years from now American genius shall have opened and maintained the Panama canal and

[26]Ibid., Dec., 449.
[27]"In the Lion's Den," *Out West*, XIX (1903), Dec., 675-78.

realized one per cent on the investment, the Lion will be glad to pull his own teeth at the first doorknob, and beg pardon of the Prophets."[28]

In his last important observation on United States imperialism, Lummis reproachfully examined the moral consequence of American policy in Panama:

If Civilization is nothing but increased opportunity for the trader to Make Money, for the strong to take from the weak, then perhaps the first day on which the canal could be opened would be the chief question. But if Civilization has some little meaning to enable people to Live Better by practicing the rules of honor that obtain between man and man; if it means Right, not Might; if it means that every man and every nation, big or little, rich or poor, shall have justice—if Civilization means these things, the Panama business is a serious setback. The "interests" of any decent Civilization can never be advanced by violating its principles.[29]

If the Lion needed to demonstrate his independence, he had certainly done so through his consistent opposition to imperialist expansion, beginning with his refusal to sanction the "splendid little war" with Spain.

Lummis' generous attention to the issue of imperialism left relatively little room for other comment on the national scene, and, generally speaking, such comment can scarcely be termed penetrating. For example, he made only casual and occasional reference to tariff policy and then only to complain of something like the tax on tobacco which made Havana cigarettes sell at an exorbitant price. Again, relating to the coal strike of 1902, the Lion praised the President's action in settling the strike but he was so busy admiring the President that he never got around to commenting on the significant issues involved.[30] Although thoroughly opposed to cheap money and free silver, that issue was largely settled by the election of 1896, and Lummis summed up his attitude in the epigram, "Speech is silver, and silence is golden; and the consistent silverite maintains the ratio of 16 to 1."[31]

The Lion loved a fight and he was prone to glorify military

[28]Ibid., 677.   [29]Ibid., XX (1904), Feb., 196.   [30]Ibid., XVII (1902), Nov., 611.
[31]"In the Lion's Den," *Land of Sunshine*, V (1896), Aug., 122.

and naval figures, yet, in 1899, he dismissed the suggestion of conscription with a remark to the effect that about a quarter of the country's population came here to avoid that very thing.[32] In discussing naval warfare, Lummis longed for the old days when frigates fought grapple-close and he lamented the fact that naval war had become mechanized and was conducted at long range. Comparing it to courting by long-distance telephone, he remarked, "In love or in war, the chief satisfaction is in Getting Alongside." This was prefatory to a criticism of the government's policy of sinking its money into five-million-dollar battleships ("floating coffins," Lummis called them), instead of investing in $2,500 torpedoes and in coastal defenses.[33]

Lummis had little to say concerning foreign affairs save in connection with British imperialism. He condemned Great Britain for her conduct of the Boer War, being careful, generally, to make a distinction between the British people, who, he asserted, were not behind the war, and British politicians like Cecil Rhodes and Joseph Chamberlain who, in the Lion's eyes, were waging a war of imperial aggression.[34] At every opportunity Lummis applauded successes in the field of the outnumbered Boer forces. When conflict reached the brutal stage characterized by concentration camps in which women and children succumbed to starvation and disease, an indignant Lummis demanded that President Roosevelt call the British off.[35] In July, 1902, the editor noted with relief the end of the "vicious and unjust war," and expressed regret that the United States did not contribute to bringing it to a close. However, apparently mellowed by the generosity of the British peace terms, Lummis closed this aspect of his anti-imperialist crusade with a toast: "Here's to them [the Boers] and to the brave nation with whom they are henceforth to be allied, and to their joint efforts to build up peace and good will and nationality where Chamberlain left the ashes of political arson."[36]

32Ibid., X (1899), Mar., 208.
33"In the Lion's Den," *Out West*, XX (1904), May, 469.
34"In the Lion's Den," *Land of Sunshine*, XII (1899), Dec., 49.
35Ibid., XV (1901), Oct., 264.
36"In the Lion's Den," *Out West*, XVII (1902), July, 86.

Few things delighted the Lion more than to catch someone in error, especially should he be an easterner mistaken about the West. One of the Lion's early victims was Professor William Libbey of Princeton who climbed Katzímo or the Enchanted Mesa, a 430-foot rock-table near the settlement of Acoma, New Mexico, which, according to Indian tradition, had once been inhabited. The professor's purpose was to ascertain whether the legend had any foundation in fact, and his findings, as reported in *Harper's*, were that it did not. Lummis noted regretfully at the time that Libbey's expedition was conducted so hurriedly and carelessly that, although his conclusion might be correct, further investigation would be necessary to dispose of the legend.[37]

In September, 1897, Frederick Webb Hodge of the Bureau of Ethnology made a similar expedition to the Enchanted Mesa, using less equipment, ascending the rock in hours rather than days, and staying longer at the top. His findings proved beyond doubt the truth of the Indian tradition and provided the Lion with sport for several months. Lummis condemned Libbey for failing to recognize authentic archaeological remains and ridiculed the elaborate precautions taken in his scaling of the cliff. When Libbey implied that Hodge "salted the claim" Lummis cried foul! Finally, when the professor asserted in the journal *Science* that he, himself, erected a monument he had originally attributed to erosion, the editor asked with heavy sarcasm, "Did this candid professor also carve the prehistoric toe-holes of the ancient trail? Why stop half-way? Is it not a fact, hidden only by the notorious modesty of him, that Professor Libbey built the Enchanted Mesa *in toto?* Nay—did he not create New Mexico? The Lion is sorry. He would rather have thought of Professor Libbey as an honest ignoramus."[38]

Lummis ranged widely in search of error. In fact, he collected mistakes like a proofreader paid for piecework. He complained of a Field Columbian Museum monograph which spoke of tigers in the New World.[39] He scoffed at a Columbia University professor for claiming to have exhumed the original

[37]"In the Lion's Den," *Land of Sunshine*, VII (1897), Sept., 166.
[38]Ibid., VIII (1898), Jan., 85.   [39]Ibid., IV (1896), May, 287.

man in the locality of Bitter Creek, Colorado.[40] He ridiculed a resident of Carmel who announced that a Spaniard named Viscan made the first white settlement in the United States at Carmel in 1602. Incidentally, in citing the founding date of St. Augustine, Florida, as 1560, Lummis himself erred by five years.[41] He scored George Wharton James for a "fake" article on the Fire Dance of the Navajos, charging plagiarism and willful mendacity. No slip was too picayune to command his attention and his correctives were frequently phrased with a vehemence which stamped them as teapot tempests. Nonetheless his function was an educative one, and although he was not above producing a false impression of his own, he corrected more than he created, especially in the sphere of southwestern history.

In most cases Lummis' victims stayed corrected, but occasionally the Lion was challenged. This happened in the case of what Lummis termed "deformed spelling." He had from time to time commented with considerable asperity on the tendency to streamline spelling by removing superfluous letters and operating on a modified phonetic basis. The Lion's reverence for etymology and for the evolutionary processes of language ill-disposed him toward any tendency to tamper deliberately with the spelling of words. He stated his position in a reference to the sanctioning of "drummer spelling" (another Lummis term) by the University of Chicago: "But this 'reform' is invariably a confession of ignorance of etymology. No man who really understands the legitimate descent of words ever did or ever will favor any project to make them vagabond bastards. The restlessness belongs only to those who do not quite know why words are spelled as they are. Their feeling is purely commercial; and while a 'drummer' is entitled to use words, he isn't the man to determine them."[42]

In 1907, in refutation of one of the Lion's forays against the Simplified Spelling Board, Brander Matthews, professor of literature at Columbia University, entered the lists on the side of simplified spelling. In a courteous, methodical, restrained

[40]Ibid., III (1895), Nov., 285.
[41]"In the Lion's Den," *Out West*, XXV (1906), Sept., 279.
[42]"In the Lion's Den," *Land of Sunshine*, XII (1900), Feb., 192.

argument he noted that words are undergoing continuous modification in the direction of simplification, and he felt that an intelligent effort to further that process was sensible and worthwhile. Matthews went on to note that the Board was composed of specialists in language, mentioning, among others, the editors of *Webster's*, the *Century*, and the *Oxford* dictionaries as well as professors of English from Oxford, Cambridge, Yale, Columbia, Johns Hopkins, and Stanford. He asked: "If these men do not understand the laws governing the growth of the English language, who does?"[43] In addition, Matthews listed other supporters of streamlined spelling, including Theodore Roosevelt, David Starr Jordan, and Mark Twain. He concluded that he and Lummis were in agreement about disliking deformed spelling but were at odds as to when spelling is deformed.

Lummis took up the challenge with relish and launched a long, detailed, and often circuitous answer. He began rather deferentially with several allusions to Matthews' erudition and training. He acknowledged the prominence of the members of the Simplified Spelling Board and then proceeded to do his best to disqualify them. First he dispatched Benjamin Smith, editor of the *Century Dictionary*, by citing the dictionary's confusion of pepper tree with the Chili pepper—an error, Lummis averred, merely indicative of many more. He doubted that either Teddy Roosevelt or David Starr Jordan were really supporters of simplified spelling. He claimed that Funk of the *Standard Dictionary* was dependent on wireless messages from the spirit world and that the secretary of the Board was a theosophist residing at the Point Loma colony. As for Mark Twain, the Lion was sure the humorist endorsed deformed spelling as a huge joke.[44]

Lummis asserted that the examples usually given as evidence of a need for spelling reform are cases which nobody questions and are words which have already been streamlined by natural processes. Citing the Board's circular as stating that many schools and periodicals use the new spellings, Lummis asked: "Does Harvard? Does *The Nation?* Does the *Boston Transcript* or the *Springfield Republican?*" He went on to claim that the changes

[43]"In the Lion's Den," *Out West*, XXVII (1907), Oct., 366.
[44]Ibid., 377.

advocated often were not logical. "Now, damn a cat that would condescend to 'pur,'" roared the Lion. "No cat ever did or could. Purring means more R's than one."[45] If words are modified naturally over a period of time, he argued, why try to speed up and perhaps pervert or misdirect the process?

The response to the controversy was largely gratifying to the editor. In the December, 1907, Den, he printed a good-natured reply from the "champion of deform" Brander Matthews, who wrote: "Well roared, Lion!" and asked for more copies of the October number. The Los Angeles *Times* gave Lummis the decision and in a qualified endorsement of simplified spelling David Starr Jordan delighted Lummis by remarking that "thru is enough to fatigue a polliwog."[46]

In January, 1896, the Lion issued a personal manifesto of literary independence. He decried the popular tendency to stigmatize any so-called provincial literary product and he pointed out that many great works of literature have been purely local, citing the *Odyssey, Don Quixote*, and Shakespeare's works. The editor deplored the dependence of American writers on foreign models but he prophesied the coming of "a day of honesty when superstition is lifted from letters and we shall have an American literature; and every man Jack of us will write of nature and of life as he sees them and not as he has been taught to imagine they look to a blind man in a London fog." He continued:

The expression of this literature should be newer, broader, less tired; more hopeful and more tolerant, since it is the first broad proving-ground of the brotherhood of man, the one land which all bloods are "making."

And amid America, the West at least should need no tag. Unless history is a fool and evolution a liar, it must produce a literature distinguishable. It has all the advantages of the East, for its people were born and bred there; with the higher education added by transplanting—not to mention the climatic aperient. There will be an American literature—even a Western literature. It will come when coherent spirit and unborrowed sight do. And no thanks to either the Western maverick or the Eastern stalled ox. . . . The same eternal truths which begot upon Greece a literature whose face is fair and clear through all the ages will give us as sure an heir—when we are fit for parentage.[47]

[45]Ibid., 374.   [46]Ibid., Dec., 532.
[47]"In the Lion's Den," *Land of Sunshine*, IV (1896), Jan., 87-89.

Such a statement echoed and reinforced the literary credo of Hamlin Garland published as a series of critical essays under the title *Crumbling Idols* in 1894.

Lummis' appraisal of Edwin Markham's "Man with a Hoe" is revealing. He praised Markham's skill as a poet but quarreled with his social philosophy, counterposing the concept of individual responsibility to Markham's deterministic implication of social responsibility for the plight of the man with a hoe. In the Lion's words: "It is a cowardly trick of the day to lay our faults to heredity and destiny, and our virtues to ourselves. This is very comfortable, but it is no more science than it is religion. The only oppressor a man can't get away from is himself."[48]

Lummis sounds like an abler critic when he evaluated Mark Twain as much more than merely a humorist. "For all his fooling," the Lion asserted, "thoughtful people have long known that he is the largest and most serious of all the Western writers."[49]

His tribute to Frank Norris, appearing shortly after that author's untimely death, indicates a mature appreciation of Norris' literary stature. In the editor's opinion, Norris was the most promising of all western fictionists for "he had two things we habitually lack in our letters — reality and power."[50]

When the name of a public figure appeared in the Lion's Den, its readers could be reasonably sure the person was mistaken, retired, or dead. In most cases the individual was characterized in a few vague, eulogistic phrases frequently followed by a kind of benediction. A sample will establish the type.

In January, 1900, Lummis mourned the death of General Henry Lawton, a soldier who "died in a war he didn't believe in — a sacrifice to imperialistic designs. His better life is forfeit for the stupidity, the blindness and the ambition of others. Friend, hero, patriot—God rest him!"[51]

On occasion the Lion could deliver a scathing personal attack. For example, in a reference to Benjamin F. Tilley,

[48]Ibid., XI (1899), Aug., 174-75.
[49]Ibid., XIV (1901), Mar., 236.
[50]"In the Lion's Den," *Out West*, XVII (1902), Nov., 614-15.
[51]"In the Lion's Den," *Land of Sunshine*, XII (1900), Jan., 114.

governor general of Samoa, Lummis cited Tilley's annual report to the Secretary of the Navy to the effect that organized government was keeping the natives quiet and happy while helping them along the path toward complete civilization, and then wrote:

Happy Tutuilians! Why not, when their great exemplar of complete civilization gets Happy early and often? . . . The "officer and gentleman" who was picked up in the San Francisco gutters a few months ago, drunk and in disguise; whom the soberest citizens and our most reputable travelers picture in Tutuila as publicly intoxicated, as debauching the natives, as gallopading through the streets on the same horse with a drunken strumpet—who else so well can teach "complete civilization" to a "gentle and simpleminded people"? [52]

Elliot Coues, Frank Pixley, Cecil Rhodes, Jessie Benton Frémont, Sacajawea, Richard Harding Davis, Frank H. Cushing, Rudyard Kipling—these names, picked at random from those which stud the pages of the Lion's Den, would seem to indicate a rich lode of biographical data. Yet the sketches, for the most part, include little specific information concerning the individuals themselves. Too often the references are brief and irritatingly general. Evidently the Lion did not intend to supply factual material concerning the persons he mentioned, but merely to bestow a journalistic accolade, usually posthumous, or issue a sharp reprimand, usually not.

The Den was to a considerable extent a mirror of Lummis' social conscience. He was outspoken in condemnation of most forms of racial prejudice. Sometimes he used the record of race violence in the South as an oblique criticism of the "benevolent assimilation" of the imperialists. Occasionally he pleaded for tolerance toward the Spanish Americans, to whose forebears he felt the United States owed so much. Once he demanded that the National Federation of Women's Clubs reinstate a chapter expelled for admitting Negroes to membership. [53] The Lion pounced on a statement in the San Francisco *Argonaut* to the effect that in the native tongue of the Negro in Africa (which of the hundreds of tongues, Lummis noted, was not specified)

[52]Ibid., XV (1901), Dec., 474-75.
[53]"In the Lion's Den," *Out West*, XVI (1902), May, 524-25.

there is no word for chastity. "There are," mused the Lion, "philologists to whom it would occur that virtue need not be defined until vice is familiar."[54] He went on to regret that a journal of the moral and mental size of the *Argonaut* should be marred by race bigotry.

The Lion became really aroused when he made references to Negro burnings in the South: "'Americans' burning 'Niggers' at the stake; skinning them, hacking them, carrying home chunks of man-meat for relics in American households! 'Americans!' Bah! They are not even dogs! Neither in morals nor in brains. For what they think they do to the Negro individual, they are in fact doing to themselves, and to their children, and to their children's children."[55]

The only instance of opposition to a racial group was Lummis' argument against unlimited immigration of the Chinese. He based his stand partly on the economic protest against cheap labor but largely on his opinion that the Chinese resist assimilation.[56]

The Lion's attitude on organized religion is perhaps best characterized as tolerance tinged with amusement. He deplored anti-Catholic sentiment and, as a commentary on the futility of religious persecution, he recalled that his father's people were flogged out of New England by his mother's people.[57] Lummis admired militant and courageous ministers, remarking at one time, "No mollusc ever shamed the devil yet."[58] He looked on theosophy, Christian Science, and kindred creeds as symptoms of dyspepsia, but he felt that any creed had more good than bad in it, more truth than falsehood.

The editor seldom expressed views on labor but when he did it is evident that his sympathies were not with the unions. He admitted that the labor union is a modern sociologic necessity but he insisted: " ... the American Union is just a leetle larger and more essential yet. If unionism is to hope to 'win'—or even to

54Ibid., XIX (1903), Sept., 316.
55Ibid., Aug., 216.
56"In the Lion's Den," *Land of Sunshine*, XV (1901), Nov., 368.
57"In the Lion's Den," *Out West*, XVII (1902), Dec., 735.
58"In the Lion's Den," *Land of Sunshine*, X (1899), Feb., 149.

exist for very long—in this republic, it must be by sticking to American methods, and earning and keeping the respect of the vast American public—by proving the unions make better workmen, and no worse citizens."[59]

Lummis harbored an abiding grudge against the daily press. He objected to its deliberate distortion of news, to its careless handling of facts, to its accent on the sensational, to its cold impersonalism, and to its tendency to cheapen the taste of the reading public. "If man really expected to go into the kind of world mirrored in his morning paper," the Lion remarked, "he would gird on a gun, a suit of armor, a life preserver, a police-man and two or three witnesses before he ventured forth. . . . Only by burrowing and searching in odd corners of the paper," he contended, "may the reader find the suggestion — fitted for American consumption by that flippancy which is supposed to be necessary sauce before you can get the reader to swallow anything solid—that there are art and scholarship and educa-tion and the fear of God in the community whereupon he pays taxes."[60] Bitter as he was about the popular press, Lummis placed the ultimate blame upon the people. He wrote: "The root of the trouble is that our taste has been degraded, our respect for Law wiped out, our ideals bartered for 'deals.' For all this, beyond doubt, our modern newspapers are damnably respon-sible—but we are responsible for our newspapers."[61]

On the issue of academic freedom the Lion's tolerance had limits. His first encounter with the problem, in the Den at least, occurred in September, 1897, over the dismissal of Presi-dent Elisha B. Andrews of Brown University for his advocacy of free silver. Lummis took the position that a man has a right to believe almost anything but that if the church to which he ministers or the college over which he presides holds his views to be vicious, it is not only entitled but it is obligated to see that he keep silent on that score or resign. In the Lion's words: "We curtail the 'freedom' of indecent and profane speech; sedi-tious speech is not wholly untrammeled; and there is no danger

[59]"In the Lion's Den," *Out West*, XIX (1903), Oct., 424-27.
[60]Ibid., XXIII (1905), Aug., 177-78.
[61]"In the Lion's Den," *Land of Sunshine*, XV (1901), Oct., 262.

that Freedom would shriek...if we were to circumscribe fool speech a little."[62] The editor failed to stipulate who was to decide what constitutes "fool speech."

Closer to home was the case involving the resignation of Edward A. Ross, professor of sociology at Stanford, at the request of Mrs. Stanford, because of alleged slurs made in class on the memory of Leland Stanford. Lummis came to the defense of Mrs. Stanford and of President David Starr Jordan, and the controversy raged for several months, sometimes spilling over from the Den into other sections of the magazine. However, the original issue of academic freedom was lost in quibbling over such things as whether or not Ross exhibited good taste in his remarks.[63]

Lummis defended at least two of his eccentricities in the Den, namely, his unorthodox use of capital letters and his habit of wearing a corduroy suit, an Indian belt, moccasins, and a sombrero.

In justifying his use of capitals, Lummis employed a familiar analogy between words and tools, explaining that every real workman respects and cares for his tools but does not make idols of them. The editor found historical sanction for the upper case in both German and Old English script. Moreover, he observed that punctuation is an indefinite art about which no two textbooks agree and that it is a matter of taste whether one shall use the overworked italics or some other device of better historic and etymologic authority. The Lion admitted that he did not own the English language but then averred that neither did it own him and since he preferred capitals he was very likely to keep on using them. "As a matter of fact," he added, "the man who shaves himself is never the one that abuses the razor. That fine, though now neglected, tool meets real disrespect at the hands of those who clandestinely borrow it to cut their corns."[64]

In reply to an item in the New York *Evening Post* which described Lummis' southwestern garb and accused him of seek-

---

[62]Ibid., VII (1897), Sept., 166.
[63]Ibid., XIII (1900), Dec., 447-48; XIV (1901), Feb., 151-54.
[64]"In the Lion's Den," *Out West*, XXI (1904), Nov., 477-80.

ing publicity, the Lion remarked that he had worn the same kind of clothes for twenty years and whether at home, or in the desert, or in any company, he was the same disagreeable and unbeautiful beast. "On the contrary," continued the editor in the third person, "he has certain frank affection for the National Costume which has been good enough for him, for his wife and children and friends through the serious part of his life. His garb is clean. It 'cost as much' as that of the Evening Post. It is paid for. And it covers so much of the Lion's cuticle as is required of law; leaving his face exposed to all men, his hands open to his friends and doubled to — those who are not." After remarking on the bad manners displayed by the New York paper, Lummis, still belligerent, concluded: "Meantime, this Distant and Sometimes Pacific beast would like to wear peaceably what few and unfashionable garments he has the honor to own; but he is going to wear them anyhow — even if he has to fight for them."[65]

In the Lion's Den Lummis left an uneven editorial record. Probably his most trenchant prose was written in the early phases of his opposition to imperialism. On this topic, where there was some excuse for passion and prejudice, Lummis at times maintained a measure of tolerance and restraint which made what he had to say all the more effective. His treatment of other national topics was often superficial and lacking in discretion.

The Lion's writing on local, state, and regional topics was most significant for the things it espoused. The genesis, in print at any rate, for the Southwest Museum, the Landmarks Club, Sequoya League, and the southwestern chapter of the Archaeological Society of America may be found in the Lion's Den. These movements, along with his campaigns for the preservation of historic place names and statehood for the territories, plus persistent efforts to educate the rest of the country in things western, gave the Lion and his editorials an influential role in the cultural and social development of the Southwest.

That Lummis sought to exert an influence in the West some-

[65]Ibid., XXII (1905), Mar. to Apr., 244-46.

what comparable to that of the *Nation* over the country at large, is indicated in his attitude on social issues. He spoke out forcefully against bigotry in matters of race and religion, but his stand on academic freedom suggests limitations to his tolerance in at least one direction.

Lummis' references to literature form a small but significant segment of his editorial comment. His literary judgments while not profound, are reasonably sound. Further, his confidence in the literary future of the West and his efforts to encourage and stimulate western literary production merit recognition.

The Lion's prose never quite attains the dignity of literature. His style is frequently arresting as well as convincing, but although it sometimes glitters, it rarely glows. It is characterized by unorthodox constructions, strange conceits, puns, mixed metaphors, and extended figures of speech. Lummis was capable of true economy of expression as his epigrams attest, but in descriptive passages he was prone to become so involved as to obscure his meaning.

Although Lummis' range of interests was broad, the Lion's Den by no means dealt with every type of topic. Comment on business and industrial developments, such as oil, railroads, and labor, rarely or never appeared, and art, music, and sports items were conspicuous by their absence. Such observations, however, are largely irrelevant, for it was never the Lion's intention to achieve comprehensive coverage. After all, the Lion's Den is nothing more or less than the record of one man's reactions to his world, and in that simple fact lies its fullest significance.

Chapter **V** CORDUROY CRUSADER

CHARLES LUMMIS was not content merely to stand for things. He worked and fought for what he believed. His was the zeal of a crusader, and to a marked degree his magazine became a crusading journal. In the pages of *Out West* Lummis and others of similar or related convictions inveighed against imperialism, pleaded for regional loyalty and pride, demanded justice for the Indian, campaigned for the preservation of the California mission, urged racial tolerance and political reform, and espoused national irrigation and the reclamation of western lands.

In a sense its editor used *Out West* to preach a single, persistent crusade – a crusade of locality. Through illustration, through verse, by means of descriptive or interpretive essay, through editorial, advertisement, story, historical sketch, promotional piece, and historical document, the journal exhibited, celebrated, interpreted, and championed southern California, the Southwest, and the West in general. Such regional preoccupation was at once so all-pervasive and so amorphous as to defy analysis. More consistent with the concept of crusade was the role of the magazine with reference to the preservation of historic landmarks and the defense of Indian rights. In these two spheres *Out West* was a positive force yielding, not infrequently, tangible results.

It was not surprising that early in his term as editor of a magazine designed to mirror and to publicize southern California, Lummis should make the preservation of historic landmarks part of the business of the *Land of Sunshine*. Nor was it remarkable that he should select the most conspicuous and romantic remnant of the region's Spanish epoch – the missions – as the focal point in his campaign to preserve the past. Although the magazine had carried several articles dealing with various missions in southern California, the first intimation of an organized effort to safeguard them appeared in the Lion's Den. Here Lummis issued a clarion call to preserve the missions not only as examples of superb architecture and buildings of true historical worth, but as magnets capable of drawing tourists to the Southland. "There is to be no accursed 'restoration'—," Lummis wrote, "*preservation* is the watchword. ...A society will be incorporated....A general campaign will be made to arouse interest in all quarters and to raise a permanent fund for the protection and conservation of the finest ruins in the United States."[1]

By December, 1895, the movement was given permanence and form by the organization and incorporation of the Landmarks Club. According to its constitution the new body's objectives were: "To preserve from further decay and vandalism the old Missions of California; to assist in the restoration of such of the Mission buildings as may be found adaptable for uses in harmony with their original purposes; and to safeguard and conserve other historic monuments, relics and landmarks of the State."[2]

Lummis was not the first to attempt to save the missions of southern California. That distinction, as Lummis himself acknowledged, belonged to Miss Tessa L. Kelso who, in 1892, while head of the Los Angeles Public Library, was instrumental in organizing, along with the help of members of the Historical Society of Southern California, the Association for the Preservation of the Missions.[3] This group conducted a number of excursions to the missions, gathered numerous pictures showing the need for the protection of landmarks, and raised funds through entertainments and subscriptions. When Miss Kelso left for the East to take a job with *Scribner's*, the association languished, to be revived a couple of years later by Lummis and cast in the corporate form. There was real continuity

[1]Vol. IV (1895), Dec., 44.

[2]MS, in Lummis collection.

[3]In turn the impetus behind Miss Kelso's efforts likely derived from the amazingly effective popularization of the mission era in Helen Hunt Jackson's *Ramona* (1882).

between the two organizations for some of the more enthusiastic of the earlier workers joined the new order, and Miss Kelso turned over to the Landmarks Club a balance of ninety dollars which the older association had raised. On the first anniversary of the Landmarks Club, Miss Kelso was elected to honorary life membership.[4]

The constitution of the Landmarks Club provided for a rather elaborate organization including an honorary president, a president, three vice-presidents, a secretary, an assistant secretary, a corresponding secretary, a treasurer, a chancellor, two architects, a councilor, an organizer, a chronicler, and a board of nine directors. This formidable array of officers was reduced in practice to President Lummis, Vice-President Margaret Collier Graham, two secretaries, a treasurer, a board of seven directors, and an advisory board.[5] The sole requisite for membership was the payment of one dollar annual dues. Lifetime memberships could be had for twenty-five dollars. The work of the Landmarks Club was financed through those dues plus voluntary contributions from persons in sympathy with its aims. Contributions were scrupulously acknowledged, and news of progress in mission rehabilitation was posted each month under a Landmarks Club department in Lummis' magazine.

The Landmarks Club was concerned primarily with those missions south of the Tehachapi most in need of attention. Missions such as Santa Barbara and San Luis Rey, which were occupied by members of the Franciscan order, or like San Gabriel and San Buenaventura under the care of secular priests, generally did not figure in the Landmarks program. Instead the Club concentrated on the mother mission San Diego, San Juan Capistrano, San Fernando, and Pala, an *asistencia* of San Luis Rey, all of which virtually were deserted and in advanced stages of decay.[6] The Club turned first to San Juan Capistrano, where it secured a lease on the buildings and ten acres of ground. Here the kitchen received attention first. Its rotting sycamore rafters

[4]"Landmarks Club," *Land of Sunshine*, VI (1896), Dec., 25-26.
[5]Ibid., IV (1896), Jan., 85.
[6]*The Landmarks Club: What It has Done, What It has to Do* (Los Angeles: Out West Company, 1903), p. 13.

were replaced with Oregon pine over which the tiles were laid, and breaches in its walls were repaired. Next, about fifty feet of the front corridor and two hundred feet of the corridor on the patio were roofed to the extent of the rafters and sheeting, while colonnades and room-walls in the same stretch were tied with bolts from side to side insuring stability. Further, some four hundred feet of cloisters were reroofed and waterproofed with asphalt as they had been originally; the crumbling pilasters which supported all that remained of the great stone church were buttressed; and the roof structure of the adobe church founded by Father Serra was replaced and covered with tiles.[7]

The initial response to the call to protect the missions was most heartening. Contributions came in from all parts of the country and occasionally from abroad. A group of Pasadena women, organized as a local committee of the Landmarks Club, staged a benefit and turned almost three hundred dollars over to the Landmarks treasurer.[8] By November, 1896, the major ravages of time and tourist at San Juan Capistrano were checked. A month later, on the Club's first anniversary, its president could declare that it had succeeded in reinforcing the mission San Juan Capistrano so that it would stand for another century, and this at a cost of approximately $1,400, raised entirely through voluntary contributions and subscriptions. Membership at the year's end stood just under four hundred.[9]

The Landmarks Club turned next to the mission San Fernando, in even worse condition than San Juan Capistrano. An estimated $2,000 would be necessary to safeguard the ruins of the monastery and the church. Since the Landmarks Club used up its funds as rapidly as it received them, it launched a campaign through the *Land of Sunshine* to raise the required sum. Lummis wrote an appreciation of the California mission system, illustrating it with photographs of the ragged roofs and gaping walls of the San Fernando mission buildings to dramatize the missions' plight.[10] Despite these efforts and the launching of a lecture series

---

[7]"Landmarks Club," *Land of Sunshine*, V (1896), Nov., 244.

[8]Ibid., IV (1896), May, 285-86.   [9]Ibid., VI (1896), Dec., 25.

[10]Juan del Rio [Lummis], "A Splendid Ruin," *Land of Sunshine*, VI (1896), Dec., 13-17.

on various aspects of early Southwest history on behalf of the Club's work, the fund-raising drive had bogged down by February, 1897, and operations at San Fernando were delayed. Gradually, however, contributions and subscriptions dribbled in and the work of repair and preservation continued. By the close of the Club's second year the major work at San Fernando was done and the *Land of Sunshine* could announce the saving of a second mission. By this time something over $2,000 had been collected and it was urged that delinquent dues be paid so the Club might start the new year clear of a debt of $75 still owed on the roof of the San Fernando Church.[11] Almost before its members could respond, however, the Landmarks Club went further in arrears when what Lummis chose to label an "unusual" December storm did $150 worth of damage to the newly laid roof.[12] Despite this setback Lummis announced the intention of preserving the façade and reinforcing the walls of the fading San Diego mission, but the onset of the Spanish-American war forced the Landmarks Club into a period of inactivity, which lasted until March, 1899, when the Club resumed its interrupted labors.

Work was carried on at San Diego, San Fernando, and later at the *asistencia* of Pala in much the same manner as before the war. The usual procedure was for the Club's architects to survey the job to be done and make a cost-estimate which the Club then set out to raise. When possible, some interested and influential member of the community wherein the mission was located was brought into the plans and used as a fulcrum in efforts to enlist the community's active support. Care was taken not to violate the original style of mission architecture, and priority was given to the principal buildings of each mission so that often the peripheral structures were ignored. Although Lummis insisted throughout most of the Club's active life that the organization's proper function was merely preservation, there were times when the Club restored essential elements such as pillars.[13] The Club's work, however, was handicapped through lack of funds. Occa-

[11]"Landmarks Club," *Land of Sunshine*, VIII (1897), Dec., 26.
[12]Ibid. (1898), Jan., 82.
[13]Arthur B. Benton to Lummis, Aug. 28, 1902, in Lummis collection.

sionally the group received an unexpected increment such as in October, 1901, when Mrs. Phoebe Apperson Hearst, the same benefactress who later helped finance *Out West*, furnished $500 to be applied in the rehabilitation of Pala.[14] Here the entire structure was reroofed and the campanile reinforced with iron rods. The people of the valley — whites, Mexicans, and Indians — volunteered their services for varying amounts of time. However, such windfalls were infrequent, and the pages in *Out West* devoted to Landmarks activity present a monotonous plea for contributions and for payment of dues. Nevertheless by November, 1903, after eight years of existence, the Club had spent over $7,000 in protective repairs including, as perhaps the major single item, the reroofing of more than 60,000 square feet of mission buildings.[15] Thanks to these efforts the remains of four mission structures — San Juan Capistrano, San Fernando, San Diego, and Pala — were reinforced and further disintegration was prevented.

For a time the Landmarks Club identified itself with a campaign to restore the Camino Real connecting the twenty-one California missions. This movement, like that of preserving the missions, stemmed from the early nineties when Miss Ana B. Picher began agitation for such a project. Late in 1903 Lummis concluded that interest in the missions had been sufficiently aroused to back an organized move to establish a highway from San Diego to San Francisco in the footsteps of the padres. He wrote the Board of Directors of the Los Angeles Chamber of Commerce to that effect, rehearsing the record of Miss Picher and the Landmarks Club and suggesting that women's clubs, historical societies, pioneer groups, highway interests, and the like "can be rallied to this work for considerations sentimental, practical, patriotic."[16] In the December *Out West* the convening of a Camino Real convention in Los Angeles to discuss plans for re-creating the historic highway from San Diego as far north as Santa Barbara was announced. Lummis argued that the most

[14]"Landmarks Club," *Land of Sunshine*, XV (1901), Oct., 260.
[15]Ibid., XIX (1903), Dec., 671.
[16]Nov. 18, 1903, in Lummis collection.

feasible way to achieve a Camino Real was to do it by halves and that northern California, goaded and encouraged by the example of the southern part of the state, would rise to the occasion and complete the project from Santa Barbara north. He went so far as to draft a tentative list of topics to be discussed at the convention. As he saw it, the undertaking should unfold in three steps. First, a popular movement should be organized since "every hotel man, every livery-stable; every railroad, every street-car line, every enterprise and every individual that plans to harvest a tourist dollar has a stake in the movement." Next, he insisted that the original route be determined as accurately as possible from a careful study of historical documents. Finally, he would sanction no patchwork affair, but called for a uniform, modern highway. He went on to predict that the plan would ultimately require state, perhaps even national, aid, but he urged that it be kept in spirit a popular movement begun with personal contributions and sustained by enlightened state and local interest.[17]

At the convention in Los Angeles in December, 1903, attended by some eighty delegates from historical societies, chambers of commerce, women's clubs, and pioneer organizations, the Camino Real project as envisioned by Lummis and the Landmarks Club was rejected, and in its place the convention voted for a Camino Real coterminous with the northern and southern boundaries of the state. Lummis claimed that selfish political and commercial interests, hopeful of snaring generous appropriations from the state legislature, were at the bottom of this travesty on California history. Their method, he contended, had been to spread the falsehood that the original Camino Real plan was a masked move for state division, thereby alarming the Native Sons and Daughters of the Golden West who controlled a majority of the convention delegates and threw their support to the state-length scheme.[18] However, the Los Angeles Chamber of Commerce repudiated the convention's action and shortly after Lummis happily noted that a second Camino Real convention held at Santa Barbara in April,

[17]"The Camino Real," *Out West*, XX (1904), Jan., 82-83.
[18]Ibid., Mar., 278.

1904, reversed the decision of the earlier body and resolved to "preserve as far as practicable, the ancient Camino Real, or King's Highway, as travelled by the padres."[19] With this change of tack Lummis of course was in hearty accord, but after the formation of an official Camino Real Association the Landmarks Club severed any direct connection it might have had with the project of a King's Highway.

Along with its temporary concern with the Camino Real movement, the Landmarks Club prevented the Los Angeles plaza from becoming the site of a public market; contributed to the preservation of the home of Pio Pico, last Mexican governor over California; and campaigned to prevent the mutilation of Spanish place names by an unenlightened postal department. These, however, were minor services. By far the most significant work of the Landmarks Club was its preservation of the missions. True, Lummis was not the first to labor in this field, nor was the Landmarks Club the first organization to campaign for the preservation of historic sites in California. As Joseph R. Knowland rather caustically pointed out in the *Grizzly Bear*, that distinction belonged to the Native Sons of the Golden West who began landmarks work in 1888.[20] Doubtless too, Lummis romanticized the role of the Franciscans in California. It is also true that in addition to stressing cultural and artistic values resident in the missions, he urged their protection on crass commercial grounds, speaking of them often as one of the state's most valuable business assets. Still, few will deny that the missions are worth preservation. While others talked and wrote about the golden mission period, Lummis and the Landmarks Club contributed substantially to salvaging the physical remains of that epoch most in danger of disappearance. Furthermore, the repeated publicity given the Landmarks program in *Out West* fed a growing awareness that southern California had a historical heritage worth conserving. Finally, since the magazine enjoyed a widespread circulation, the example of the Landmarks Club stimulated the launching of similar movements in northern California, in

[19]"In the Lion's Den," *Out West*, XX (1904), Apr., 390.
[20]"Native Sons' Landmarks Work," *Grizzly Bear*, XX (1917), Jan., 7.

Texas and in Wisconsin, as well as in other parts of the country.[21] Shortly after Charles Lummis left *Out West* to head the Los Angeles Public Library, the Landmarks Club lost its sole important and continuous publicity channel. The monthly department with its news of the Club's plans and activities, and its steady acknowledgment of contributions to the cause, had given the movement a currency and a permanence vital to its success. When this visible evidence of the Club's existence and progress was cut off, ostensibly the body was defunct, although Lummis claimed in 1916 that there had never been a year when landmarks work was not being done by the Club. In that same year, at Riverside, the Landmarks Club was reorganized on a state-wide basis and it sponsored a celebration at the San Fernando mission, commemorating the Spanish discovery of the valley, which netted approximately $3,500, all of which was to be expended in repairing the mission.[22] Also, the revived organization had taken over La Purísima near Lompoc, California, as a gift from the Standard Oil Company, with the provision that the Club undertake repairs amounting to $1,500.[23] The Landmarks Club was in the midst of these two projects when the country's entry into World War I apparently choked off the comeback attempt before it was well begun. In view of the body's tenuous existence after 1906 and excepting the brief rejuvenation just mentioned, it can be said that the Landmarks Club died as an effective force when its ties with *Out West* were cut.

More dramatic than the steady efforts to preserve historic landmarks was the crusade of Lummis and his magazine on behalf of the Indians of California and the Southwest. Lummis marshaled rather widespread but unorganized sympathy for the Indian, and, by its compression within an incorporated league and its promotion through the pages of *Out West*, he forged an effective instrument of reform.

From the start Lummis' magazine reflected its editor's interest

[21]"Landmarks Club," *Out West*, XVIII (1903), Jan., 88-89.

[22]Lummis to Miss Elizabeth W. Johnson, Sept. 11, 1916, in Lummis collection.

[23]Mrs. Alice N. Yates to Herbert Fleishhacker, Oct. 27, 1919, in Lummis collection.

in Indians. Almost every number of the journal carried an article or story or poem on some aspect of Indian life, but for nearly five years there was little indication of anything other than a general historical or cultural interest in the Indian. Then, in August, 1899, Lummis began a series of seven articles which he called "My Brother's Keeper." This was the opening shot in a long campaign waged by Lummis and his magazine in protest against the treatment of the Indian by the government. In these papers Lummis penned a severe indictment of the Indian School Service, not on the basis of its corruptness, for he felt much of the skulduggery of earlier days had been eliminated, but largely on grounds of indifference, stupidity, and incompetence.

The incident that provoked this crusade was a national convention of Indian educators meeting in Los Angeles in July, 1899. Lummis subjected the proceedings to scathing criticism: first, because he felt the papers presented, with few exceptions, revealed no awareness that the work of scholars was available to those who were dealing with the Indian and that such data could contribute invaluably to their understanding and appreciation of the first Americans; and second, because the 315 delegates were completely dominated by one man — Major Richard H. Pratt of the Carlisle Indian School.[24] Major Pratt, observed Lummis, was an "undiluted materialist," a man of tremendous force but a man completely incapable of comprehending that an Indian has a soul. To Lummis, the system of educating the Indian by taking him from his family and confining him in government schools, a system which he believed Pratt epitomized, had scarcely a redeeming feature. That such a plan of education was even attempted was due, Lummis contended, to the absence of scientific knowledge on the part of the officials responsible for forming the Indian policy. The only bright spot Lummis could find in the proceedings of the convention was the paper read by Miss Estelle Reel, new superintendent of Indian schools. Her apparent willingness to learn and her recommendation of patience as being essential in any attempt to civilize the Indian drew high praise from Lummis in an otherwise negative and pessimistic report of the convention.[25] In subse-

[24]"My Brother's Keeper," *Land of Sunshine*, IX (1899), Aug., 139-40.
[25]Ibid., Sept., 213.

quent essays Lummis embellished his theme, decrying the ignorance and brutality of government agents on reservations at Zuñi and Moqui, stressing the essentially tractable nature of the Indians, and explaining the destructive effects of separating children from their parents for purposes of education.

Lummis' solution was simply the application of common sense. As a first step, he suggested the employment of no one within the Indian service professionally ignorant of Indians; second, an earnest and sustained attempt to adapt the education of the Indian to his capacity and to his needs. This second objective, the editor thought, meant teaching him to read and write, and to handle the English language. It meant imparting some comprehension of the nation's laws and its history. But above all else, it meant equipping the Indian to adjust to a new situation which called for his becoming a farmer rather than a hunter or trapper.

The editor's sustained attack drew a response from Major Pratt who met the Lion's charges by calling the *Land of Sunshine* "a thin little magazine" and Lummis a "fantastic litterateur." Lummis admitted that his magazine was thin, but so, he pointed out, is a razor; he added that "a leaf from the fifth chapter of Matthew is less paper than a volume of the *Congressional Record*, but I presume it can be just as truthful."[26] The series ended with further comment as to Major Pratt's fundamental unfitness for the job he held. These articles struck a note which sounded persistently throughout Lummis' demands for reform in Indian policy—that the Bureau of Indian Affairs was administered by men who did not know their business and who were concerned with the Indians as statistics rather than as human beings.

In the spring of 1901 Lummis shifted his attack from general criticism of Major Pratt and the Indian School Service to a case much closer to home. He became actively concerned over the plight of some 300 Mission Indians in San Diego County who faced eviction from their ancestral lands as a result of an adverse decision of the United States Supreme Court

[26]Ibid., XII (1900), Jan., 92-93.

which deprived them of title to the land they occupied.[27] Lummis was not the first to become interested in the conditions prevailing among the Mission Indians. As their official reports attest, southern California Indian agents had long been aware that their charges needed attention. In 1883 Helen Hunt Jackson and Abbot Kinney made a field trip among the Mission Indians and compiled a report on their status which appeared in all editions of *A Century of Dishonor* subsequent to 1883. The appearance of *Ramona* in 1884 created a wave of interest in the Mission Indian, but had any reader of Mrs. Jackson's romance visited the Mission Indians in the eighties seeking the prototype of Ramona or Allesandro, he would still be looking.

Aside from sporadic contributions of food and clothing on the part of scattered sympathizers, the first overt action on the Mission Indians' behalf was taken by the Indian Rights Association with headquarters in Philadelphia. In June, 1897, the executive council of that organization furnished an indemnity bond of $1,600 to permit appeal to the California supreme court by the Indians of an adverse decision in a contest with white claimants over title to Warner's Ranch in the San Diego back country.[28] In October, 1899, the court rendered a decision against the Indians and the case was appealed to the United States Supreme Court.[29] Again the Indians lost out, when in May, 1901, the Supreme Court sustained the judgment of the state supreme court on the basis that the Indians forfeited title by their failure to present their claims for confirmation to the

[27]Mission Indians is a term which has become fastened on the southern California Indians in the aggregate, largely because in the Spanish period the bulk of the natives south of Tehachapi and along the present San Diego-Imperial county line were missionized. To a degree continued use of the name is inaccurate, for, according to Carey McWilliams, the thoroughly missionized Indians such as the Chumash, the Gabrieliño, the Luiseño, and the Juaneño are now wholly extinct; whereas those having had least contact with the missions, such as the Cahuilla and the Dieguño, are the only groups to have survived even in limited numbers.

[28]*13th Annual Report of the Executive Committee of the Indian Rights Association, 1897* (Philadelphia, 1897), in Charles L. Partridge collection, Bancroft Library, Berkeley, California. Hereafter cited as Partridge collection.

[29]Ibid. (1899).

Board of Land Commissioners created by act of Congress, March 3, 1851.[30]

Meanwhile Charles Lummis prepared to take a hand. In the Lion's Den of May, 1901, he criticized the government for apathy and incompetence in dealing with the Mission Indians. He cited a report by Constance Goddard DuBois, a summer resident of southern California and a contributor to his magazine, which he claimed would open many eyes to the deplorable conditions existing among the Mission Indians. Other southern Californians who were concerned with the Indian's welfare included Right Reverend Joseph H. Johnson, Bishop of the Episcopal Church in the Los Angeles diocese, Horatio N. Rust, former agent for the Mission Indians and a contributor to *Out West*, and Charles L. Partridge of Redlands. With this sort of support the Lion hoped to launch a movement on behalf of the Indians.[31]

On November 22, 1901, at Lummis' home, fifty persons voted to form a permanent league to begin and maintain systematic work to protect and aid the Indians, particularly those of southern California.[32] A memorial addressed to W. A. Jones, Commissioner of Indian Affairs, called attention to the status of the Mission Indians and recommended the appointment of a commission to make an investigation of the reservation lands and to submit a report of its findings. The document went on to analyze briefly the situation on a number of specific reservations placing special stress on the Warner's Ranch case as demanding immediate action. The memorial closed with this statement:

So serious and so protracted has been the mismanagement of the Mission Indians of Southern California that a permanent association of citizens is now arranging to incorporate . . . for the sole purpose of remedying—and keeping remedied—as many as possible of these abuses. . . . We earnestly hope for your aid in the adjustment of these matters. As to the necessity of action—and competent action—we believe there can be no two opinions among those who inform them-

[30]Ibid. (1901).
[31]"In the Lion's Den," *Land of Sunshine*, XIV (1901), May, 421.
[32]Lummis Journal, Nov. 22–28, 1901.

selves as to the facts. We will gladly, both personally and as an organization, render you any assistance in our power toward a just and adequate solution of problems which for more than a generation have been neglected, evaded or muddled in a manner discreditable alike to our humanity and our common sense.[33]

Lummis attached great significance to names and he confessed to some difficulty in fixing upon an appropriate title for the new association. His insistence upon a one- or two-word label narrowed the possibilities to three—Wampum League, Calumet League, and Sequoya League. The Lion favored the name Sequoya because "the Indian Cadmus is a good godfather."[34] The objection that it might be confused with a movement to protect the California redwoods he considered invalid because he planned to make the new organization so well known that there would be no reasonable doubt as to its objectives. Besides, in the unlikely event of confusion, Lummis saw little harm in the League being associated with so laudable a cause as preservation of the redwoods. At any rate, the name of the inventor of the Cherokee alphabet was applied to the new society and the label Sequoya along with the League's constitution appeared in *Out West* for March, 1902. From that date the magazine became the League's official organ.

The League's executive committee and advisory board included, among others, David Starr Jordan; George Bird Grinnell, editor of *Forest and Stream* and authority on the Plains Indians; Major John W. Powell, director of the Bureau of Ethnology and formerly of the United States Geological Survey; United States senator from California, Thomas R. Bard; Frederick W. Hodge of the Smithsonian Institute; and Hamlin Garland. The Sequoya League was to be national in scope and its slogan was "to make better Indians and better treated ones." Among its avowed intentions were: to co-operate with the Department of the Interior and with the Indian Bureau in shaping Indian policy; to supply "specific, responsible, authen-

[33]"In the Lion's Den," *Land of Sunshine*, XIV (1901), Dec., 460.

[34]Lummis to W. J. McGee, Bureau of American Ethnology, Washington, D. C., Dec. 31, 1901, in J. Manuel Espinosa, "Some Charles F. Lummis Letters, 1897-1903," *New Mexico Quarterly Review*, XI (1941), May, 152-53.

tic and disinterested information" concerning the Indians; and to encourage the revival of native arts and crafts as a means of supplementing the Indian's income. League membership was two dollars annually and life membership cost fifty dollars. Local councils, taking their charter from the League, might be formed in any town or city in the United States on petition from three responsible persons.[35] Contributions were solicited and acknowledged when received through the Sequoya League department in *Out West*. This department reported League activities each month until Lummis severed his connection with the magazine.

The Sequoya League's chances for success were greatly enhanced by the fact that Lummis had discussed its plans and objectives with President Roosevelt, Secretary of the Interior Ethan Hitchcock, and Indian Commissioner Jones, and had received their promise of assistance and support.[36] In addition, the two United States senators from California, Thomas Bard and George C. Perkins, along with Senator Boies Penrose of Pennsylvania, were backing the movement.

Once formed, the Sequoya League turned immediately to the plight of the Mission Indians. In the Den, in the League's department, and in personal correspondence Lummis put steady pressure on the government either to prevent the imminent eviction of the Warner's Ranch Indians or to provide accommodations for them once eviction had occurred. Persistent publicity in *Out West*, the influence of Senator Bard, and the personal interest of President Roosevelt contributed to the decision to appoint the special investigating commission advocated by the Sequoya League.[37] Lummis announced this as the first victory. Then he launched into a chest-beating, shadow-boxing tirade against all who had taken unfair advantage of the Indian. Included in his blanket condemnation were: the white trash squatter who drove the Indian off his own property at the point of a gun; the ranch company that hired compliant sur-

[35]"The Sequoya League," *Out West*, XVI (1902), Mar., 297-300. Actually only three such councils took form: one in New York, one in Connecticut, and one in Los Angeles.
[36]Ibid., 298.   [37]Ibid., Apr., 412-13.

veyors to push its fences a little farther when it found a half-acre the Indians had not already been robbed of; and the rancher who ran his stock over Indian fields. "These worthies," wrote Lummis grimly:

. . . will no longer be able to "make it stick." Neither will the legal officers who connive at violation of the law in favor of a white against an Indian. These gentlemen have had their day for 25 years—and most of them have made hay. But their harvest is past and their summer ended. The League is in deadly earnest; and it has the government at its back, as well as all decent public opinion.

The general plan of the League is to let bygones be bygones. It is not vindictive. The history of our dealings with the Mission Indians thus far is a disgrace; . . . *Now*, the government understands the case, and there is a legal organization which will include the foremost people in California, and tens of thousands throughout the country to stop this shame. . . . If there are people who think they are strong enough to fight this organization . . . let them try; if there are people who think they are foxy enough to fool this organization, let them try. But if they will take a fool's advice they will save money and credit by accepting the inevitable. The League has on its side the law, the equity and the numbers; and so it expects that it will find no permanent opposition. People who really knew better have maltreated the Indians just because it was no one's organized business to stop them; but now it is someone's business.[38]

The tone of these remarks was hardly conciliatory but perhaps Lummis can be permitted some pyrotechnics since, for the first time in a long record of official indifference toward the Mission Indians, he was getting results.

Before the commission was appointed, Lummis visited the Indians on Warner's Ranch and a report of his tour appeared in *Out West* in May, 1902. The back country of San Diego County, where Warner's Hot Springs are situated, Lummis described as lonely, picturesque and interesting "a consecutive wilderness as big as the State of Massachusetts, threaded by hundreds of leagues of good country roads, . . . with little oases here and there; . . . with sparse forests and groves of noble trees, and vast reaches of chaparral — but in its overwhelming majority an irremediable waste of crumbling granite and barren peaks."[39]

[38]Ibid.
[39]"The Exiles of Cupa," *Out West*, XVI (1902), May, 465.

The Agua Caliente or Hot Springs lie at an altitude of about 3,000 feet on the east side of Warner's Ranch, walled from the desert by a narrow mountain range. The Indian village or *rancheria* of 154 men, women, and children, under a leader or captain, consisted of some forty houses, most of them adobe, a small adobe chapel, and a new $1,200 schoolhouse. These Indians were known as Cupeños since their name for the Hot Springs was Cupa. The springs well up from the bottom of a rocky cleft and at the time of Lummis' visit the water was conducted in wooden flumes through rough-board bathhouses to form several bluish pools, before it trickled down the arroyo, irrigating a few score acres. In all, several hundred acres were under cultivation by the Indians, watered by irrigating ditches stemming from a reservoir. Lummis valued the improvements the Indians would have to abandon at $10,000. The Hot Springs themselves brought the Indians a substantial income by attracting tourists and health seekers. They were also useful as a natural laundry and in softening the materials which went into the weaving of baskets and rugs.

At several *juntas*, or meetings, held in the schoolroom, Lummis went over the significance of the court decision. He explained there was practically no possibility that the government would purchase the Indians' own land for them since the principal white claimant, J. Harvey Downey, refused to sell the 900 acres occupied by the Indians, or any less than the entire 30,000 acres for which he asked $245,000. Lummis suggested they consider the surrounding country and decide where, outside of the Hot Springs, they would like to live. At the second *junta*, held the next day, the Indians talked back through Celsa Apapas, a young woman who could speak Spanish, English, and Cupeño. According to Lummis, she rendered the captain's answers better than he spoke them, yet with complete fidelity to the spirit in which they were uttered. A fragment of the reply follows:

We thank you for coming here to talk to us in a way we can understand. It is the first time anyone has done so. You ask us to think what place we like next best to this place where we always live. You see that graveyard out there? There are our fathers and our grandfathers. You see that Eagle-nest mountain and that Rabbit-hole mountain?

When God made them, He gave us this place. We have always been here. We do not care for any other place. It may be good, but it is not ours. We have always lived here. We would rather die here. Our fathers did. We cannot leave them. Our children born here—how can we go away? . . . If Harvey Downey say he own this place, that is wrong. The Indians always here. We do not go on his land. We stay here. Everybody knows this Indian land. These Hot Springs always Indian. We cannot live anywhere else.

. . . We do not want you to buy any other place. If you will not buy this place we will go into the mountains like quail, and die there, the old people and the women and the children. Let the government be glad and proud. It can kill us. We do not fight. We do what it says. If we cannot live here we want to go into those mountains and die. We do not want any other home.[40]

The attitude of the Indians was unmistakable and it changed very slowly if at all.

Not long after his return from Warner's Ranch Lummis received the telegraphic notice of his appointment as chairman of the Warner's Ranch Indian Advisory Commission which he had obviously expected. Serving with him were Russell C. Allen and Charles L. Partridge. When the commission took the field on June 2, 1902, equipped with stage, cook-wagon, and a saddle horse, the party included William Collier, special attorney for the Mission Indians; Richard Egan, of San Juan Capistrano, a director of the Santa Fe Railroad and an experienced appraiser; Miss M. E. Haskins, stenographer; a cook; the chairman's little daughter, Turbesé; and two representatives of the Indians. Lanier Bartlett of the Los Angeles *Times* accompanied the party for ten days as an independent onlooker.[41]

The Warner's Ranch commission did a thorough job. Traveling an aggregate of nearly 2,000 miles by rail and 943 miles by wagon, the commissioners inspected 106 ranches totaling approximately 110,000 acres, and made 42 measurements of flowing waters. Numerous photographs were taken of the sites inspected.

The commission's major recommendation was that the government buy the Pala properties of 3,438 acres for $46,230,

[40]Ibid., 472-76.
[41]"The Sequoya League," *Out West*, XVII (1902), July, 83.

rather than the Monserrate Ranch, recommended by an agent of the government, of 2,370 acres for $70,000.[42] In justification of this selection a convincing case was presented. The properties which the commission examined were rated on a chart under headings such as: available gravity water; distribution of water; area arable; area irrigable; variety of crops; value of timber; market for products; market for labor; rainfall; native wild foods; basket materials; immediate income available; and reaction of the Indians. Each of these qualities or conditions was assigned a point value with a total of 400 points equivalent to a perfect score. On this scale the Pala property scored 372. Its nearest competitor was the Las Flores area with 293 points, followed by Descanso with 281.[43]

Of the 3,438 acres at Pala, the commission found over 2,000 acres to be arable and more than 700 acres irrigable with prospects of the irrigable area being increased at relatively small expense. In comparison with the Monserrate holdings Pala offered about fifty per cent more land; sixty per cent more arable land; and six hundred per cent more irrigable land. Moreover, there were at Pala 316 acres already under irrigation as compared to none at the Monserrate Ranch. Monserrate had the advantage in hard timber, but there was so much more acreage in timber at Pala as to make the total value considerably greater. At Pala it was estimated the government would have to build twelve to fifteen houses, at Monserrate nearly fifty. The quality of the land at Pala was the best in the San Luis Rey Valley in the judgment of the commission and averaged far better than on the Monserrate.[44] Further, in the variety of crops growing, the Pala region enjoyed a decided advantage over the ranch favored by the agent of the government. With

[42]"Preliminary Report of the Warner's Ranch Indian Advisory Commission" (Los Angeles, 1902), pp. 16-22, in Lummis collection. Purchase of the Monserrate Ranch had been recommended by government inspector James McLaughlin before the appointment of Lummis and the commission. It was partly because Lummis considered the Monserrate Ranch inadequate that he had urged the selection of a special investigating commission.

[43]Ibid., 5-6.

[44]Charles F. Lummis, "Turning a New Leaf," *Out West*, XVIII (1903), Apr., 441-55.

the exception of the Las Flores area, no other property examined by the commission was at once so accessible to civilization and so safe from aggression. The Pala Valley is bowl-shaped with exits east and west along the stream, and north and south by passes. The configuration, the commissioners asserted, precluded occupation of lands adjacent to the Indians except in the east and west narrows of the valley. In the light of the history of the relations between Indians and whites in California, such a consideration was of real importance. With regard to the possibilities of immediate income to be realized should the Indians be established at Pala, the commissioners emphasized a large stand of alfalfa and considerable timber resources. Further, the report stated that 200 men could find work eight months in the year within 40 miles of Pala and 100 within 16 miles. It was assumed, however, that the government was more interested in the Indians' becoming self-sustaining farmers than itinerant laborers. The commissioners found the water supply at Pala to be one of the strongest features in the site's favor with measurements taken of flow in the two irrigating ditches in use yielding 149.974 miner's inches — by far the largest body of gravity water seen anywhere by the commissioners except at Jurupa. Moreover, this flow could be increased by construction of a diverting dam.

The commission also suggested that should the government purchase the Pala site, it contribute some 5,000 acres of vacant government land adjoining Pala to the reservation.[45] Finally, it was recommended that, provided Pala was acquired, the savings realized be used to purchase lands adjoining some of the other reservations which were deemed inadequate to support their Indian populations.[46]

The preliminary report of the commission was approved on August 15, 1902, and abstracts of title and deeds were requested for examination.[47] The Sequoya League had clearly won a vic-

[45]On the commission's recommendation, the General Land Office withdrew from entry these public lands on three sides of Pala by order of Jan. 24, 1903.
[46]"Preliminary Report of the Warner's Ranch Indian Advisory Commission," pp. 3-4.
[47]Thomas Ryan, Acting Secretary of the Interior, to Charles F. Lummis, Aug. 19, 1902, in Partridge collection.

tory and Lummis claimed that for the first time in the history of Indian-white relations west of the Mississippi, the Indians had been furnished a superior home to the one from which they had been removed.

However, the actual transfer of the Warner's Ranch Indians was not completed without sadness, confusion, and delay. Lummis complained of meddlers, some of them well-meaning, some of them vicious, who, he claimed, were arousing false hopes among the Indians that something might yet be done to save Warner's Ranch for them. Lummis exposed a San Bernardino lawyer named John Brown as having accepted fees from the Indians with the understanding that he would save their home. Brown, fumed Lummis, knew little or nothing of the case, for he had not even read the Supreme Court decision that conferred the reservation lands on Downey. Later on Brown made partial amends by using his influence to induce the Indians to move peacefully.

Three of the leaders among the Indians made an eleventh-hour trip on horseback to San Bernardino in a fruitless attempt to prevail upon President Roosevelt to intervene. In their absence James E. Jenkins, one of the eight government Indian inspectors, arrived from Oklahoma to supervise the eviction. He was assisted by L. A. Wright, agent of the Mission Indians. According to the account of Grant Wallace representing the San Francisco *Bulletin*, Jenkins found the Indians determined to "stay and die in their homes," although a few months before they apparently had no thought of resisting removal. After a series of *juntas*, however, the Indians bowed to the inevitable. Perhaps the return of the unsuccessful trio from San Bernardino brought home to the Indians the futility of further appeal. At any rate, in the first installment, ninety-eight of the Warner's Ranch Indians were moved to Pala, but they went reluctantly and with open manifestations of malice.[48] The last group of Indians was moved to Pala in September, 1903, and the eviction which had been decreed in May, 1901, was at last completed.[49]

[48]Grant Wallace, "The Exiles of Cupa," *Out West*, XIX (1903), July, 31-41.
[49]Charles F. Lummis, "The Last Eviction," *Out West*, XIX (1903), Nov., 489-90.

Lummis had predicted in *Out West* that after a short period of adjustment the Indians would settle down at Pala and realize a happier and more profitable existence than had been true at the Hot Springs. Events proved him overly optimistic. In response to the commission's contention that the water supply at Pala could be increased, George Butler was sent by the Commissioner of Indian Affairs to develop an irrigation system. Butler found the Indians unco-operative, sullen, and unpredictable. He was singularly unimpressed with the general caliber of the Mission Indians, rating them below the local Mexican element in industry, thrift, and intelligence. He complained that work on the irrigation project was seriously impeded by the unreliability of the Indian labor. His labor troubles he attributed to the fact that the captain, holding his commission from Washington, was dictatorial, insubordinate, and rebellious and that his word was absolute law to the Cupeños. Butler was of the opinion that the Indians might move off the reservation at any time, and he suggested that it might be better "to resort to the baneful ration system and issue to them the regulation amount of subsistence supplies until harvest time next year when they could be self-sustaining, rather than to pay them for a half-hearted pretence of labor at doing nothing."[50]

Lummis complained of the situation at Pala to Commissioner Jones, asserting that things had been "hoodoed" since the acquisition of the new reservation. He noted, late in July, that no crops had been planted, although there had been ample time to put in communal crops for fall harvesting. He also found Butler's call for $25,000 for an irrigation system unreasonable, claiming that adequate irrigation works could be installed for $8,000.[51]

Nothing was said of the difficulties at Pala in *Out West*, but Lummis by no means gave up his campaign for the improvement of the Mission Indians. He kept after the Bureau of Indian Affairs and the Department of Interior to provide other Mission Indians with lands. With the aid of Senator Bard he gained an

[50]Sept. 5, 1903, in Partridge collection.

[51]Lummis to W. A. Jones, July 22, 1903, in Partridge collection.

[124]

arrangement whereby the money saved through the purchase of Pala would go to buy additional land for several reservations in San Diego County. It was estimated that at least 700 Mission Indians would benefit directly from such action.[52]

According to the Lion, out of more than 3,000 Mission Indians on more than 30 reservations, not half were in even tolerable circumstances. "With the exception of Moronga and Pala," he insisted, "there is not a single Mission reservation which is not a disgrace to the Government and to Civilization. With two or three other exceptions, there is not a reservation whose Indians are not in actual want." "Since nothing else seems to serve," he concluded, "the campaign will be begun over again; and the matter of the present condition of the Mission Indians will be taken up with the Department, with Congress, and with the President, by organized public sentiment in California; and the thing will be hammered away at until there is relief."[53]

To redeem this pledge, a Los Angeles Council of the Sequoya League was founded in May, 1904. An attendance of nearly 1,000 at this body's first public meeting indicated that the Indian problem had become a live issue in Los Angeles.[54] The line of the Council's attack was to work for the elimination of red tape and incompetence; to urge the desirability of consulting scholars like those in the Bureau of Ethnology in the determination of policy; and to encourage the revival of native handiwork.

The chance to take specific action came in the fall of 1904. Again Constance Goddard DuBois was the inciting influence. On learning of the coming visit to southern California of Colonel John S. Lockwood, president of the Indian Industries League of Boston, she prevailed upon him to visit the Campo *rancheria*, the smallest of the villages in the Mission Indian system, and one where the natives were most destitute. A report of this visit and of a follow-up investigation made by Edward H. Davis, who had served as guide to Colonel Lockwood, found its way into

[52]Ibid., Mar. 19, 1903.
[53]"Sequoya League," *Out West*, XX (1904), May, 464-65.
[54]Ibid., June, 556-57.

Lummis' hands and was published in *Out West*. It showed the Indians of Campo to be on the edge of starvation due to failure of the pine nut and acorn crops which formed their main items of diet.

Davis' report led Lummis, as chairman of the executive committee of the Sequoya League, and Wayland H. Smith, secretary of the Los Angeles Council of the League, to make their own thorough investigation of the Campo reservation and surrounding area between November eighth and fifteenth. On the five reservations visited, the two men found cases of actual starvation, and it was estimated that at least twenty-five of the older, more infirm Indians would be dead by spring unless aid was forthcoming. An emergency fund was set up for the relief of Campo. San Diego citizens responded quickly and generously with money to buy seed grain for the next season, and a mass meeting in Los Angeles wakened public sentiment to the need for immediate aid. Under the direction of Wayland Smith a scheme for the systematic relief of the Indians was devised. There was initial distribution of clothing and food with rations issued every two weeks thereafter. In January a belated but welcome $500 appropriation by the Indian Bureau was acknowledged.[55]

Looking toward more permanent relief, the Los Angeles Council sponsored a co-operative enterprise which arranged for marketing the basketwork of the Mission Indians without resort to a middleman, thus allowing the Indians full benefit of the sale except for a slight deduction to pay for shipping charges. Also the Council redoubled its efforts to achieve the government purchase of arable land to be added to the Campo reservations so as to make the Indians self-sufficient. This was land, Lummis noted, which should have been purchased with the $23,000 the Warner's Ranch commission had saved the government.

In September, 1904, Lummis had visited Washington, D. C., and had talked with President Roosevelt, the new Commissioner of Indian Affairs, Francis P. Leupp, whom Lummis held in high

[55]Wayland H. Smith, "The Relief of Campo," *Out West*, XXII (1905), Jan., 21-22.

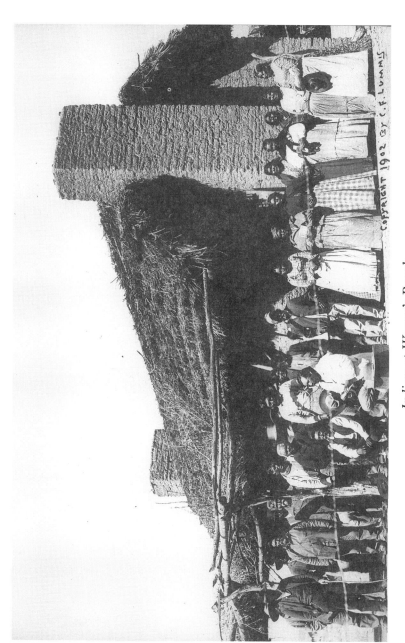

Indians at Warner's Ranch

esteem, and with the chairman of the Indian committees of both houses of Congress looking to the purchase of new and adequate land for the five reservations of Campo. Another mass meeting was held in Los Angeles in February, 1905, to urge action of Congress in this direction. However, the desired appropriation was not forthcoming. Still the agitation continued, and real encouragement was derived from an inspection of the Campo reservations by Senator Frank P. Flint in the fall of 1905. Senator Flint was convinced by his visit that the government should do something about furnishing satisfactory lands to the Indians.[56] Once more the Mission Indians in the Campo area were succored by public contributions largely solicited and distributed by the Sequoya League, enabling them to survive the winter. Then in February, 1906, C. E. Kelsey was appointed special agent for the California Indians. Kelsey was an experienced San Jose lawyer who for a number of years had been active in the cause of some 14,000 northern California Indians who were in a position similar to that of the Indians of San Diego County. Following Kelsey's inspection, Senator Flint prepared a bill calling for an appropriation of $100,000 to purchase lands for California Indians who were unable to support themselves on their present reservations.[57] The Los Angeles Council of the Sequoya League prepared a resolution endorsed by the city chamber of commerce to the effect that for two years running the people of California had contributed about $4,000 in support of the starving wards of the government, and that since the annual suffering of the Indians might be permanently relieved by allotting them lands on which they could make a living, it was respectfully requested that this be done. Copies of this memorial were dispatched to the President, the Secretary of the Interior, the Commissioner of Indian Affairs, and to the Indian committees of the Senate and the House of Representatives. Hundreds of letters to these officials were sent by southern Californians and others interested in alleviating the suffering of the Indians. Further, both Senator Flint and Inspector Kelsey testified before Congress to the need for additional lands. Such action, co-ordinated with

[56]"Sequoya League," *Out West*, XXIII (1905), Oct., 375-76.
[57]Ibid., XXIV (1906), Mar., 239-40.

agitation along similar lines by the Northern California Indian Association, must have contributed substantially to getting the appropriation through Congress, and Lummis, the Sequoya League, and its local Los Angeles Council could claim a decisive part in improving the lot of the California Indians.[58]

During the prolonged Warner's Ranch eviction case, the attention of Lummis and the Sequoya League was not confined to the Mission Indians. In the spring of 1903 Lummis struck a direct blow at the educational system he had criticized so bitterly in "My Brother's Keeper." Charles E. Burton, Superintendent and Disbursing Agent of the Hopis and Navajos stationed at Keam's Canyon, Arizona, bore the brunt of Lummis' attack. In what he termed the Sequoya League's second crusade, Lummis set out to expose and reform the Burton regime over the Moqui.[59] The announcement of this crusade in the April *Out West* came rather suddenly, but apparently a special agent of the Sequoya League had been scouting the Hopi reservation for several months gathering data on which to base a complaint. In addition, Lummis possessed an affidavit sworn to by Belle Axtell Kolp, a former teacher in the government day school at Oraibi, Arizona, who had resigned in disgust with the methods employed by John L. Ballinger, the school administrator, who was backed by Superintendent Burton.[60]

A formal complaint against Burton was drafted and addressed to the Commissioner of Indian Affairs, requesting an official investigation of conditions on the reservation under his supervision. The League's charges against Burton were grouped under four headings: general incompetence; arbitrary and despotic conduct; illegal violence; and violation of the rules of the service. These general categories, Lummis held, covered a multitude of specific sins. Burton, it was contended, commanded neither the respect nor the good will of his wards. In his determination to

[58]George Wharton James, "Charles F. Lummis: A Unique Literary Personage of Modern America," *National Magazine*, XXXVII (1912), Oct., 136, reprint in Lummis collection.

[59]Hopi and Moqui are used here interchangeably. Actually Moqui refers to the collection of eight villages wherein the Hopis live.

[60]"Affidavit of a Teacher," *Out West*, XIX (1903), July, 47-55.

fill the government schools he was accused of resorting to raids on Hopi homes in search of truants. These raids were made by armed Navajo police and led, the charge read, by Burton or by brutal subordinates. The Superintendent was charged with censoring those in his employ who seemed to be earning the love and confidence of the Indians, and with refusing the offer of a citizen to increase the inadequate water supply of the Indians. Burton's administration was said to be marked by the habitual use of intimidation and physical violence, thereby establishing a "reign of terror," and directly violating the rules of the Indian School Service prohibiting the resort to corporal punishment. A subordinate named H. Kampmeyer was the principal offender in this respect. After four years' service with Burton, Kampmeyer had recently been transferred, but Ballinger, who replaced him in the government school at Oraibi, was alleged to be little better. Moreover, Burton was accused of using hair-cropping as a punitive measure against the Hopis, despite the fact that an original policy of the Bureau of Indian Affairs designed to compel the Indians, especially those in government employ, to cut their hair had been modified to the point of virtual nullification.[61] The formal accusation closed with a request that witnesses be assured of and given complete protection so they would feel free to testify accurately and openly as to the conditions that prevailed under Burton's administration. This document was signed by the Executive Committee of the Sequoya League and appended to it was a strong endorsement by scientists, travelers, teachers, and others familiar with the Moqui case.[62] The Sequoya League's request for an investigation was granted, and United States Indian Inspector James E. Jenkins, supervisor of the Warner's Ranch eviction, was placed in charge. He was assisted by Charles Amadon Moody of the staff of *Out West*, who served as representative of the Sequoya League.

The findings of the official investigation by no means fully

[61]The so-called "hair-cut order" had been greeted with widespread derision. Lummis, among others, had objected strenuously, and apparently President Theodore Roosevelt had called for its revision. The result was an official interpretation which for all practical purposes emasculated the original directive.

[62]Lummis, "Bullying the 'Quaker Indians,'" *Out West*, XIX (1903), Aug., 171-75.

substantiated the charges made by Lummis and the League. The preliminary inquiry of the League, it was admitted, had been sincere and searching, but hardly impartial. No evidence was found to indicate that Burton was hostile to employees who were sympathetic to the Indians. No proof was obtained that Burton had hampered efforts to aid the Moquis. The offer to increase the water supply he could not accept, since only the Bureau had that power. The investigators found no indication that the Moquis objected to the use of Navajo police. It was asserted that the Superintendent's failure to clip the hair of Navajos as well as Hopis, which had left him open to the charge of cowardice, was dictated by discretion, not fear. If Burton had imposed a "reign of terror" it was apparent neither to Jenkins nor Moody; nor was there evidence that the schools were filled at the point of a gun as a matter of general practice. Finally, the investigators found Burton kindly, conscientious, courteous, and "anything but a brutal bully." The first impression of Jenkins and Moody alike was that on the whole the charges were unfounded and never should have been made.[63]

Despite the fact that a good many specific complaints appeared to be groundless, a number of the essential charges were substantiated. There was no doubt that rule 249 of the Indian School Service which stated: "In no case shall the school employees resort to . . . corporal punishment . . ." had been repeatedly violated. The charge that Burton's administration was marked by physical violence was true. The evidence showed clearly that Kampmeyer, former head of the school at Oraibi, was a man of violent temper and that he had been guilty of actual brutality in handling the Indians. Further, his replacement Ballinger admitted to wearing a revolver, "pushing with his foot" an Indian boy, and to cutting a gash in the head of another Indian with his revolver because the man protested the removal of his sister to attend the government school. Burton, it was pointed out, bore full responsibility for these and similar actions of men under his supervision. Finally, it was proved that in at least one instance Indian children were rounded up and taken from their homes

63"The Moqui Investigation," *Out West*, XIX (1903), Sept., 303-305.

by a squad of armed police led by Superintendent Burton. As a matter of fact, Burton had submitted a report of this action to the Commissioner of Indian Affairs and had received formal approval of the measures he had taken.[64] He justified his methods on the grounds that, although the children of other Indian mesas on the reservation had been in regular school attendance for nearly two years, the hostile faction at Oraibi had held out and that extreme measures were necessary to get their children into school.

Although the main objective of Lummis and the Sequoya League — to get rid of Burton — was not realized, the Bureau of Indian Affairs did take action. Kampmeyer, clearly the villain of the piece, was summarily dismissed from the Indian service and Ballinger was demoted. Burton was reprimanded for his sufferance of both Kampmeyer and Ballinger, but otherwise he was declared competent and was maintained in his position.

Lummis was certain that both the government agent and Moody had been deceived. He pointed out that Burton had plenty of warning that an investigation was imminent and thus was fully prepared for the inspection. The editor also reminded the Commissioners that the Indian's deep-seated fear prevented him from testifying against his superiors even when assured of protection. He insisted that the Indians would talk frankly only to those whom they felt they could trust. Moreover, Lummis was of the opinion that Jenkins and Moody had emphasized the unproved allegations of the League with the result that they tended to minimize what was proved.[65] In summarizing the affair Lummis contended that the investigation proved that the rules forbidding physical punishment were violated; that Burton resorted to hair-cropping as a punitive measure; that the Superintendent retained brutal and incompetent assistants; that on at least one occasion Indian houses were invaded and children taken to school by force; in short, that the major allegations of the League were upheld. Lummis went on to apologize to Burton for "whatever injustices have been done him personally." The

[64]Ibid., 307-309.
[65]Lummis to E. A. Hitchcock, Secretary of the Interior, Aug. 24, 1903, in Lummis collection.

Lion admitted that too many of the charges directed mainly at his administration were "lapped over" upon the Superintendent himself.[66] On the whole, Lummis was satisfied that the League's major contentions with respect to the Burton regime were borne out by the official investigation.

It is difficult to make a fair appraisal of the Moqui case. From the evidence available it is apparent that Lummis was injudicious in drawing up the charges against Burton. He relied on the testimony of persons who bore grudges against Burton. He couched even the formal accusation in intemperate language. His characterization of Burton's administration as a "reign of terror" was extreme. He was prone to label techniques used once or twice as habitual. Lummis weakened the League's case by indiscriminate use of terms such as "pin head," "coward," "bully," and "bigot," and by failing to make a clear distinction between acts committed by Burton's subordinates and actions of the Superintendent himself. Perhaps Lummis could not overcome his penchant for overstatement. It may be he believed overstatement was necessary to get action. Whatever the explanation, it seems evident that the charges brought against Burton by the Sequoya League were distorted and extreme. On the other hand, a careful reading of Moody's report reveals several instances of naïveté in accepting at face value statements from witnesses which a more discerning investigator would question or at least probe into further. Moreover, Lummis' claim that the Indians would not talk freely to agents of a government they had little reason to trust seems reasonable. Enough truth inhered in the major charges leveled against the Burton regime to justify the investigation. It is clear that the League's plan to expose the evils of Burton's administration and to secure his removal never quite came off. However, the dismissal of Kampmeyer and the demotion and transfer of Ballinger were concrete gains, and the chances that the harshness of the Burton regime would be tempered seemed excellent. All in all, the crusade of Lummis and his League on behalf of the Hopis might with accuracy be considered a qualified success.

[66]"Sequoya League," *Out West,* XIX (1903), Oct., 420.

Like the Landmarks Club, the history of the Sequoya League is vague after Lummis left *Out West*. Occasional reports of contributions received were printed in the magazine until the Christmas number for 1909, when the Sequoya League heading appeared for the last time. Lummis did not lose his interest in the welfare of the Indians, but the organized work of the League he had founded was done.

The contribution of the Sequoya League to Indian relief was substantial. It secured the Indians evicted from Warner's Ranch a vastly better home at Pala and one to which they eventually became adjusted. It achieved partial reform in Indian education through persistent editorial complaint and by bringing about an investigation of conditions among the Hopis in Arizona. It brought organized relief to the destitute Indians of the Campo reservations for two winters, and was a significant factor in securing a $100,000 appropriation for the purpose of procuring additional land for the reservations in San Diego County. The Sequoya League was neither the first nor the only association which worked for the well-being of the Indian; but by all odds it was the most efficient and most successful champion of the Indian in southern California and the Southwest.

Chapter **VI** APOSTLES OF THE WEST

U NDER EDITOR CHARLES LUMMIS the title page
of *Out West* displayed a large roster of far western
intellectuals beneath the pretentious and mislead-
ing heading "Staff." As a matter of fact, many
who were regularly listed as staff members scarcely merited
even the less ambitious designation of contributor. For example,
Joaquin Miller, Ina Coolbrith, Charles Warren Stoddard, Edwin
Markham, Theodore H. Hittell, and George Hamlin Fitch —
all persons of note in western letters and some of international
reputation, and all consistently listed among the staff — could
claim among them less than twenty contributions over a ten-
year period. It would have been more realistic, although less
impressive, had Lummis substituted the names of Julia Boynton
Green, Eugene Manlove Rhodes, Arthur B. Bennett, Juliette
Estelle Mathis, Nora May French, and Sui Sin Far. These
writers never rated staff listing, yet they accounted for nearly
a hundred contributions over the same ten years. There were,
of course, contributors regularly cited on the title page who
were worthy of the staff label including, among others,
Margaret Collier Graham, William E. Smythe, Sharlot Hall,
Charles and Louise Keeler, David Starr Jordan, Elizabeth and
Joseph Grinnell, Charlotte Perkins Gilman, Grace Ellery Channing, and Mary Austin.

Actually a school of writers never developed in Los Angeles
around Lummis' magazine in the same sense that the *Overland*
school existed in San Francisco a generation earlier. During
Lummis' tenure as editor more than six hundred individuals
contributed to the magazine. Of these, well over three hundred
appeared but once. Less than fifty could claim five or more
entries in *Out West*. A good share of the contributions to
Lummis' journal came from far beyond the city limits. Moreover, a survey of the *Reader's Guide* over the decade of Lummis'

dominance indicates that for a number of contributors *Out West* was by no means the principal publication channel.

On the other hand, shapeless and unwieldy as was the body of *Out West* contributors, within it were traces of homogeneity. After 1899 enrollment in Lummis' League of Western Writers provided a kind of cohesion. Then too a cluster of creative artists formed around the editor, seeking his criticism and gathering informally in his unusual home in the Arroyo Seco to participate in a western version of the European salon. Margaret Collier Graham, L. Maynard Dixon, Julia Boynton Green, Sharlot Hall, Eugene Manlove Rhodes, Idah Meacham Strobridge, Grace Ellery Channing, Charlotte Perkins Gilman, and Mary Austin were among those who, at one time or another, sought stimulation and encouragement at El Alisal. The editor also exercised a loose control over contributors through energetic and persistent correspondence. However, none of these centralizing tendencies alone, nor all of them combined, justifies the application of the term "school" to the contributors to *Out West*.

Nevertheless it is possible to draw a distinction between major and lesser contributors. On the basis of frequency of appearance and by virtue of distinctive handling of western materials, five writers — Sharlot Hall, Mary Austin, Eugene Manlove Rhodes, William E. Smythe, and Lummis himself — stand out boldly from among those who contributed to the monthly.

Lummis was incontestably the primary contributor to his own magazine. No one remotely approached him in linage. His performance in the Lion's Den and his writings in connection with western reforms have been treated. As for poetry, his contribution to *Out West* was negligible. It remains, however, to consider contributor Lummis as interpreter of California and the Southwest and in the capacity of reviewer and critic.

Lummis produced some of his most effective prose in his earnest attempts to describe and interpret the Southwest. A good example is the series of sketches published under the heading "The Southwestern Wonderland." This was a familiar text for the editor. Similar studies had appeared under his name in the nation's magazines in the eighties, and in the first half of the next decade he wrote several books dealing with the people and customs of the Southwest.

The first article in the series outlined what was to come by cataloguing the marvels of the region—the Grand Canyon, the Petrified Forest, the Moqui snake dance, the crucifixion ceremony of the Penitentes, Inscription Rock, the Natural Bridge, and like phenomena of man and nature. In sixteen essays, richly illustrated for the most part with photographs taken by himself, Lummis displayed to excellent advantage the results of long study and exploration in New Mexico and Arizona. His purpose plainly was to depict the most unusual and spectacular features of the Southwest, so as to compel interest in a neglected corner of the country. In these pieces, Lummis' touch is deft and sure. He is obviously dealing with a subject he knows and loves, and the outcome is at once entertaining and convincing. For the most part his prose is lucid, direct, and relatively restrained. The sketch dealing with the anachronistic rites of the Penitentes, accompanied by photographs, the description of the cliff city of Acoma, and the account of Inscription Rock are especially well done. Frequently the illustrations in this series were the first photographs of various aspects of the "Southwestern Wonderland" to be published.

In June, 1902, Lummis began a succession of articles focused on California and entitled "The Right Hand of the Continent." This series terminated abruptly in June, 1903, for, despite the promise "To be Continued," the thirteenth proved to be the final installment. "The Right Hand of the Continent," which referred of course to California, is not solely history, essay, propaganda piece, or sociological treatise, but possesses elements of all four. The central theme is simply the superiority of California to all other places in the world and that theme is given rambling, elaborate, repetitious, yet frequently striking statement. At times the editor became enmeshed in extended figures of speech. In one place, struggling desperately to confine a description of the wonders of his adopted state within a single sentence, he resorted to twenty-three lines of type fragmented by dashes, semicolons, and parentheses, not to mention commas.[1]

[1]*Out West*, XVII (1902), July, 4-5.

Moreover, his enthusiasm sometimes betrayed him into absurd generalizations, extravagant claims, and unlikely prophecies. Lummis launched the series by elaborating on the figure of speech embodied in the title:

In sober fact, it *is* the Right Hand, with all the name implies; and with triceps, biceps, forearm, wrist, fist and fingers full sinewed for its office. The passing prophecy, seven years ago, that in time this member must come to be realized of the rest—though to this day the self-sufficient left hand "outscriptures scripture, and as little cares as it little knows what the Right Hand doeth"—has fulfillment sooner than should have been expected. We have decided (officially, at least) to be a "world power."

From California we have reached out to pocket the Hawaiian orphans and the Philippine "rebels" (begging the dictionary's pardon); from California we shall continue to administer them at their proper cost, in so far as we shall carry out the contract. Even should a certain rather American reaction from emotion to figures, and from the voice of the siren to the voice of the Fathers, serve to put a hitch in our gallop, we can never again forget (though it may take us some time fully to remember) our actual national anatomy. Nothing can put us back so left handed as we were in 1897.[2]

Suddenly Lummis changed the figure of speech from right hand to tail and had California wagging the rest of the nation. California, he insisted, repeating claims already made in the Lion's Den, put the United States on a gold standard by adding tremendously to the nation's gold supply. Further, he held California directly responsible for delivering the West to the Union. "There were not many people with Webster's brains," he wrote, "but plenty who could imitate the limp of his provincialism. The United States was mostly content to remain a narrow huddle of provinces when California, suddenly and almost empirically, unrolled our trivial half-way map to another ocean, and gave us a national span, and pulled along population enough to vindicate the map."[3]

Proceeding from the material to the cultural, Lummis was convinced that California had made over the American mind. The golden state, he argued earnestly, brought mystery and

[2]Ibid., XVI (1902), June, 569-70.
[3]Ibid., 576.

romance to the nation and fostered the flowering of a national imagination. The impact of the gold rush, he believed, had changed the temper of the American mind forever, since it taught a low-aiming generation "to raise its sights for riches on the wing — and we have forgotten how to shoot low."[4] True, he admitted, California had produced no man of heroic national stature, but this he explained by noting the state's comparative youth.

After these and other introductory statements in a similar vein, the editor outlined his intentions relative to the future articles in the series on California. He did not propose to insist on 300-pound squashes and 150-pound watermelons and other productive prodigies even though he admitted most of them existed. Instead he would examine the state in its own and the nation's development and attempt to explain how and why it was evolving a civilization unique in the United States. Further, he would inquire what this new sociologic trend meant and was likely to mean for California and for the rest of the federal family. In short, he desired to discuss California as "a factor, not as a freak."[5]

Editor Lummis confessed a strong bias at the outset, admitting that he was an unabashed lover of his adopted state. The superlative he agreed was a dangerous weapon and subject to abuse, but on the other hand he felt it was not "a thing to skulk from since a scientific maximum was as true as a scientific minimum." There is no "skulking" from the superlative in the following passage:

... And it is not to be reckoned folly to count as of some big import ... a State which has twice been populated faster than any other on the continent, with classes respectively as unlike as buccaneers from professors; which was the most Western, and is now the most Eastern, State in the Union; the most foolish once, and now I believe, the wisest—in any event, the most potent. Nor can there fail to be, aside from economics, a certain human interest in the State which was our only transient hotel, and is now the most ineradicable home; the only State so many Americans ever sought in fever, and so few ever abandon in any temperature.[6]

[4]Ibid., 587.   [5]Ibid., 592.   [6]Ibid., 595.

Early in his treatise Lummis considered the weather. Climate he held to be the foremost influence in shaping the conditions which prevailed in California, but he quarreled with the term semitropic as applied to the state. The only valid resemblance he could find between California and the tropics was that in neither did one freeze to death. Temperate, he felt, was a better term, but "so long as New England is in the temperate zone, California cannot politely be." Equable zone Lummis finally selected as most appropriate, but, he insisted, the critical fact was that "it is the Land of the Golden Mean . . . as tonic as Maine (and with incomparably vaster pine forests), but without pneumonia; as fertile as Panama, but minus equatorial fevers."[7] Such a climate, he declared, produced superior physical specimens, and he paused to cite statistics on the chest expansion of Wellesley and University of California girls in which the Berkeley coeds were clearly out in front. As for the men, of the 1,300 students in Stanford University, Lummis pointed out, one third came from the East, but no one from the wrong side of Colorado got on the football team.[8]

Leaving the climatic factor, the Lion launched into a recital of sociological and cultural advantages which California enjoyed over older parts of the country. He claimed that New York had a larger percentage of illiteracy, poverty, and crime than California and a smaller percentage of people who owned their own homes. California, he crowed, had twice as many newspapers as New England. Moreover, he insisted, no state had better average schoolhouses for city and county, nor more of them in proportion to population. Furthermore, no other state paid its teachers so well on the average. California, concluded the editor, had all the comforts that money would buy in other localities and one comfort, its incomparable climate, that money could not buy.[9]

A distinctive feature of the editor's enthusiastic essay was the development of his own frontier hypothesis. Lummis argued

[7]Ibid., July, 9.

[8]Lummis would have had difficulty to explain the superiority in recent years of midwestern over California schools on the gridiron.

[9]*Out West*, XVII (1902), July, 23-29.

that a race derived real vitality from frontier conditions and that the Old World and a good part of the New was declining for want of a frontier. Although he noted that ruggedness was a characteristic of most frontiers, he did not consider it an essential quality. Elbow room and proximity to nature were, in his eyes, the *sine qua non* of a frontier and should nature be gentle rather than obstreperous, so much the better.

It was the lure of the city, Lummis asserted, that had sapped the strength of the New England frontier, and that lure was effective because the people of the East turned to "urban cushions" for shelter and comfort from the stony soil and harsh climate of rural New England. California, he suggested, was the last frontier, and man might trust that frontier to endure where others had disappeared simply because it was endurable.

The Lion mentioned the security California farmers enjoyed through the development of irrigation. He envisioned an agrarian environment where the population remained close to the soil and thus preserved the freshness of the frontier. In this affinity between man and the earth, Lummis argued, "lies the longest — perhaps the imperishable — vitality of California. Its newness will fade; its remoteness is already reduced sixty fold— from six months to three days — its roughness has disappeared forever; its refinement is already sensitive. But it is not in the usual civilized drift to over-refinement and ingrowing and anemia, because it will be always the outdoor country, always a temptation to tickle the grateful earth that we may see her smile."[10] This was the Lummis frontier hypothesis—naïve, opinionated, narrow, and smug, but withal refreshing, sincere, and doubtless plausible, perhaps intriguing, to the prospective settler.

In subsequent articles in the series, much of the discussion revolved around San Francisco and Los Angeles. Each city was considered apart in the light of its history, its personalities, and its material assets, and then the two were closely compared. Lummis found the northern metropolis essentially western in character and Los Angeles decidedly eastern.

By the time the Lion reached the final chapter in his California encomium he had sandwiched in a good deal of history;

[10]Ibid., 289-91.

biographical sketches of men such as James Lick, Adolph Sutro, William Keith, and John Muir; copious and sometimes tiresome statistics on immigration, natural resources, industrial and agricultural output; and a thorough inventory of the man-made facilities of the state. The series was richly illustrated by photographs, not necessarily correlated with the text, depicting various aspects of California ranging from shots of a residence in Berkeley or the Pacific Ocean from a La Jolla cave, to the tower arch at Stanford or a close-up of a horned toad. Thus did Lummis develop his dominant theme of California *über alles.*

Two special contributions Lummis made to his magazine were detailed reviews of works produced in the early modern era of European history. The first was a treatise written in 1646 by Ferrarius of Siena on the culture and use of the orange, lemon, and lime.[11] The second dealt with mining methods and appeared first in 1550 under the hand of Georg Agricola.[12] Lummis analyzed each work and reproduced a number of the illustrations — copper plates in the case of Ferrarius' treatise and woodcuts in the work by Agricola.

The editor's main object in these two reviews was to call attention to the fact that in neither the propagation of citrus fruits nor in mining methods had California and the West made spectacular progress over that of 250 to 350 years earlier. In support of this contention he quoted instructions from Ferrarius as to the proper means of fertilizing, ditching, irrigating, and pruning the orange, and he reproduced woodcuts from the book on mining depicting chain pumps, stamp mills, and a variety of "long tom." Both works he praised highly as masterpieces of thorough and scholarly research. Lummis derived patent satisfaction from delivering a shock to New World complacency through this demonstration of Old World expertness in two fields in which he claimed Californians considered themselves far advanced. Such satisfaction, hardly consistent with Lummis' customary attitude toward the Far West, may have come from his feeling he had scored a personal historical coup.

[11] "Citrus Fruits 250 Years Ago," *Out West*, XVI (1902), Feb. to Apr.
[12] "Mining 350 Years Ago," *Out West*, XX (1904), Jan. to Mar. An English translation of this work was later prepared by Herbert Hoover and his wife.

The Lion also functioned as book reviewer, critic, and general arbiter on matters of western culture. For several years, in a monthly department called "That Which Is Written," Lummis passed judgment on books that came to his attention, according priority to those with western themes. After 1902, this task was largely assumed by assistant editor Charles Amadon Moody, but frequently Lummis invaded the department to evaluate a new book dealing with Spain in America or with the American West. Generally his comments were short, giving the department the form of a monthly collection of book notes, but sometimes more extended notices appeared. A characteristic feature of Lummis' review technique was his tendency to point out errors of detail. Often an author drew a sound drubbing for the barbarization of Spanish terms, for incorrect dates, for ignorance of western geography, or some similar misdemeanor, but he might escape with little or no comment on the broader aspects of his book — its organization, success in achieving objectives, or the relation of the work to its field.

Lummis made no attempt to disguise his prejudices in his reviews. Writers such as Reuben Gold Thwaites, Charles Elliott Coues, Ernest Thompson Seton, and Rudyard Kipling received unfailingly sympathetic treatment. His dislikes were largely confined to lesser-known writers, especially to those who wrote carelessly or mendaciously about the West. Two exceptions to this were Hubert Howe Bancroft and Henry James. In the former instance, whenever opportunity arose, Lummis made slurring comment on the man whom he contemptuously dismissed as a book salesman and co-ordinator of historical hack work.[13] In the case of Henry James, reviewer Lummis recognized the subtlety of his work but deplored its lack of human warmth. "Now probably no educated person alive has read James," he wrote, "without being tickled mentally by his unhuman cleverness; but he has lived nigh three-score years and spent his mature life in writing, and never yet has bitten one human heart. Is that smart, after all? And smartness is the only leg he ever had to stand on. . . . It would be a pity to be dull to

<hr>

[13]"A New League for the West," *Land of Sunshine*, VIII (1898), Apr., 208.

Charles F. Lummis in 1928
Probably the last picture

his astounding cleverness; but it is a greater pity not to be sorry for a man who is too clever to be human and not clever enough to be divine."[14]

Lummis' treatment of Bancroft and James, however, was mild compared to the type-lashing he administered Edwin Markham. After the spectacular reception of "Man with a Hoe," Markham had committed, in Lummis' eyes, the cardinal sin of moving east to capitalize on his sudden rise to fame. Of Markham in Oakland, the editor asserted, California and the West might justly be proud:

But Markham in Brooklyn, regurgitating How I Wrote It, and two-bitting from Hoboken to Rahway to relieve the natural anxiety of other mothers and spinsters as to the details of his gestation; plastering the visible walls, tables and what-nots of his rented habitation with clippings of It in all the varieties of newspaper "art"; pink-teaing on this flattery, instead of Doing Something—ach!

The Lion was especially aroused over an elaborate snapshot interview of Markham in *Everybody's Magazine* portraying the poet in various poses. After sarcastic reference to what he considered a vulgar display, Lummis turned directly on Markham:

Shame, Oakland schoolmaster! Shame, California poet! Do you know how you look Yorking? Will you go on posing on your Accident, or will you Do Something? Let go the tinkling brass, Man! You can't play on it! The thinnest, meanest, laziest, cowardliest capital in the world for a man to go on is What he Has Done—particularly when it was a scratch. The only vital thing about any man is what he is Going to Do. It's nobody's Manhattan business How you Did it; and nobody worth the alum to tan his hide cares. The Would-bes, the Mentally Unemployed are your audiences now. The only interest you or any other writer commands with people who have visible means of support is—Can you Do it Again—and a little better? If you cannot, do not think to put off the day of Forgottenness. If you can, *do* it—and you will never do it footlighting. You are in *Everybody's Magazine*—Now re-enter *Somebody's*.[15]

If somewhat intemperate, the advice was sound. However, only in "Lincoln, the Man of the People" did Markham approach his performance in "Man with the Hoe."

[14]"That Which Is Written," *Land of Sunshine*, XIII (1900), Dec., 453.
[15]"In Western Letters," *Land of Sunshine*, XIII (1900), Aug., 151-53.

Lummis exercised his function as critic in other ways, including a series of articles appraising western artists such as William Keith, Maynard Dixon, and Ed Borein; a group of biographical and critical sketches of authorities on the Southwest, among them Adolph F. Bandelier, Washington Matthews, George Parker Winship, and Frederick Webb Hodge; and a department called "In Western Letters," where the editor welcomed new contributors, printed news notes of western literati, and occasionally took a writer to task as he had Edwin Markham.

Charles Lummis was a fearless, energetic, and sincere critic. His over-all judgments were generally reliable. He was an alert and tireless defender of accuracy in detail, especially in matters involving the treatment of western materials. On the other hand, he was neither dispassionate nor penetrating in his criticism. His prejudices often colored his judgments. Moreover, some of his book notices and most of his evaluations of authors and artists contain so many generalities and ambiguities that upon analysis they yield little more substance than does cotton candy.

After editor Lummis, William E. Smythe was the most frequent contributor to *Out West*. With Smythe the magazine acquired a new evangelist for the region it represented. His chief text was national irrigation as the key to the coming kingdom of the arid West. Beginning in July, 1901, and for two and a half years thereafter he conducted a department in Lummis' magazine averaging about twenty pages and entitled "20th Century West." Here Smythe wrote enthusiastically and persuasively on irrigation, colonization, and co-operation — the cornerstones, he insisted, whereon might be raised out of aridity a civilization greater than anything a humid environment had yet produced.

William Ellsworth Smythe, like Charles Lummis an uprooted Yankee, was born in Worcester, Massachusetts, December 24, 1861.[16] Like Lummis, too, he selected journalism as an early calling, graduating from printer to reporter at seventeen. While he was serving as an editorial writer on the Omaha *Bee* in 1890 the plight of drought-stricken Nebraska farmers kindled in him an interest in irrigation as a means of relieving their distress, and

[16]*National Encyclopedia of American Biography*, XVII (New York, 1927), 444.

he wrote a series of articles in the *Bee* exploring irrigation possibilities in Nebraska. This self-imposed assignment apparently changed his life. "I had taken the cross of a new crusade," Smythe testified. "To my mind irrigation seemed the biggest thing in the world. It was not merely a matter of ditches and acres, but a philosophy, a religion, and a programme of practical statesmanship rolled into one."[17]

Out of these articles in the *Bee* emerged an organized irrigation movement, beginning with a series of local conventions in western Nebraska followed by a state gathering at Lincoln which made Smythe chairman of a committee to arrange for a national irrigation congress. The first such congress met at Salt Lake City in 1891 and delegates from ten western states and territories emphatically advocated outright cession of the public domain, except mineral lands, to the several states in which they were located. Two years later a second convention in Los Angeles gave birth to the first public sentiment in favor of national irrigation works.[18] During subsequent congresses the trend grew stronger in favor of the participation of the federal government in irrigation projects. The first official advocacy of governmental construction of irrigation works appeared in a report compiled in 1897 by Captain Hiram M. Chittenden of the Corps of Engineers in which reservoir sites in Colorado and Wyoming were surveyed. In the same year a National Irrigation Association was formed at Wichita, Kansas.[19] Then, in 1900, a congress meeting in Chicago issued a forceful declaration for national irrigation works with water rights determined on the basis of beneficial use.[20]

Meanwhile Smythe had left the Omaha *Bee* to found at Denver in 1891 a unique magazine, *Irrigation Age*, for the propagation of his gospel of irrigation. Several years later Smythe's first and most important book appeared. In *The Conquest of Arid America* (1899) he looked at the United States as cut

[17]*The Conquest of Arid America* (New York, 1905), pp. 266-67.

[18]William E. Smythe, "20th Century West," *Land of Sunshine*, XV (1901), Nov., 380.

[19]Walter Prescott Webb, *The Great Plains* (New York, 1931), p. 361.

[20]Smythe, "20th Century West," *Land of Sunshine*, XV (1901), Nov., 381.

into halves by the 87th meridian. The better half, he insisted, lay west of that line and its outstanding characteristic was its essential aridity endowing the soil with an incredible fertility which only irrigation could release. According to Smythe, Salt Lake in Utah, Greeley in Colorado, and Anaheim and Riverside in California were the utopias of the arid West created by the miracle of irrigation. The application of this miracle on a grand scale throughout arid America, he contended, would inaugurate a new and crowning era in the nation's history.[21] Briefly, this was the background and these were the views of the man who joined the *Land of Sunshine's* staff in July, 1901. Lummis gave the irrigationist free rein, asking only that he make his writing as near literature as the subject matter would allow.

The three crucial questions of the West according to William Smythe were: how to get the water on the land; how to get the landless man to the manless land; how to make the man prosperous and secure once on the land. The answer to the first, Smythe claimed, lay in a system of public works and the exercise of public authority over the distribution of the water supply. New Zealand's system of scientific colonization he felt answered the second question. The key to the third he put in a single word—co-operation.[22] These three questions and the attempts to answer them comprise the significant content of "20th Century West."

Smythe maintained a running and critical commentary on the progress of national irrigation and on the status of water-law reform in California and in other western states; he printed papers by authorities dealing with successful irrigation experiments in the West; he wrote essays on irrigation ethics; he analyzed government reports pertaining to the water problem; he struck out against projected legislation if he believed it tended to subvert the cause of public irrigation; and he reviewed important books in the irrigation field. He was against the doctrine of riparian rights and he deplored the laxity of laws governing the distribution of water which often permitted overappropriation. He fought private monopoly of water, achieved through the

[21]*The Conquest of Arid America*, passim.
[22]"20th Century West," *Out West*, XVI (1902), Mar., 317-22.

divorcement of water from land ownership, because it usually led to speculation in water rights. On the other hand, he was for government construction of reservoirs; he favored state control over distribution of water made available through government works, provided that distribution was equitable and went to bona fide settlers on the land. Moreover, he demanded that ownership of water attach to the soil; that the right to the use of water for irrigation be vested in the user and become appurtenant to the land irrigated; and that beneficial use be the basis for the distribution of water rights.

Smythe's immediate concern was the status of California water laws and he worked hard to achieve their reform. He urged, among other things, that a state board of control of water be empowered to fix equitable rates for the sale of water rights and for the sale of water for irrigation by private companies; that use of water for domestic purposes take precedence over all other uses; that the state legislature outlaw the doctrine of riparian rights in California, except to make riparian owners on streams preferred users of natural stream flow for domestic and stock purposes; and that all unappropriated waters be made public property.[23]

Although he wrote long and earnestly on California's water problem, Smythe wrought no immediate change in the water laws nor did he inaugurate an age of national irrigation. Rather, it is in the role of propagandist and precursor that Smythe's influence is to be measured.

Closely aligned with his interest in irrigation was Smythe's belief in what he termed scientific colonization, the essence of which was co-operation. He claimed that California was not being colonized successfully due largely to expenses involved in the activities of numerous land companies and because of distrust in the East created and fostered by rival and conflicting claims as to the richness of California and the opportunities offered. Smythe suggested a single co-operative association financed by subscriptions to its capital stock and selling land upon terms designed to return profits to be prorated among stockholders, with owners of the land disposed of receiving

[23]"20th Century West," *Land of Sunshine*, XV (1901), Dec., 499-500.

individual profits besides. He estimated that it would cost about $50,000 to test the plan and he suggested this could be raised partly by stock subscription and partly by donation.[24] Smythe also proposed a model co-operative colony plan that the colonizing association might employ to get the settlers on the land.[25]

Actually Smythe was working up to a more radical proposal. Was it necessary, he inquired, to leave the destinies of California to be worked out by private enterprise? Might not institutions and methods tried elsewhere with success be transferred to the arid West, especially to California? In answer to these questions, Smythe described New Zealand's policy and suggested its adaptation to California. In New Zealand, Smythe explained, great tracts of fertile soil had passed out of the hands of the government to become lordly private estates. A roughly analogous situation prevailed in California, he contended, where some holdings traced back to Spanish and Mexican land grants and others had been acquired during the American period under United States land laws. New Zealand, he informed his readers, dealt with private holdings by requiring them to pay their full share of taxation or by buying them up from their owners and applying them to higher public uses. Once acquired, the state developed them by irrigation projects, road-building programs, railroad construction, and the like. Having obtained the great estates and having provided them with public improvements, New Zealand leased them to settlers. The leasehold seemed a wiser public policy than the freehold to Smythe because it made farming land available to families of poor or moderate means, because land speculation was prevented, and because the clotting of land into large estates once more was rendered impossible.[26] Smythe considered this an infinitely shrewder plan than the haphazard policies of private capital that prevailed in California.

Up to this point Smythe appears to have been conducting a paper crusade. However, combined with neat plans for planting co-operative colonies, essays on irrigation ethics, and papers

[24]Ibid., Oct., 279-85.
[25]Ibid., Nov., 383-90.
[26]"New Zealand Institutions," *Out West*, XVI (1902), Feb., 203-204.

smacking strongly of socialist leanings, was an attempt to organize actively for the betterment of California. To this end Smythe founded the California Constructive League in February, 1902. In his words: "We are going to have a popular crusade. Its purpose —TO BUILD THE STATE! . . . its champions will go forth to slay the dragon of Public Indifference and start an intellectual friction which will result in Bringing These Things To Pass."[27] The plan was to establish debating societies called Constructive Clubs to be combined in the state League. Their function was to discuss current practical questions in an attempt to revive the village lyceum as it existed in Horace Greeley's day. The League was nonpartisan but frankly and deliberately political. It began the crusade with one fixed objective — to send men to both branches of the state legislature who would work for reform in water laws.

Smythe put up a brave front in *Out West*, but the League had little genuine cohesion. He aimed at the establishment of not less than 100 clubs in California and possibly others in other Pacific states. Actually at no time was there more than a handful of active groups.[28] Constructive Leaguers were admonished to exert their influence at the polls, but only with respect to irrigation was any of the League's ambitious program heeded by either of the major political parties.

When the Republican and Democratic platforms emerged from the state conventions in 1902, each contained commitments on irrigation, and Smythe pointed out that for the first time irrigation had risen to the proportions of a first-class state issue. He confidently assumed credit for such progress on behalf of the California Constructive League, and with some justice, for he had served on the committee on resolutions at the Democratic state convention.[29] He then urged members of the League to concentrate on electing friends of the constructive movement to both houses of the state legislature. Smythe himself was nominated by the Democrats to run for congressman from the newly formed eighth district, but he was badly beaten.

[27]"California Constructive League," *Out West*, XVI (1902), Feb., 197-99.
[28]Ibid., XVII (1902), July, 118-19.
[29]Ibid., Oct., 507-508.

The California Constructive League limped along until June, 1903, when an attempt was made at reorganization. The plan was to incorporate, and to drop the word California from the title so its work might be extended throughout the country. Six months after the announcement of reorganization, Smythe closed the "20th Century West" department and the Constructive League was dead.

Smythe's parting message to the readers of the magazine was an earnest affirmation of faith:

I do not know when all the things I have fought for shall come true; I do not know when the last vestige of water monopoly shall disappear, and, in its place, a system erected on foundations of everlasting justice shall arise to endure forever and bless the unborn millions who are to follow where we have led the way. I do not know when the hideous institution of monopoly in land shall perish and when God's green earth shall be divided among those who earn their bread in the sweat of their faces. I do not know when the pitiful strife of man against man shall give place to noble forms of cooperation. . . . But I know that these things *shall* come in the progress of civilization. And if what I have written for *Out West* has hastened by a day or an hour the consummation of this logical and inevitable development of Western institutions I thank God it was given me to write it.[30]

Smythe's farewell to *Out West* was also a farewell to politics, and he turned to experimentation with land colonization. The plan he developed came to be known as the Little Landers movement because its underlying idea was the establishment of groups of families upon small land holdings, containing from one to five acres.[31] Smythe organized three distinct Little Lander colonies in California between 1908 and 1919. All three ventures finally failed, largely because in each case the land provided was of poor quality.[32] In 1919 Smythe dropped out of the movement he had founded and became associated with Secretary of the Interior Franklin K. Lane in connection with a plan to extend the reclamation movement throughout the United States.[33] He died in New York on October 27, 1922.

[30]"20th Century West," *Out West*, XX (1904), Jan., 103, 104.
[31]Henry S. Anderson, "The Little Landers' Land Colonies: A Unique Agricultural Experiment in California," *Agricultural History*, V (1931), Oct., 140.
[32]Ibid., passim.
[33]Ibid., 149-50.

It is impossible to measure the influence of William Smythe and his department with precision. Probably it was slight. By most criteria Smythe was a failure throughout his connection with *Out West*. To many of his contemporaries his views must have seemed at best chimerical, at worst subversive. The League he led to accomplish his reform program was handicapped by inadequate funds, journalistic ridicule, and an organization so loose as to be generally ineffective. His personal foray into politics ended in rout. He was a man with a cause but with a shadowy and unreliable following. As Smythe explained: "I fear I must be classified as a conservative among radicals and a radical among conservatives."[34]

Yet the man and his department are not without significance. Smythe was a pioneer in the national irrigation movement, and "20th Century West" represented an extension and elaboration of his thinking on this and related subjects. He himself observed that if ordered to strike from the record all he had said and done since he became interested in western development, his contribution to five volumes of the magazine would not be the first to go.[35] Second, his writings reveal an early awareness of the need for modification of economic and political institutions to meet the demands of an arid environment. Third, the formation of a nonpartisan league to effect reform at the local and state political level in a sense foreshadowed the Lincoln-Roosevelt League which paved the way for the successful reform movement led by Hiram Johnson. Fourth, although admittedly they were ephemeral, some interest inheres in Smythe's writings because they display originality, independence, and considerably more tolerance than those of many better-known reformers of the period. Finally, through "20th Century West" Smythe gave Lummis' magazine a positive, refreshing, and courageous voice in discussing California's most vital issue — water.

Sharlot Hall was one of *Out West's* most loyal and dependable contributors, and she served for several years as associate editor of the monthly. Miss Hall's experience was firmly set in

[34]"20th Century West," *Out West*, XVI (1902), May, 538.
[35]Ibid., XX (1904), Jan., 103.

the tradition of the West. She was born October 27, 1870, the first white child in what became Lincoln County, Kansas. Her first twelve years were spent in Kansas. Then, in November, 1881, her family started by wagon train over part of the Santa Fe Trail to join her uncles in Arizona who had drifted down from the mining camps of Colorado soon after Arizona achieved territorial status. The Halls were on the trail for months and arrived in the territory early in 1882, establishing a ranch home on Lower Lynx Creek in the Yavapai hills about twenty miles from Prescott.[36]

Sharlot Hall had only a limited formal education, including grammar school near Dewey, Arizona, a term in high school at Prescott, and another in the Cumnock School of Expression in Los Angeles. Duties at Orchard Ranch, as the Hall residence came to be called, absorbed much of Miss Hall's time, but the recurrence of a hip injury caused by a fall from her pony on the trek to Arizona, confined her to bed for about a year and gave her a chance to try her hand at writing verse for publication. Two of her poems saw print during this period, one in a farm journal and the other in the *Great Divide*, a magazine published by the *Rocky Mountain News*. Meanwhile she had formed a literary contact with Charles Lummis through familiarity with his work in the national magazines, and not long after he assumed editorship of the *Land of Sunshine* Miss Hall submitted verses and articles which he accepted and published. Later, on a trip to the West Coast, she visited the Lummis home, and this led to an intermittent associate editorship which called her to Los Angeles to help edit the magazine when Lummis was away.[37]

Before and during her connection with Lummis' magazine, Sharlot Hall was largely responsible for operating the family ranch since her father was crippled. She also developed a keen interest in the Southwest and she built up an intimate knowledge of its history and its peoples. Her appointment as Territorial Historian of Arizona in 1909 terminated her relationship

---

[36]Charles Franklin Parker, "Out of the West of Long Ago," *Arizona Highways*, XIX (1943), Jan., 8.

[37]Ibid., 9.

with *Out West*. This office she held until 1912, when she returned to Orchard Ranch because of the illness of her mother. Here she remained until 1929, when she sold the ranch and acquired the property in Prescott known as the First Governor's Mansion. This she transformed into a museum of pioneer history, a task which occupied her until her death in 1943 at the age of seventy-two.[38]

Sharlot Hall's contributions to the magazine were truly representative of the writer's works. Many of the poems which made up *Cactus and Pine*, her only published volume, and a fair share of her verse included in various anthologies, appeared first in the pages of *Out West*. Her offerings to the magazine included poems and articles in about equal number and a handful of short stories.

The short stories are generally undistinguished. All are sentimental, but the restraint with which they are written coupled, in almost every case, with a tragic twist, keep them from being maudlin. In one of her better stories Miss Hall explores a common theme in western writing — the effect of isolation and the desert upon a sensitive woman. The tale deals with the wife of a renderer of quicklime whose first child dies a few hours after birth. The tragedy, combined with continual isolation and the indifference of an unimaginative husband, drives the woman to seek solace in the deserted cliff dwellings near their cabin, where she falls victim to hallucinations involving the "little people." At length her husband decides to have her committed to an institution, but before his return with a physician she takes refuge in the cliff caves where the "little people" claim their friend.[39] The other stories have widely varying plots, but all are set in the Southwest and most of them contain carefully drawn descriptions of the region.

In her articles Sharlot Hall combined the functions of historian, promoter, and essayist. Her interest centered on Indians, mining, and on the land itself. One of her most effective prose pieces deals with the cremation of a Mojave chief in the vicinity of Needles, California. In it Miss Hall captures much of the

[38]Ibid.

[39]"The Friend of the Little People," *Out West*, XXIV (1906), Mar., 217-21.

dignity, sternness, and resistance to change of the Mojave people.[40] Other papers deal with the flora of the Arizona desert, with the history of pioneer towns such as Prescott and Tombstone, with the origin and development of some of the richest Arizona mines, and with irrigation and forest conservation in Arizona.

Sharlot Hall best interpreted the Southwest through her poetry. The verse she contributed to Lummis' magazine over a period of ten years shows a steady growth both in conception and execution. Her first attempts were short, simple love or nature lyrics with a happy, optimistic motif and frequent classical allusions. "Wind Song," the last of this type, is the best, and although it treats of death, in spirit it is essentially optimistic. The second stanza follows:

> But I would go when strong winds blow
>   Full-throated down the heaven
> And on the blast like pennants cast
>   The wild black hawks are driven.
> Oh, kith and kin are they to me,
>   Wild-winged my soul shall pass
> With them, as their own shadows drive
>   Across the wind-swept grass.[41]

As the years passed, Sharlot Hall's poetic contributions to *Out West* grew longer, more earnest in statement, more western in flavor. Some of them like "The Santa Fe Trail," "Arizona," and "Out West" have an epic quality. The last was written to dedicate and commemorate the change in the magazine's name from *Land of Sunshine* to *Out West*. Lummis had asked both Edwin Markham and Joaquin Miller for a poem for the occasion, but since neither responded, the assignment fell to Miss Hall. The poem was printed on heavy cardboard along with a painting by Maynard Dixon, and it was sent to every periodical of importance in the country with announcement of the change in name. Later the poem was used in a choral arrangement and given at the Festival of Western Songs in Minnesota. The poem epitomized the qualities which Sharlot Hall believed

[40]"The Burning of a Mojave Chief," *Out West*, XVIII (1903), Jan., 60-65.
[41]*Land of Sunshine*, XIV (1901), Jan., 3.

made the West great—sternness, vitality, freedom, breadth—and it strongly underwrote the concept of manifest destiny.

However, it was in her narrative poems that Sharlot Hall produced her most distinctive verse. Here she was at once historian and poet, taking authentic western material and working it into ballad form. Two poems published in *Out West* represent Miss Hall at her best in balladry. The first, "Two Bits," tells the story of an ex-race horse stationed at Fort Whipple, Arizona Territory, who bore his rider through Indian country toward Fort Wingate, New Mexico, to bring aid to the post which was under Apache attack. After outrunning a band of Apaches, and receiving a ball in the chest, Two Bits reaches Fort Wingate and leads the soldiers back to where his wounded rider fell. The man lives but the horse dies and is buried beside the overland road a few miles west of the fort.[42]

In the "Mercy of Nah-Ne," Sharlot Hall exploits the tale of Felix Knox, tinhorn gambler. Knox, while driving with his wife not far from Silver City, Arizona, finds they are pursued by a band of Apaches. He stands them off with a Winchester long enough to allow his wife to drive the buckboard to town and safety. Knox is found dead the next day, but he is unscalped and his body is covered with the blanket of an Apache chief in tribute to his sacrifice.[43] In romantic narrative poems such as these, Sharlot Hall gives compelling expression to some of the West's legends of bravery and selflessness, often on the part of decidedly imperfect human beings.

When Miss Hall died she left behind a volume of verse, a museum of pioneer history, and forty contributions to *Out West* bearing witness to the love and loyalty she bore the Southwest and to her ability to understand the region and interpret it for others.

Charles Lummis and his magazine can claim a modest part in producing one of America's most distinguished women of letters—Mary Hunter Austin. Mary Hunter was born and spent her youth in Carlinville, Illinois. She was graduated from Blackburn College in 1888. She came to California with her mother and

[42]*Out West*, XVI (1902), June, 617-19.
[43]Ibid., XXIII (1905), July, 3-4.

two brothers in the same year, and the Hunter family home-steaded in the vicinity of Bakersfield. Here began Mary's experiences with the land which formed the background for her early stories and novels. While teaching in a ranch school below Tejon Pass she met and, in 1891, married Stafford W. Austin, a teacher and sometime promoter. The next year a child, Ruth, was born to the Austins and in the same year Mary's first story was accepted by the *Overland Monthly*.

During the nineties the Austins lived in various towns of the Owens River Valley and Mary cultivated a deep interest in the government Indian school at Bishop. Besides teaching she devoted much time to painstaking and penetrating observation of nature and the people about her. These were years of deepening sorrow and frustration. Her marriage was threatening to end in divorce, and the child proved mentally retarded.

Mrs. Austin became increasingly determined to write and she went to Los Angeles in the summer of 1899 to join the group which had formed around Charles Lummis. She received more encouragement from Eva Lummis than from the editor who felt she had talent, industry, and "a certain kind of knowledge," but no real genius.[44] Nevertheless, through the Lummises, Mrs. Austin was admitted to the inner circles of writers both in Los Angeles and in Carmel, and when she wrote to the house that was publishing her first book, *Land of Little Rain*, she cited Charles Lummis as her first and warmest friend in the West.[45]

Except for a personal report on the San Francisco earthquake and fire of 1906, all of Mary Austin's offerings appeared in Lummis' magazine between 1899 and 1904. During this time she was working hard to master her craft. Out of these years came *Land of Little Rain* and *The Basket Maker*. Also, she was publishing in *St. Nicholas*, *Cosmopolitan*, and the *Atlantic Monthly*. The stories and poems she sent to Lummis were probably not her best, but they were a part of her training,

[44]Mary Austin, *Earth Horizon* (New York, 1932), pp. 290-292.
[45]Mary Austin to Messrs. Houghton, Mifflin and Company, Nov. 5, 1902, in Helen MacKnight Doyle, *Mary Austin: Woman of Genius* (New York, 1937), p. 200.

and they served to give her an opportunity to see how her knowledge of the desert and its people looked in print. In her offerings to the western monthly both in poetry and prose there is evidence of growth in technique as well as in assurance.

The verse that Mary Austin wrote for *Out West* was either narrative or descriptive, and she produced both with equal facility. It is difficult to generalize about her poems. Each was distinct. Each was an expression of an individual mood or told an independent story. In "The Burgher's Wife" she wrote hotly of British herding of Boer women and children into concentration camps with consequent high incidence of disease and death. The poem ends:

> It is not for you, O England, to give me back my sons,
> We have paid the tale twice over by the coughing, spitting guns,
> But the small graves of the children, they are yawning in the sod—
> Deep enough to gulf your glory—high to witness unto God[46]

Mary Austin turned to a wilderness theme when she wrote "The Song of the Bow," a simple poem with an easy swing detailing the function of an Indian's bow. Two stanzas will illustrate its nature:

> The wood was the heart of a juniper tree
>   On a strong, sea-sloping hill,
> And the things it learned in the young green bough
>   The bow remembered still;
>
> For it learned of the wind, it learned of the sea
>   And it learned of the spotted snake,
> And their threefold sting was loosed from the string
>   When the will of the bow would wake.[47]

Love and affinity for nature are evident in this fragment from "A Twilight Hill":

> Some beams still light the far, dark, tapered firs,
> A Quail belated to its covert whirrs
> In nestling hollows where a warm wind stirs
>   The lupins everywhere.

[46]*Land of Sunshine*, XV (1901), Dec., 423-24.
[47]*Out West*, XX (1904), Jan., 55.

The hill folk have no fear of such as I,
The questing night hawk hurtles dauntless by,
I hear the speckled owlets hoot, and spy
    Their matings unaware.[48]

Four short stories and a novelette in five installments constitute Mary Austin's output in fiction to the magazine. All exploit
western topics — a lost mine, a sheepherder's revenge, the courage
of a crippled Indian boy — and all are informed by an intimate
knowledge of the setting and characters of the stories. The
novelette suffers mainly from mechanical defects. The plot
unfolds sluggishly; some of the characters, the villain in particular, are painfully stereotyped; and the dialogue is frequently
stilted.

Mary Austin is more effective in the short stories and despite
touches of sentimentality the tales are plausible. One of the most
entertaining is an involved and tragic story of Guadalupe,
daughter of a miner and a Paiute woman. The girl falls in love
and forms a liaison with a faro dealer. After a time the two
are separated when the gambler is forced into hiding to avoid
the consequences of an old crime. Guadalupe learns of the
whereabouts of a lost mine from an ancient Indian who has
befriended the deserted girl. Hoping to use the wealth to locate
her lover, Guadalupe uses a young Indian who loves her to help
her find the mine and take out the gold. Once the rich vein
is located, the misapprehending Indian seeks to claim Guadalupe
and she stabs him. However, the strain is too much for the girl
who loses her mind and lives out her days a half-wit.[49]

Such stories leave much to be desired, but they are markers
on Mary Austin's path to literary maturity. They may also
have had a certain therapeutic value by providing a catharsis
for her unhappiness and frustration. The insight and authority
with which Mary Austin later wrote of the desert country
are suggested in these stories.

The years following Mary Austin's association with Lummis
and his magazine were busy ones. She traveled abroad and in
this country, writing continually, and gradually she fulfilled

[48]*Land of Sunshine*, XIV (1901), Mar., 181.
[49]"The Lost Mine of Fisherman's Peak," *Out West*, XIX (1903), Nov., 501-10.

the promise shown during her literary apprenticeship. In 1924 she made her home in Santa Fe, where she crusaded for the preservation and rehabilitation of Indian and Spanish arts and crafts, and assumed aggressive leadership in a number of other regional movements. Her death, August 13, 1934, ended the career of a unique and forceful figure in the life of the Southwest but her influence survives in her writings.

If *Out West* can advance proprietary right to any contributor it is to Eugene Manlove Rhodes, the only man, in the opinion of Bernard De Voto, who attained the level of genuine art in writing fiction about the cowboy.[50] The first short story Rhodes wrote was sold to Lummis for ten dollars, and was published in the January number in 1902. A few poems by the New Mexican cowboy had already appeared in Lummis' monthly. Gene Rhodes received encouragement from the editor and he came to Los Angeles to meet Lummis. Rhodes wrote May Davison, his wife-to-be, of his visit to El Alisal, describing how at his knock, Lummis stuck his head out of the window of his study tower and shouted, "Who are you? I think I can lick you whoever you are."[51] Rhodes, who loved a fight and a fighter, could appreciate such a hail, and in the friendship which developed, Lummis, although about the same age, assumed a relationship to the cowboy somewhere between that of an experienced uncle and an elder brother.[52]

As for Gene Rhodes's background, let him speak for himself here in an autobiographical sketch written in the third person:

Came to New Mexico in 1881 as a boy of twelve. From 1881 to 1888 he worked for several cattle outfits known respectively as the Ky, KIM, John Cross, Bar Cross and 7TX—longest for the Bar Cross on the Jornada del Muerto. In earlier days did a little mining and freighting; later set up a ranch of his own on the San Andres. Held four aces in El Paso, 1893; in Organ, New Mexico, 1896; in New York, 1908. Held straight flush in New York, 1913. Mr. Rhodes wrote his first stories for Out West in 1902 and 1904. He went East in 1906 to

[50]"Horizon Land," *Saturday Review of Literature*, XIV (1936), Oct. 17, 8.
[51]May Davison Rhodes, *Hired Man on Horseback: My Story of Eugene Manlove Rhodes* (Boston, 1938), p. 150.
[52]Ibid., 151.

write some more stories. Arrived in New York with a guitar, a scrap-book and $3.50 in cash, with indebtedness of $2500. Returned to New Mexico in 1926 with three scrapbooks and a family, the guitar being broken. In the interim wrote seven books and about a hundred short stories, all except five of the stories dealing with New Mexico and New Mexicans.[53]

Some gaps need filling. Gene Rhodes was a Nebraska boy born in Tecumseh, January 19, 1869. He began work with a cattle outfit at thirteen, serving as wrangler. Although never a "top hand" he was competent, and he had the liking and respect of the men he worked with.[54] Perhaps his passion for reading prevented his reaching the top bracket of the profession. Rhodes was said to carry a book instead of a gun, and he had the habit of reading while riding. One time his horse slipped off a trail, tumbling Rhodes from the saddle. To the anxious inquiries of his companions if he was hurt, Gene retorted, "Well, he lost my place."[55] When he was twenty, Rhodes went to school for a couple of years in the University of the Pacific at San Jose, California, where he made his first writing efforts.

Gene Rhodes married May Davison Purple of Apalachin, New York, a widow with two children, in 1899. They had known each other only three weeks, although a two-year court-ship by correspondence had preceded their meeting. He greeted her in New York with gifts — a book of Kipling's verse and a pearl-handled six-gun — and a joke about his cheap New York-bought suit: "('I was a stranger and they took me in!')"[56] He and his wife returned to New Mexico where Gene resumed writing. After three years of ranch life in Tularosa, Mrs. Rhodes returned East for a visit with her family. Gene joined her in Apalachin in 1906, where, in his phrase, he "got snowed in for twenty years."

[53]"They Know New Mexico" (Passenger Department, Atchison, Topeka, and Santa Fe Railroad, 1928), p. 40.

[54]J. Frank Dobie, "Gene Rhodes: Cowboy Novelist," *Atlantic Monthly*, CLXXXIII (1949), June, 75.

[55]Eddy Orcutt, "Passed By Here: A Memorial to Gene Rhodes," *Saturday Evening Post*, CCXI (1938), Aug. 20, 21.

[56]Joseph Henry Jackson, *Saturday Review of Literature*, XVIII (1938), Oct. 15, 7.

During these years of exile Rhodes earned his living by his pen. Most of his stories appeared in the *Saturday Evening Post*, although *Out West* published one or two of them. That Lummis was still an influence in the cowboy-author's life is indicated by the editor's comments on the appearance of Gene's first book in 1910. "You have done a very extraordinary thing, very uneven, in places hazy. Not entirely pulled together in a final Drawstring. A novel made up of episodes. But you have made the Best talking book that ever came out of the mouth of the West. The language they use on occasion is frequent and painful and free. . . . I never saw any work of yours I didn't admire. I never saw any of it that I didn't want to kick you for not doing it better as you are perfectly competent to do."[57]

In 1926 the Rhodes family returned to New Mexico, but in 1931, in deference to Gene's poor health, they moved to a little cottage at Pacific Beach near San Diego. Here in his last years Rhodes turned out some of his best work, including *The Proud Sheriff*, which was published posthumously. Gene Rhodes died of a heart attack June 27, 1934. He lies on the top of San Andres Mountain in New Mexico beneath the simple legend *Paso por aquí*. Equally appropriate would have been an epitaph he once composed, signed "Mine by Me":

> Now hushed at last the murmur of his mirth.
> Here he lies quiet in the quiet earth.[58]

Gene Rhodes began his writing career with verse. Five of his poems were printed in Lummis' western monthly. One of them was a clumsily constructed but bitter denunciation of imperialism in the Pacific. Its concluding lines read:

> The words of Christ our armies spread and bid His Church increase—
> The kind and gentle, the meek and mild, the lowly Prince of Peace—
> For the holy name of Freedom and the Glory of our God,
> The blood of Luzon's children smokes up from Luzon's sod;
> And o'er their swollen corpses the vultures wheel in glee
> Who dared to die for the ancient lie that God made all men Free![59]

---

[57]Lummis to Rhodes, quoted in Rhodes, p. 151.
[58]Orcutt, p. 53.
[59]"Te Deum Laudamus," *Land of Sunshine*, XIV (1901), Jan., 55.

The other four poems develop southwestern themes and are generally mediocre. Verse was not to be Gene Rhodes's most effective medium.

The short stories are a different matter. Here the cowboy could better express his sentiments, and he had much to say. Most of Rhodes's stories deal with his experiences, with the experiences of men he knew, or with those of men who had become a part of western folklore in tales told around campfires under the night sky. They dealt with situations that gave the New Mexican word-wrangler full opportunity to exploit the legendary qualities of the cowboy breed—courage, self-sacrifice, veneration for women, generosity, humor, independence, stamina, terseness, nervelessness, and competence. Then too Rhodes had a message to get across to the East. He wanted to open the eyes of citified men to the fact that the range produced men of honor and of worth. He sought to demonstrate that often the alleged lawlessness of the westerner was nothing worse than practical adjustment to the realities of an existence that eastern law ignored or made no provision for. He tried to show that humble, illiterate men—thieves, and professional gamblers, and killers—could rise to acts of courage and unselfishness that made better men of all who witnessed them, and that by such acts their names lived in the land as symbols of high valor and devotion, commanding respect instead of hatred or dread.

All these elements appeared in Gene Rhodes's stories, together with a dry humor and a knack for reproducing the cowboy vernacular that went far to mitigate the sentimentality of the stories. A few phrases, even when wrenched from their context, reveal the pungency and aptness of the range idiom as set down with uncompromising fidelity by Rhodes: "Uncork him for me if he pitches"; "He broke his ribs pretty plenty"; "They've got me watering at night" (running from the law); "He'll stand without bein' tied"; and, "I've been hopin' he'd take on fat and shed off slick."

Of course Rhodes's stories have their faults. His women for the most part are too good to be true. However, as De Voto points out, that was exactly how the westerner felt about women.[60] A defect in many of Rhodes's early stories is a tendency to make the point of the tale too explicit. For example, in "The Bar Cross Liar," a story taken out of Rhodes's own experience, the hero, a young horse-wrangler, has been thought a miser by his comrades because he dresses poorly and intends to stay away from a Christmas dance. The boy has been treated coldly by the other hands and is in danger of being fired, when the men learn that not only has he been sending every spare cent to his destitute folks, but he has been writing them of the kindness and generosity of his fellows to ease his family's mind as to how their boy is faring. Thoroughly shamed, the outfit stages a Christmas banquet with the boy as surprise guest of honor and his parents in attendance. An effective speech is made by one of the "top hands" and the wrangler is warmly welcomed into the group. Here the story might well have closed, but Rhodes adds:

The tumult falls on heedless ears and deaf. Life's sweetest cup is trembling at his lips. Whatever gifts the years may hold for him, there shall be no triumph so dear as to eclipse this moment; no shame to wash away its benediction. Not wealth, nor fame, nor power, nor vengeance long-delayed, shall thrill his heart so deeply. Not love itself, nor love's first clinging kiss can yield a rapture keener than now awaits him—a mother's tears of pride and joy over her first born.[61]

This emotional, sentimental excess is the more difficult to understand because it violates the cowboy's proverbial reticence.

Rhodes worked hard to make himself a successful writer and he did not arrive overnight. His first story for the *Saturday Evening Post* had been submitted six times over a period of two years, varying in length between 3,500 and 22,000 words. Nevertheless the qualities that make Rhodes one of the finest writers of western fiction — his honesty, his knowledge and love of his subject, his ear for speech patterns — these were all present in the first stories he wrote, stories that appeared in *Out West*, and in the laconic but potent praise of the cowhand, "they'll do to take along."

[60]De Voto, p. 8.
[61]*Out West*, XVI (1902), June, 619-25.

Chapter **VII** OTHER CONTRIBUTORS

I N SELECTING REPRESENTATIVES from the lesser contributors for special treatment it is necessary to be somewhat arbitrary, although a number of considerations have
influenced the choices made. Some, like Joaquin Miller,
are selected largely on the basis of earlier achievement. Theodore H. Hittell, Washington Matthews, Elizabeth and Joseph
Grinnell, and L. Maynard Dixon appear primarily because they
were experts in fields which the editor emphasized. Julia Boynton Green, Charlotte Perkins Gilman, John Vance Cheney, and
Nora May French deserve attention as representative poets,
while Grace Ellery Channing, David Starr Jordan, and Charles
and Louise Keeler merit inclusion as essayists. Sui Sin Far's concern with the Oriental in the West qualifies her for consideration.
These criteria are not necessarily mutually exclusive. The common denominator among the writers selected is that all dealt
almost exclusively with western themes.

Lummis' magazine fell heir to some of the members of the
Overland school who were still active even though California's
golden era of literature was done. Joaquin Miller, Charles Stoddard, and Ina Coolbrith appeared briefly in the pages of *Out
West*.

By 1895, when he contributed his first poem to Lummis'
western monthly, Joaquin Miller had settled down to a life of
quiet eccentricity on about one hundred acres in the hills
overlooking Oakland. From "the Heights" he continued his
literary flow and occasionally a trickle reached the southern
California magazine. Miller's half-dozen pieces published by
Lummis dealt with varied themes. The first, a poem, struck a
contradictory note when the poet of the Sierra wrote from his
hilly fastness where he had planted thousands of trees:

[164]

Give me the desert! I should trust
Nor sea nor ship nor mountain chine.
Nude nature, ashen, prone in dust;
So like this bittered life of mine.
Give me the desert, emptied quite
Of all that maketh man's delight.

The desert! dust, bone, stone for me,
And there companioned but by Him
Behold my faith shall grow a tree
So bright all others shall grow dim;
So tall no serpent eye can sight;
So green no slander tongue can blight.[1]

A few months later another verse was forthcoming from "the Heights" in the form of a brief tribute to Frémont in which the poet offered the Pathfinder poppies for his "bed and bier."[2]

In June, 1898, the *Land of Sunshine* carried a rambling, petulant report of life in the Klondike by Joaquin Miller. There were one or two comparisons of conditions in Alaska in '98 with those which had prevailed in California in the days of '49, but for the most part the article focused on problems of keeping clean and preparing meals in the diggings.[3]

There is general agreement among critics of American literature that on occasion Joaquin Miller produced poetry which will live. It is safe to say that none of this variety found its way into Lummis' monthly. However, by depicting phases of western life, the poet faithfully reflected the magazine's major emphasis.

The other two survivors of California's pioneer literary period contributed so sparsely to the magazine as to warrant little more than mention. Charles Warren Stoddard wrote a reminiscent sketch of the "old days" that revolved around Ina Coolbrith, and he also contributed two inconsequential poems.[4] Ina Coolbrith, in "The Cactus Hedge," penned a delicately

---

[1]"Give Me the Desert," *Land of Sunshine*, III (1895), Aug., 103.

[2]"Frémont," *Land of Sunshine*, IV (1895), Dec., 18.

[3]"Daily Life in a Klondike Cabin," IX, 16-23.

[4]"Amber," *Land of Sunshine*, X (1899), Jan., 72-76; "California," *Land of Sunshine*, X (1898), Dec., 3; "Revery," *Land of Sunshine*, XII (1899), Dec., 3.

worded invitation to romance proffered by a Spanish girl to her lover.⁵ Less frivolous was her poetic tribute to the California landscape artist, William Keith, which appeared in *Out West* in April, 1903.

In the fall of 1902 Jack London made an appearance in the western monthly with two short stories. At this time he was living in Piedmont, California, not far from the poet George Sterling. London, whose tales of the Far North were drawing encouraging critical comment, was on the brink of a period of rich literary productivity. The two stories which Lummis published dealt with Alaskan Indians, and in them London drew on his experiences in the Klondike in 1897-1898. The stronger of the two tales tells how a Tlingit shaman outwits a rival medicine man from a neighboring village and then disposes of a skeptic within his own tribe. London's characteristic preoccupation with brute force is present but subordinated in this story. Here the feeble but wily shaman prevails over enemies of superior physical prowess, although, significantly, the disbeliever's destruction is accomplished by a tribal stoning incited by the shaman.⁶

In both stories London wrote realistically of the Northwest Indians. His unflinching approach to life's grimness and barbarity prevented the tales from falling into the sentimental and artificial pattern of so many Indian stories of the day.

In the next year or so, with the appearance of books such as *The Call of the Wild*, *The Kempton-Wace Letters* with Anna Strunsky, *People of the Abyss*, and several collections of Alaskan stories, Jack London achieved literary renown, and his brief appearance in *Out West* was not repeated.

It was only proper that the man whom Lummis considered the foremost historian of California should be represented in the magazine. Theodore H. Hittell, son of a Pennsylvania physician, was born at Marietta in Lancaster County, April 5, 1830. The boy was raised in Ohio where at fifteen he entered Oxford College, now part of Miami University. He went from there to Center College in Danville, Kentucky, and then on to Yale where

⁵*Out West*, XVII (1902), Oct., 429.
⁶"Master of Mystery," *Out West*, XVII (1902), Sept., 330-339.

he was graduated in 1849. After several years of law practice in Ohio, Hittell came to San Francisco by way of the Isthmus in 1855. He served as law reporter for the San Francisco *Bulletin* and he supported the revival of the Vigilance Committee in 1856. After 1860 he entered into law practice and became an authority on the complicated question of land titles in California. In the eighties Hittell ventured into politics, serving as state senator. Having achieved prominence and wealth through his legal practice, Hittell devoted increasing time to research and writing. His first published work, *Adventures of James Capen Adams*, was off the press in 1860, and in 1872 he produced a paper-bound criticism of Goethe's *Faust*.[7]

In 1871 Hittell began a study of California upon which his reputation as a historian rests. After fourteen years the first two volumes were published in 1885, and twelve years later the concluding two volumes appeared. The four-volume work generally received cordial treatment from reviewers. Lummis gave it enthusiastic endorsement and at the same time cast disparaging remarks in Bancroft's direction. "Hittell," the Lion observed, "is not a 'drummer' but a student; not a hirer of reporters, but a historian. Not by the sweat of irresponsible and alien brows, but by personal research for more than a quarter of a century, he has come into ripeness of knowledge. With more conscience, sounder judgment and better style, he has made the four great volumes of his monumental *History* coherent, attractive, trustworthy; and the work has promptly supplanted Bancroft's colossal failure."[8]

In the opinion of less biased reviewers such was not the case. Josiah Royce claimed that Bancroft was still the best authority for the Spanish period, although he recognized Hittell's superiority for the epoch after 1850. Royce found fault with Hittell for making too few generalizations and he also criticized his lack of perspective and inclusion of endless detail.[9]

---

[7]G. W. Dickie, Leverett Mills Loomis, Ransom Pratt (committee), "In Memoriam: Theodore Henry Hittell," *Proceedings of the California Academy of Sciences*, 4th ser., VIII (1918), June 17, 3-8.

[8]"A New League for the West," *Land of Sunshine*, VIII (1898), Apr., 208.

[9]*American Historical Review*, IV (1896), Oct., 184-86.

Although the *Nation* regarded Hittell's study as "the largest result yet obtained by any one man's unaided work in historical writing of California," it cautioned that Bancroft had not been superseded and that students must consult the works of both historians. Along with Royce, this reviewer found Hittell "lacking in the courage to draw striking conclusions."[10]

At any rate, an article or two by Theodore Hittell would clearly help raise the tone of Lummis' young monthly, and the editor welcomed a paper on the "Big Bonanza" which he printed in two installments in the *Land of Sunshine*.[11] This was a careful, scholarly discussion of the discovery and exploitation of the Comstock Lode and despite an annoying tendency toward repetition, the article makes interesting and reliable reading.

When Lummis pressed for another contribution, historian Hittell submitted a paper on the geographical peculiarities of California, written, he confessed, some years earlier but never published.[12] In this article Hittell pointed out California's central position with respect to the Pacific Coast of North America. He went on to consider the topographical symmetry of the state, comparing it roughly to one felly of a wagon wheel with its outward rim toward the ocean. In the middle of this outer rim, he observed, lay the bay of San Francisco, "the mouth of perhaps the most symmetrical and interesting natural drainage system on the face of the globe."[13] Somewhat carried away by his theme, Hittell concluded that the geographical balance carried over into such fields as mining and agriculture, and that the same kind of symmetry prevailed between the people of the north and south of California, binding them into one undivided and indivisible state. On this provocative note the paper ended. Although Hittell had a number of productive years left, this was his last contribution to *Out West*.

A more frequent contributor than Hittell was Washington Matthews, whom Lummis labeled "Dean of American Ethnolo-

[10]Vol. LXVIII (1899), Jan. 5, 15-16.

[11]Vol. XI (1899), Sept., Oct., 214-22; 276-82.

[12]Theodore H. Hittell to Charles F. Lummis, San Francisco, Nov. 13, 1900, in Lummis collection.

[13]Vol. XV (1901), Sept., 154.

gists." Matthews was born in Killiney, Dublin County, Ireland, July 17, 1843. His father, Dr. Nicholas Blayney Matthews, brought Washington and his brother to Wisconsin Territory in 1847 shortly after the death of their mother, and then moved to Iowa where Washington grew up. He began the study of medicine under his father when he was seventeen, and he received an M.D. degree from the University of Iowa in his twenty-first year. He volunteered for service in the United States Army where he served as a doctor for the next thirty years, much of the time on the frontier.[14] Despite long military service Matthews' more significant career lay in the scientific study of North American Indians, beginning with the Hidatsa, Arikara, and Mandan, and culminating with the Navajo on whom he became a recognized authority.

Matthews' outstanding contribution to ethnology was his thorough study of legend and ceremonial among the Navajo. In 1895 his *Navajo Legends* was published. Here the surgeon-ethnologist carefully related the traditional history of the Navajo intermingled with the people's mythology and presupposed in their ritual. Eight years later Matthews' work was crowned with an exhaustive explanation of a single Navajo ceremony – the Night Chant. In the words of a competent judge, this study provided "a record of at least one rite of a tribe, in which scientific accuracy is united with poetical perception, to make thoroughly comprehensible the religious belief which has so long remained mysterious."[15]

Matthews contributed to *Out West* both as ethnologist and poet, but in the latter capacity his offerings are inconsequential. He first entered the pages of Lummis' magazine in October, 1896, with an introductory paper on the types and meanings of Navajo songs. He vigorously refuted the views of Dr. Jona Letterman of the army, who claimed that the singing of the Navajos was little more than a succession of grunts. Matthews translated several Navajo chants and pointed out the Indians'

[14]J. M., "In Memoriam: Washington Matthews," *American Anthropologist*, VII (1905), Sept., 514-15.

[15]H. W. Newell, *The Journal of American Folk-Lore*, XVI (1903), Mar., 613-15.

deliberate and effective use of repetition, antithesis, climax, and irony.[16] In this and in other articles that followed, Washington Matthews helped to make the scientific study of the Southwest Indian interesting and intelligible to the magazine's readers.

From time to time editor Lummis relied upon his close friend David Starr Jordan, then president of Stanford University, for material to publish in his magazine. Jordan, a native of New York and a student of Louis Agassiz at Cornell, achieved early distinction as an ichthyologist and later recognition as an educator, lecturer, and crusader for the peaceful settlement of international disputes.[17]

Jordan's first contribution was a discussion of the ideals of Stanford. After taking stock of the first seven years of the school's life, its president attempted to state clearly what the university stood for. The essence of the Stanford ideal of education, he believed, was the building of character and personality through emphasis upon the needs and capabilities of the individual.[18] Jordan had some pertinent comments on higher education and he stated them well. Much of his philosophy of education is contained in these excerpts from his article:

It is not brick and mortar, books and laboratories that make a university. These are its vegetative organs. Its spirit is given by its teachers. It is not what is their fame, what their degrees, what have they published, but *what can they do?* . . . The best teacher, other things being equal, is the one most human. The ultimate end of education is the regulation of human conduct. Its justification is the building up of an enlightened common sense. It is to help make right action possible and prevalent that the university exists. . . . The search for truth is more to us than the truth we win in searching. Self-direction is more important than innocence. Any fool can be innocent; it takes something of a man to be virtuous.

That the university may have freedom, it must exist for its own purposes alone. . . . Partisanship and truth cannot get along together. "It can acknowledge no master in human form," if it is to be loyal to its highest purpose.[19]

[16]"Songs of the Navajos," *Land of Sunshine,* V (1896), Oct., 197-201.

[17]Walter V. Woehlke, "Our Twelve Great Scientists: XI, Dr. David Starr Jordan," *Technical World,* XXIII (1915), Mar., 108-12.

[18]Vol. IX (1898), June, 5-6.

[19]Ibid., 10-12.

In line with the extension of the magazine's scope, Jordan turned to the problem of the administration of Hawaii. Without offering a solution, he pointed out the difficulties in the application of democratic forms of government to a backward area possessing differences in racial traits and interests which were bound to persist for several generations.[20] In this article and in a later piece published in 1907 that was critical of agitation against Japanese immigration, Jordan demonstrated his willingness and ability to discuss controversial issues with tolerance and restraint.[21]

Jordan's contributions, infrequent though they were, identified Lummis' magazine with Stanford, and the editor consistently displayed partiality to that institution when discussing education in the West. Lummis took pride in the University of California, too but his interest in Stanford was more personal. He and David Starr Jordan had much in common. Both were converts to the West, both were staunch individualists, both were reformers, and when Lummis named his second son Jordan, the tie between the two men was further strengthened. In his two-volume autobiography, *Days of a Man* (1922), a rich, sprawling, informal record of his life and times, David Starr Jordan writes with affection of Lummis and his magazine.

In June, 1896, the *Land of Sunshine* published a short story by Sui Sin Far. This was the pen name of Edith Maude Eaton, daughter of an English artist and his Chinese wife whom he had met and married in Shanghai. The Eatons returned to Macclesfield, Cheshire, England, where Edith was born in 1868.[22] In the middle seventies the family came to the United States. They lived for a time in New York and then moved to Montreal. According to her own testimony, Maude Eaton's childhood and youth were unhappy. More sensitive than her three sisters and two brothers, the stream of unpleasant incidents imposed on the half-caste by society created tensions

[20]"On Certain Problems of Democracy in Hawaii," *Out West*, XVI (1902), Jan., Feb., 25-32; 139-49.

[21]"The Japanese Problem in California," *Out West*, XXVI (1907), Mar., 224-30.

[22]Lummis, "In Western Letters," *Land of Sunshine*, XIII (1900), Nov., 336.

within her which she was able partly to discharge through writing for publication. Miss Eaton supported herself as a stenographer and drifted west seeking the lowest level of prejudice. Apparently she found it in Seattle at the turn of the century after stays of varying lengths in Montreal, Chicago, Jamaica, and San Francisco.

In an autobiographical article Miss Eaton described her first personal contact with editor Lummis thus: "I meet some literary people, chief among whom is the editor of the magazine who took my first Chinese stories. He and his wife give me a warm welcome to their ranch. They are broad-minded people whose interest in me is sincere and intelligent, not affected and vulgar."[23]

Sui Sin Far contributed nine stories and one article to Lummis' magazine. All her work dealt with the Chinese in America and particularly with the plight of the Eurasian. All but two of the stories end tragically, and translation into print of the writer's suffering and frustration is patent. The stories themselves have little literary polish. The dialogue, which is usually western, clashes with the statement of the theme and the spirit of the story which are essentially eastern. Thus the conflict within Miss Eaton between her occidental environment and her oriental heritage produces an evident dichotomy in her stories disruptive of their unity. Miss Eaton stated her basic and irremediable dilemma succinctly: "I give my right hand to the Occidentals and my left to the Orientals, hoping that between them they will not utterly destroy the insignificant 'connecting link.' And that's all."[24] It is her bold and poignant statement of the problem of the Eurasian in America and her repeated refusal to find a happy solution that make her work noteworthy.

The passion for southern California which pervaded so much of Lummis' editorial and promotional prose found belletristic expression in the poems, stories, and essays written for the magazine by Grace Ellery Channing.

Miss Channing, granddaughter of the Reverend William Ellery Channing, was educated in private schools in Rhode

[23]Sui Sin Far, "Leaves from the Mental Portfolio of an Eurasian," *Independent*, LXVI (1909), Jan., 128-30, 132.
[24]Ibid.

Island. At eighteen she was teaching the first kindergarten in Providence.[25] A scholarly atmosphere which was her birthright, combined with semi-invalidism imposed by tuberculosis, led her into literary production. She began by editing the notes of her famous grandfather, and *Dr. Channing's Note-Book* appeared in 1889. The next year she went to Europe, living there for a time, particularly in Italy. On her return to the United States she took a position on the editorial staff of the *Youth's Companion*.[26] In June, 1894, she married Charles Walter Stetson, a Providence artist, only recently divorced from another contributor to Lummis' magazine, Charlotte A. Perkins. The Stetsons joined the Yankee exodus and established a home in Pasadena, although by 1897 they had settled in Italy, he to paint, she to write. Meanwhile Grace Ellery Channing, retaining her maiden name for literary purposes, had produced a collection of short stories, *A Sister of a Saint* (1895). This was followed by a book of verse, *Sea-Drift*, in 1899, and another cluster of stories, *The Fortune of a Day*, the next year. Throughout these years, and after, Miss Channing's name appeared often in the national magazines.

To judge from the selections in *Out West*, poetry was Miss Channing's weakest genre. Her verse is consistently romantic, sentimental, superficial, and sometimes with imperfections in cadence which strike a jarring note in the conventional rhyme patterns her poetry assumed. Throughout, her verse is tinged with nostalgia. The following is typical:

> I watched the petals of the snow
> Cover New England's breast; and "So,"
> I said, "I've seen my almond trees
> Snow down their blossoms when the breeze
> Blew soft as breezes used to blow
> In that sweet season long ago,
> In the dear Land of Sundown Seas.[27]

In her early short stories Grace Ellery Channing's desertion of New England for southern California is much more evident

[25]Lummis, "In Western Letters," *Land of Sunshine*, XIII (1900), July, 86-87.
[26]"The Lounger," *Critic*, XXXVII (1900), Nov., 391.
[27]"Memory," *Land of Sunshine*, VII (1897), July, 43.

than in her verse. The first story which appeared in the *Land of Sunshine*, "The Madness of the Rector," is an implausible tale about a young Connecticut rector visiting southern California to recoup his health. During his stay he becomes so enamored of the climate and the scenery, and only incidentally, it would seem, of an attractive mission teacher, that he literally leaves his congregation waiting at the church on Easter Sunday. He has run away intent upon embracing nature (and presumably, after a decent interval, the teacher) in the little village of the Mission Indians.[28] Other stories follow in the same vein although as the stories gain in literary finish, the promotional accent fades.

Miss Channing's essays carry her ideas more gracefully and more convincingly than either her poems or short stories. In these essays, all of them written in Rome, she is fascinated by the parallel between Italy and California, between Rome and Los Angeles, and she foresees a flowering of civilization and culture around the latter, richer and more lasting than that of the ancient city. She finds the southern Pacific coast superior to the eastern shores of the Mediterranean with respect to climate and fertility, but she is certain that southern Californians can learn from Rome. This is the central theme of her essays.

The two great sins of the easterner transplanted to the land south of the Tehachapi, Miss Channing suggests, are first, his failure to combine beauty with utility, and she contrasts the ugly iron pipe lines of Los Angeles with the aqueducts of Rome;[29] and second, the refusal of the easterner in southern California to adapt himself to a life out of doors.[30] Both the Italian and the Spaniard, she asserts, in the use of the interior court and the patio, and in the development of gardens, offer styles of home architecture and landscaping which, if followed, would allow the southern Californian to take full advantage of the climate. Her point of view is partly expressed in the following passage:

[28]Vol. IV (1896), Mar., 175-78.

[29]"What We Can Learn From Rome: 'Water Out of the Rock,'" *Out West*, XIX (1903), Oct., 366-67.

[30]*Out West*, XIX (1903), Nov., 473.

Tree for tree, bush for bush, flower for flower, we have all that Italy has; subtract the stonepine and the laurel, and all is said; and for these count us up a score of things which Italy has not. And we have it all, incomparably *more*—larger, richer, more riotously. One who walks dreaming through these Italian gardens which have been so many centuries the delight of mankind, seeing beyond their vistas California's larger spaces, her far more rapid growth of vegetation, her deeper skies and more splendid color—such a one must feel that he can in truth *but* dream what gardens here might be, and what their influence upon a race growing up amid these "thoughts of God."[31]

While not of conspicuous literary worth, Miss Channing's essays were appropriate and probably not ineffective carriers of the monthly's promotional text.

Only one writing partnership appeared among the contributors to *Out West* during Lummis' period as editor. This was Elizabeth and Joseph Grinnell, a mother-and-son combination. Elizabeth Grinnell, another New Englander, this time from Maine, married Dr. Fordyce Grinnell, a government physician to the Plains Indians, in 1874, and spent ten years with him in Indian territory. There were three sons, of whom Joseph was the eldest. In the middle eighties the family settled in Pasadena, and Joseph entered Throop Polytechnic Institute, taking his B.A. in zoology in 1897. An M.A. from Stanford followed and ultimately, in 1913, he received the doctorate. His specialty was ornithology. Mrs. Grinnell studied birds along with her son, and she also found time to write books for young people.[32] Young Joseph made an early reputation as an authority on Pacific Coast birds and in 1896, and again in 1898-1899, he was a member of scientific expeditions to Alaska. For most of his mature life he served as professor of zoology at the University of California.

The Grinnells produced a number of natural history sketches over their six-year period of association with the magazine. These essays, dealing almost exclusively with the birds of southern California, are unpretentious, informal, and usually laced

[31]Ibid., 483.
[32]Lummis, "In Western Letters," *Land of Sunshine*, XIII (1900), June, 21.

with delicate humor. Beginning with the third paper, the Grinnells illustrated their bird studies with portraits of their subject. Many of these are superior examples of bird-life photography. The Grinnells' purpose was to familiarize the reader with western birds, to provide reliable guides to bird identification, and, on more than one occasion, to come to the defense of a misunderstood bird resident such as the "Butcher Bird" or the linnet.[33] Although the mother-son literary alliance was broken in 1902, Elizabeth Grinnell continued to contribute western nature pieces.

There was another partnership among the magazine's contributors, but it was only fifty per cent literary. Charles A. Keeler and his wife, Louise Mapes Bunnell, niece of the founder-editor of *St. Nicholas*, collaborated on a number of articles for *Out West*. He did the writing and she provided the illustrations. Like Joseph Grinnell, Keeler had a keen interest in ornithology. As a boy in Wisconsin he had evinced a love of nature and during high school days in Berkeley, California, that love was centered on birds. Before Charles Keeler was twenty-one the California Academy of Sciences had published his monograph on the evolution of color in birds.[34] About this time he met Louise Bunnell, a student of entomology and art, and the two were married.

The Keelers' contact with Lummis began in 1897 when Charles Keeler's health failed and the editor invited the couple south, arranging for them to set up housekeeping in a spare room in the Mission San Juan Capistrano. Lummis also used his influence to secure a contract from the Southern Pacific Railroad for the Keelers to collaborate on a pamphlet descriptive of southern California[35]

Along with his study of birds Keeler had been developing a poetic talent. For a time these parallel interests were maintained, and his *Bird-Notes Afield* was balanced by *Idyls of*

---

[33]"That Damn-Bird," *Land of Sunshine*, XIII (1900), July, 90-97.

[34]Torrey Connor, "A Poet in the Making," *Overland Monthly*, N. S., LXXXII (1924), Sept., 105, 432.

[35]George Wharton James, "Charles Keeler: Scientist and Poet," *National Magazine*, XXVII (1911), Nov., 42.

El Dorado, a collection of verse. Gradually the poet and writer in Keeler emerged dominant over the scientist, although his style maintained a precision suggestive of his scientific training.

Aside from one uninspired poem of cumbersome cadence, Keeler's offerings to *Out West* were essays. One of the best of these was a critical appraisal of his personal friend and his wife's teacher, the California landscape artist William Keith. Keeler's is a scholarly, penetrating analysis and evaluation of the man and his work and this passage suggests his competence as critic:

His landscapes, painted after returning from abroad were good, straightforward pictures of Western scenery. They were accurate and pleasing glimpses of mountain, stream, and plain; but had he never done other work he certainly would not be entitled to a place among the great landscape painters. There was gradually dawning in him a feeling for something more in nature than he had hitherto expressed. Thus far his work had dealt with the facts of nature, poetically chosen and well rendered, but still literal facts. He now began to realize that nature was not a dead fact, but a living reality. He began to see nature as a part of himself, and to express his own joy and sorrow and reverence in terms of mountain, tree and sky. It is the work of this last period which I believe will one day rank on a par with the greatest landscape paintings of the world.[36]

In 1900 and 1901 Keeler, his wife, and their five-year-old daughter spent eleven months cruising in the South Seas. A collection of poems, *A Wanderer's Songs of the Sea* (1902), resulted from the trip as did the series of essays which appeared in *Out West*. These essays represent a high type of travel reporting. In them Keeler conveys an impression of a simple, generous people living a serene existence in an idyllic setting. Because he avoided sentimentality, his writings carry conviction. In one of the best of his sketches Keeler traces the course of a three-week friendship between a Samoan chief and himself. This gives the essayist a chance to describe the natives and their customs in good taste and in discriminating detail. The drawings by Louise Keeler which accompany this piece enhance the impression of the Pacific islands which the essays present.

[36]"The American Turner; William Keith and His Work," *Land of Sunshine,* VIII (1898), May, 257.

There was relatively little need for artists to serve *Out West* because the overwhelming majority of its illustrations were photographs. L. Maynard Dixon, however, deserves consideration, for he received encouragement from Lummis at the start of his artistic career and he supplied the magazine with striking illustrations of western life. On more than one occasion Lummis gave Dixon favorable notice in his monthly as a western artist whose work was informed by knowledge of his subject matter gained through experience.

Lafayette Maynard Dixon was born in Fresno, California, in 1875. He came of a Virginia family with a well-established military tradition. Dixon manifested artistic leanings early in life; at sixteen, with some encouragement from Frederic Remington, his family took him out of school so that he might devote himself wholeheartedly to drawing. He attended the San Francisco School of Design for a few months and then in 1893, he began working for the *Overland Monthly* where he gained a knowledge of process engraving.[37] More important than these items in his art education was the schooling he gave himself in a conscientious study of western life. "My object," he once said, "has always been to get as close to the Real Thing as possible — people, animals and country. The melodramatic Wild West idea is not for me the big possibility. The more lasting qualities are in the quiet and more broadly human aspect of Western life. I aim to interpret for the most part the poetry and pathos of the life of Western people seen amid the grandeur, sternness and loneliness of their country."[38]

In the work he did for *Out West* the broadly human aspect of western life is most apparent in his sketches of Indians and Mexicans. The few illustrations he provided for short stories or serials give little hint of the artist's future development. Only in the imaginative drawing that accompanied Sharlot Hall's dedicatory poem at the time the magazine changed names is there an indication of the draftsmanship and breadth of conception

[37]Lummis, "A California Illustrator: L. Maynard Dixon and His Work," *Land of Sunshine*, X (1898), Dec., 8-10.

[38]Hill Tolerton, "The Art of Maynard Dixon," *International Studio*, LV (1915), May, Supplement, xcii-xcv.

that later helped make Dixon a top-ranking western muralist. The artist's work for the magazine and for other periodicals represented only a phase in his development. Limitations of editorial and subject demands in this field irked him and he went on to more serious work, traveling widely throughout the plains region and constantly studying out the land and the people. According to one critic, Dixon "has seized the essentials of both land and race and rendered them with truth."[39] This judgment of the artist's mature work is applicable to the better examples of his magazine art.[40]

Another western illustrator who, early in his career, received encouragement from Lummis was Ed Borein. Like Dixon, Borein was largely a self-taught artist. His only formal training consisted of a month in a San Francisco art school.[41] Edward Borein was born in San Leandro, California, in October, 1872. As a youth he worked briefly in an architect's office, spent a year as a carpenter's apprentice, and then turned to punching cattle on the Jesus Maria Ranch in Santa Barbara, California. Much of his spare time was spent in sketching western men and scenes. He seems to have worked for the fun of it at first and then, influenced perhaps by the interest in his work of men like Lummis and Dixon, with increasing earnestness.

A representative group of the cowboy's drawings appeared in the *Land of Sunshine* for August, 1899, together with brief biographical and critical comment by the Lion.[42] Most of the sketches were a product of Borein's wanderings in Mexico the previous year. The drawings were simple, direct, and honest. What the artist may have lacked in technique he made up for in sincerity.

[39]Ruth Pieldovo, "Dixon, Painter of the West," *International Studio*, LXXVIII (1924), Mar., 472.

[40]Dixon's paintings hang today in some of the foremost galleries of the West, such as the San Francisco Museum of Art, the De Young Museum of San Francisco, the Southwest Museum, Los Angeles, and the Pasadena Art Institute. In 1939 Dixon was selected by the United States Department of the Interior to paint the Indian as he is today and as he was at the close of the period of military conquest.

[41]Carl Zigrosser, "An Etcher of the Far West," *Sunset*, XXXVIII (1917), June, 66.

[42]"A Cowboy's Pencil," XI, 159-67.

In later years Borein served as staff artist for the San Francisco *Call,* and later still, he went to New York to study etching at the Art Students League. Borein invariably dealt with south-western types — Indians, vaqueros, *rurales,* horses, and cattle. The cowboy etcher died in Santa Barbara in the spring of 1945. His work is known and valued within a select circle of far western enthusiasts.[43]

Charlotte Perkins Gilman was one of the most unusual individuals to be associated with Lummis and his monthly. Great-granddaughter of Lyman Beecher and grandniece of Harriet Beecher Stowe and of Henry Ward Beecher, she continued in the militant tradition of such New England forebears. Her long life was given over to fighting for the social and economic liberation of her sex, and she pushed the battle from the lecture platform, through the newspapers and magazines, and in her books of prose and verse.

Charlotte Perkins' formal schooling was slight, but she did extensive reading in anthropology, sociology, and economics. Her marriage to artist Charles Walter Stetson in 1884 lasted just ten years. After their divorce she demonstrated noteworthy tolerance by maintaining friendship with Stetson and his new wife, Grace Ellery Channing.[44] It was about this time that she became a contributor to the magazines and began to produce the satiric verse which first brought her recognition in the East. In her poems she protested vigorously but cleverly against woman's enslavement by means of the washtub and the "Holy Stove." In 1899 *Woman and Economics* was published. This was Charlotte Perkins' most important contribution in the field of social reform. Here she presented an incisive analysis of the evils of family and social life of her day, at the same time pointing out the advantage certain to accrue to the individual and society from the economic independence of women.[45] The *Nation* viewed this work as "the most significant utterance on the subject since Mill's *Subjection of Women*."[46]

[43]Santa Barbara *News-Press,* Sept. 17, 1950.
[44]*Newsweek,* VI (1935), Oct. 26, 40.
[45]Mabel Hurd, *Political Science Quarterly,* XIV (1899), Dec., 712-13.
[46]Vol. LXVIII (1899), June 5, 443.

With one exception the verse of Charlotte Perkins which appeared in the *Land of Sunshine* was representative of the woman who wrote it only in an occasional cleverly turned line or a flash of humor. With the same exception, hers were essentially promotional poems. The first bits of verse were quietly descriptive of southern California, distinguished by little more than a pleasant lilt. Then came more aggressive verse deriding the East and inviting immigration to the West. Typical of her sometimes satirical style is the following:

> They say we have no grass!
> To hear them talk
> You'd think that grass could walk,
> And was their bosom friend—no day to pass
> Between them and their grass!
>
>   *   *   *
>
> But come now! How does earth's pet plumage grow
> Under your snow?
> Is your beloved grass as softly nice
> When packed in ice?
> For six long months you live beneath a blight—
> No grass in sight.
> You bear up bravely. And not only that,
> But leave your grass and travel. And thereat
> We marvel deeply, with slow Western mind,
> Wondering within us what these people find
> Among our common oranges and palms
> To tear them from the well-remembered charms
> Of their dear vegetable. But still they come,
> Frost-bitten invalids, to our bright home,
> And chide our grasslessness, until we say—
> But if you hate it so—why come? Why stay?
> Just go away!
> Go to—your grass![47]

Eight years separated Charlotte Perkins' verse from her next and last appearance in Lummis' magazine. Much had happened to the poet in the interim. She had remarried, becoming the wife of her cousin, George N. Gilman, a New York lawyer. She had become a professional feminist, a socialist, and an

[47]"Their Grass," VII (1897), July, 64.

advocate of subordination of the female sex instinct so that women might take an unfettered and effective part in the world as first of all, human beings. Her last poem reflects these changes. The light touch, the humor, even the rhyme is gone. The mood is defiant, the tone earnest and aggressive, and the theme is the glorification of work and progress. The following fragment expresses Mrs. Gilman's rugged independence and furnishes a more reliable clue to the personality of the writer than do the examples of her earlier verse:

> Something does ail the procession?
> Some men stopping and waiting,
> Some men wriggling backwards,
> And praying—or urging to praying—
> That God will move the procession!
> Would you be wound up like a puppet?
> Marionettes of High Heaven?
> Or like a recalcitrant baby,
> Dragged by the arms—heels rebellious!
> Pray to yourself—that you travel!
> Or—without praying—just travel![48]

Charlotte Gilman kept on writing and preaching her feminist creed of independence and industry. In 1909 she founded the *Forerunner*, a monthly magazine of social reform, and, as publisher, editor, and sole contributor, she kept it running for seven years. After the death of her husband in 1934 she joined her daughter by her first marriage in Pasadena. In August, 1935, Mrs. Gilman, at the age of seventy-two, made her last independent move by taking her own life. The note she left was characteristic: "I have preferred chloroform to cancer."[49]

In distinct contrast to the verse of Charlotte Perkins Gilman stands that of Nora May French. Born in Aurora, New York, in April, 1881, Miss French came to Los Angeles when she was six.[50] Her first offering was accepted by Lummis when she was eighteen, and she continued to contribute delicate verse to the magazine for about five years. There is an even quality about

[48]"Labor Is Prayer," *Out West*, XXII (1905), June, 407.

[49]*Newsweek*, VI (1935), Oct. 26, 40.

[50]*Biographies of California Authors and Indexes of California Literature*, ed. Edgar Hinkel (Oakland, California, 1942), I, 78.

Miss French's poetry which prevents any single poem from standing out from the rest. All are short. All are simple and conventional in rhyme scheme. Most of them reveal definite lyric skill and a marked capacity for imagery. Her verse contains a melancholy strain. There is seldom any hint of protest, but rather a passive acceptance of sadness. The titles of her poems are self-revealing — "Mist," "By Moonlight," "Rain," "The Old Garden," and the like. "Rain" shows to fair advantage the lyric quality of her verse:

> The rain was grey before it fell,
>   And through a world where light had died
> There ran a mournful little wind
>   That shook the trees and cried.
>
> The rain was brown upon the earth,
>   In turbid stream and tiny seas:
> In swift and slender shafts that beat
>   The flowers to their knees.
>
> The rain is mirror to the sky—
>   Oh, passing words, a blue so dear!
> And drifting in the shining pools
>   The clouds are white and near.[51]

There is beauty in many a line written by Nora May French, but her pen was soon stopped, for she died at twenty-four, a suicide while visiting in the Carmel home of George Sterling and his wife.[52]

Julia Boynton Green was a frequent contributor of verse to *Out West*. Her work is somewhat similar to that of Nora May French but lacks its depth or distinction. Miss Boynton was a native of New York who came to Los Angeles in the nineties shortly after her marriage to Levi Worthington Green. She had already published a slender volume of poems called *Lines and Interlines*.[53]

Mrs. Green specialized in nature verse frequently featuring flowers or trees or a southern California landscape. In an early

[51]*Out West*, XXII (1905), Apr., 212.
[52]"Recent Poetry," *Current Literature*, XLIX (1908), June, 679.
[53]Lummis, "That Which Is Written," *Land of Sunshine*, III (1895), Nov., 286.

poem she portrays the various moods of the sea through the eyes of a lover as he walks the beach each day for a week, awaiting the arrival of the ship bearing his sweetheart. Lummis was so impressed with the poem that he broke a precedent of publishing one-page poems only. The following stanza, one of the best of the eight, is an argument against precedent breaking:

Ravenous waves, O fierce and ravenous waves,
　How can I think today of her who is far from home!
　Far toward the sky-line, trouble and danger and inky gloom,
　Throbs of fury, hither, and mountainous shocks that come
And hiss and shriek on the sand in a pallid passion of foam.
Cruel swells that shape in a merciless mock of graves;
　They scoop the bed, then swiftly spread a mound like a new-made
　　tomb,
Then scatter it o'er as a last scoff more with a white profusion
　　of bloom.[54]

"The Yucca" is more representative of this poet's verse:

　　Noon on the desert; still and hot and sweet;
　　The dry twigs snap and crackle under feet;
　　The eyes close dazzled, seeking shade in vain,
　　And must refuse to see, since sight is pain.

　　The lupines and the larkspurs and the host
　　Of fairy blooms that dyed the sand with waves
　　And waves of gold and amethyst are lost,
　　And is there naught to mark their myriad graves?

　　Lo! yonder yucca, vigorous and tall
　　Erects her ivory obelisk for them all.
　　Bravely she rears, nourished by unknown wells,
　　Her snowy pillar carven all of bells.[55]

In the verse he submitted to *Out West*, John Vance Cheney made use of southwestern materials and worked to give them a genuine western ring. In only one or two instances does he appear to have succeeded. His failure perhaps can be laid to his New England upbringing and to a strong aura of urbanity which surrounds much of his poetry.

[54]"The Voyage," *Land of Sunshine*, III (1895), Oct., 213-14.
[55]*Out West*, XVII (1902), Aug., 213.

The poet, a New Yorker, was trained for the bar, but after practicing briefly in Massachusetts and New York, he decided that legal work was not to his liking and came to California in 1876. Three years before, he had begun to write, and he ground out magazine verse in a steady stream for years although he never realized enough from his efforts for self-support. To keep alive he turned to library work, serving as head of the San Francisco Free Library in the late eighties and early nineties, and then moving to the Midwest to assume the librarianship of the Newberry Library in Chicago where he remained until 1909. Cheney sprang into fleeting fame when he won a prize offered by Collis P. Huntington for the best answer in verse to Edwin Markham's "Man with a Hoe."[56] He returned to the West to spend his declining years in San Diego. Aside from his prolific output in the nation's magazines, he published several collections of verse which rapidly went out of print and two volumes of critical essays, more distinguished for their conservatism and scholarly tone than for their originality or brilliance.[57]

Cheney's first two offerings to *Out West* attempted — rather ineffectually — to handle Spanish themes. When he shifted his emphasis to the American West he improved. The following poem is among the best this poet produced for the western monthly:

> A dim, pale shape moves over the mesa,
> Roves with the night wind up and down;
> The light-foot ghost, the wild dog of the shadow,
> Howls on the levels beyond the town;
>   Cry, cry, Coyote!
>
> No fellow has he, with leg or wing,
> No mate has that spectre, in fur or feather;
> In the sagebrush is whelped a fuzzy thing,
> And mischief itself helps lick him together—
>   Up, cub Coyote!

[56]"Recent Poetry," *Current Literature*, XL (1906), Feb., 218-19.

[57]F. M. Hopkins, "American Poets of Today: John Vance Cheney," *Current Literature*, XXIII (1898), Feb., 112-13.

The winds come blowing over and over,
The great white moon is looking down;
In the throat of the dog is devils' laughter;
Is he baying the moon or baying the town?
　　Howl, howl, Coyote!

The shadow-dog on the windy mesa,
He sits and he laughs in his devil's way;
Look to the roost and lock up the lambkin—
A deal may happen 'twixt now and the day:
　　Ha, ha! Coyote![58]

These, then, are representative of the bulk of contributors to *Out West* — poet and promoter, scholar and story-teller, artist and essayist. They and others too numerous for treatment here helped to keep Lummis' monthly going, and they made of it in no small part a composite of their tastes and talents.

[58]"Coyote," *Land of Sunshine*, V (1896), Aug., 95.

Chapter **VIII** POR ÚLTIMO

THROUGH HIS MAGAZINE Charles Lummis served the cause of regionalism for little more than a decade. Yet in that short span the energetic editor, together with the journal's contributors, compiled a remarkably rich and varied record of the "lands of the sun." That record, of course, has an interest in its own right, but it is also useful in suggesting the nature of the literary and intellectual tastes of southern Californians and of the readership in general. There is considerable evidence within the magazine that these tastes were on the whole pedestrian, conformist, a trifle precious, and not particularly exacting. The artificiality, sentimentality, and mediocrity of many of the belletristic pieces in the journal tend to support such a view. The articles, although generally of greater substance than much of the imaginative writing, are usually more descriptive than analytical; more diffuse than penetrating; more competent than profound. Further, even though the booster note was muted under Lummis, the magazine never lost its promotional purpose and the Southland during the Lion's editorship was a haven for tourists and recent "refugees" from the East and Midwest, lending credence to a conception of commercial and commonplace tastes.

But such a judgment is not entirely fair either to Lummis and *Out West* or to the magazine's readers. Doubtless the literary standards of the average reader were relatively unelevated but this does not mean he was entirely devoid of discernment. Moreover, as has been indicated in earlier chapters, not all of the fiction and verse published in Lummis' monthly is second-rate. Offerings of writers such as Mary Austin, Jack London, Nora May French, Robinson Jeffers, and Eugene Manlove Rhodes, while seldom representative of their authors' best work, often have enough originality and literary merit to raise them above the level of many of the offerings in the national magazines.

A more varied and impressive indication of reader tastes than the work of these imaginative writers suggests may be gained from the articles, editorials, and reviews. These reveal an appetite for historical and scientific treatment of the Southwest and its peoples, an appreciation of nature and of natural history, and a continuing interest in education, literary criticism, the fine arts, and other cultural and intellectual aspects of life in the Far West. Topics of this sort usually receive treatment that is sober, careful, sometimes rather specialized, but not often dull. Semipopular in style but accurate in detail, perhaps is a fair characterization of the bulk of nonfictional material in *Out West.*

Careful reading of *Out West* over the years of Lummis' dominance yields the impression that its readers were in the main educated people from the middle and upper-middle class, inquisitive about southern California and the Southwest, seeking to construct a new historical and cultural orientation, interested in the creative arts, and responsive to a restrained promotional emphasis when balanced by substantial attention to things of the mind.

To a considerable degree *Out West* made an effective appeal to such readers because Lummis thoroughly understood the nature of the southern California immigration and was interested in promoting more of the same. He was convinced that sober, successful husbandmen and well-to-do business and professional people could best be attracted out west by pointing out the Southwest's spectacular scenic and climatic assets, stressing current cultural attainments, and featuring aspects of the relatively remote Indian and Spanish past. The recent past in the Southwest was too sordid to touch. Lummis was anxious to forget that the Los Angeles of the sixties was a tough little town, perhaps, as has been said, the toughest in the country, and he was prepared to overlook its shootings, its "Nigger Alley," its violence culminating in 1871 with the murder of about a score of Chinese which was sufficiently spectacular to give the obscure far western community its moment of national notoriety. Such was not the stuff out of which to shape a western image that would find favor in eastern eyes. In another part of the West and in an earlier day the Lion might have exploited the romance of the western crossing. But although he may have walked across half a continent to Los Angeles, most southern Californians were Pullman or chair-car migrants and there was no way to make of their coming an epic. So Lummis and his contributors exploited a different and relatively little-known West. They turned to history and to archaeology and to ethnology; to scenery and to nature trails; to diaries and documentary accounts of padres and *Conquistadores;* and to strange corners of the Spanish borderlands. Instead of the Colt and the Winchester, the more peaceful and permanent southern California mission and the southwestern mesa were the symbols that the magazine evoked. Its Indians were likely to be either subjects of ethnological research, or ragged, starving, dispossessed Mission Indians, fit objects of humanitarian concern and popular reform. Even the western hero of the short stories of Eugene Manlove Rhodes was apt to be as literate as Rhodes himself and was a working cowhand rather than a gun-toter. When *Out West* dealt with the contemporary scene, the accent was on southern California and its refinements: its colleges and universities, its libraries and public schools, its artists, scientists, and writers, its women's clubs, its museums and archaeological society, and its churches. Clearly, here was a home for people of education, means, and discrimination.

Such fare was highly palatable to the winter tourist or to the recently arrived local resident who had left behind his historical heritage but who carried with him his essentially middle-class cultural predilections and who was looking for reassurance that not all of the West was wild.

Helpful as is the magazine as an index to literary tastes and successful as Lummis may have been in stimulating a selective westward movement, the factor that, perhaps more than any other, makes *Out West* distinctive is the embodiment in print of its editor. To a marked degree Lummis was the magazine and the magazine was Lummis. There was scarcely a facet of his flamboyant, complex personality that was not mirrored in his monthly. The journal helped satisfy Lummis' desire to be a force in the community. It gave him a chance to give permanent and persuasive form to his passion for California and the Southwest. It permitted him unfettered expression of certain deep-rooted convictions, most notably his hatred of imperialism. Many of the scholars, creative writers, and artists who contributed were drawn by Lummis' compelling personality, and through their offerings the Lion was able to confront the East month after month with representative samples of cultural and intellectual achievement coming out of the Southwest. Moreover, through his western monthly, Lummis could boast a share in the shaping of several regional writers. One of *Out West's* most characteristic features was its refreshing independence, a direct reflection of the attitude of an editor who refused to truckle to popular taste or be swayed by mere majority opinion.

Three western crusades were launched in the magazine: Lummis' drive to preserve historic landmarks; his agitation for better treatment of the Indians; and the campaign for national irrigation sponsored by William E. Smythe. Each movement possesses intrinsic interest as a type of regional reform. All three have broader significance, for they not only conformed to that national pattern of reform of the early twentieth century, but each of them, to some degree, influenced national crusades of similar or related nature. Further, all three crusades were inextricably linked with Lummis' magazine. His journal expressed their aims, reported their progress, and extended their scope. Without such a publicity outlet, none of the reform movements could have been sustained. By virtue of its vital part in promoting the western crusades of Charles Lummis and William Smythe, *Out West* served as a constructive influence within the region it represented, thereby establishing a modest title to inclusion in the company of the crusading journals of the nation.

Finally, *Out West* furnished Lummis with an effective means of realizing the ambition he had once expressed to Bandelier of humanizing scholarship and science. Through its pages Lummis was teacher and interpreter, and he sought to instruct its readers in many aspects of the Southwest — its scenic wonders, its climate, its business opportunities, its cultural potential, and its rich and romantic archaeological and historical past.

Confined to a phrase, Lummis' primary purpose was to produce a genuine magazine of the Southwest that would measure up to eastern journalistic and intellectual standards. This he did, but because *Out West* reflects its editor so fully and so forcefully, Lummis left in it a highly personal and diversified record of a man and his allegiance to a region.

The memory of the man is built into the Southwest Museum with its unique Lummis Carocol Tower rising above the Arroyo Seco Parkway; into El Alisal, the rambling stone and adobe house that has become a state historical monument; and into several southern California mission structures that stand today thanks, in large measure, to the work of Lummis and the Landmarks Club. The Lion lives too in a handful of his books, some of them considered classic among writings on the Southwest. The magazine is less conspicuous but the files of *Out West* are securely housed in libraries across the land and in them lies a valuable reservoir of regional lore. Thus have Charles Lummis and his magazine become a part of the southwestern heritage they did so much to promote, record, and preserve.

BIBLIOGRAPHY

MANUSCRIPT MATERIALS

The major manuscript sources consist of the personal journals of Charles F. Lummis in the possession of his daughter Mrs. Turbesé Lummis Fiske of La Jolla, California, and a mass of correspondence which forms a part of the Lummis collection in the library of the Southwest Museum, Highland Park, California. Much of Lummis' voluminous correspondence is preserved under topical headings in file boxes in the museum library. Other useful manuscript materials in the Lummis collection include a brief biography of Lummis in typescript by Mrs. Fiske, copies of the constitutions of the Landmarks Club and of the Sequoya League, a number of poems, stories, and essays by Lummis in manuscript, and the "Preliminary Report of the Warner's Ranch Indian Advisory Commission."

For the early history of the *Land of Sunshine*, the Charles Dwight Willard papers (450 pieces) in the Henry E. Huntington Library are indispensable.

In the Bancroft Library the William Keith Miscellany yielded bits of correspondence touching on the editor and his magazine. The Charles E. Partridge collection in the same library is rich in information relating to the Warner's Ranch episode.

A personal history form completed by Charles Lummis when he assumed the headship of the Los Angeles Public Library is on file in the library's department of western history material. Also in the Los Angeles Public Library there is a bound typescript copy of the letters and diary of Charles Lummis covering the period from 1911 to 1917 which the editor sent to his friend Maurice H. Newmark. Since many of the references go back in time to the years of Lummis' association with his magazine this source was of greater use than the inclusive dates indicate.

The pages of Lummis' magazine constitute the most important single source. *Out West* in incomplete or broken sets is in eighty-five libraries in the United States. The Los Angeles Public Library has the only complete file. However, virtually complete sets of the magazine may be found in the Library of Congress; in the state libraries of California, Washington, and Michigan; in the public libraries of San Francisco, Kansas City, Providence, and Boston; in the libraries of the University of California at Berkeley and Los Angeles, of Stanford, and of the Claremont Colleges, California; and in the Southwest Museum Library, the Huntington Library, the Lloyd Library and Museum, Cincinnati, the Newberry Library, Chicago, the Carnegie Library of Pittsburgh, the Rosenberg Library, Galveston, and the Wisconsin State Historical Society Library, Madison.

Other periodicals of the period of particular value in connection with this study include the *Overland Monthly, Pacific Monthly, Sunset, Current Literature*, and the *Nation*.

PUBLISHED WORKS OF CHARLES F. LUMMIS

Lummis, Charles F. *Birch Bark Poems*. Cambridge, 1879.

————. *A New Mexico David and Other Stories and Sketches of the Southwest*. New York, 1891.

————. *A Tramp Across the Continent*. New York, 1892.

————. *Some Strange Corners of Our Country: The Wonderland of the Southwest*. New York, 1892.

————. *The Land of Poco Tiempo*. New York, 1893.

————. *The Spanish Pioneers*. Chicago, 1893. A new and enlarged edition appeared in 1929 under the title *The Spanish Pioneers and the California Missions*. An edition in Spanish was published in Barcelona in 1917.

————. *The Man Who Married the Moon and Other Pueblo Indian Folk-Stories*. New York, 1894. Published in 1910 as *Pueblo Indian Folk-Stories*.

————. *The Gold Fish of Gran Chimu*. Chicago, 1896.

————. *The King of the Broncos and Other Stories of New Mexico*. New York, 1897.

_____. *The Enchanted Burro.* Chicago, 1897.

_____. *The Awakening of a Nation.* New York, 1898.

_____. *My Friend Will.* Chicago, 1911.

_____. *In Memory of Juan Rodriguez Cabrillo, Who Gave the World California.* Chula Vista, California, 1913. Also published in Spanish and Portuguese.

_____ and Frederick Webb Hodge, eds., Mrs. Edward E. Ayer, translator. *The Memorial of Fray Alonso de Benavides, 1630.* Chicago, 1916.

_____. *Spanish Songs of Old California.* Los Angeles, 1923.

_____. *Mesa, Canyon and Pueblo: Our Wonderland of the Southwest.* New York, 1925. An expanded version of *Some Strange Corners of Our Country.*

_____. *A Bronco Pegasus.* Boston, 1928.

_____. *Flowers of Our Lost Romance.* Boston, 1929.

REMINISCENCES, AUTOBIOGRAPHIES, AND BIOGRAPHICAL WORKS

Austin, Mary. *Earth Horizon: Autobiography.* Boston, 1932.

Bandelier, Adolph F. *The Delight Makers.* New York, 1916.

Davis, William Heath. *Seventy-five Years in California.* San Francisco, 1929.

Dell, Floyd. *Women as World Builders: Studies in Modern Feminism.* Chicago, 1913. Contains chapter on Charlotte Perkins Gilman.

Doyle, Helen MacKnight. *Mary Austin: Woman of Genius.* New York, 1937.

Gardner, Esther. "A Study of the Life and Works of Charles F. Lummis." Unpublished master's thesis, University of New Mexico, Albuquerque, 1941.

Gilman, Charlotte Perkins. *The Living of Charlotte Perkins Gilman.* New York, 1935.

Jordan, David Starr. *The Days of a Man: Being Memories of a Naturalist, Teacher and Minor Prophet of Democracy.* 2 vols. New York, 1922.

Neuhaus, Eugen. *William Keith: The Man and the Artist.* Berkeley, 1938.

Newmark, Maurice H. and Marco R., eds. *Sixty Years in Southern California, 1853-1913, Containing the Reminiscences of Harris Newmark.* New York, 1926.

Noel, Joseph. *Footloose in Arcadia: A Personal Record of Jack London, George Sterling, Ambrose Bierce.* New York, 1926.

Pearce, T. M. *The Beloved House* [Mary Austin in New Mexico]. Caldwell, Idaho, 1940.

Peterson, Martin S. *Joaquin Miller: Literary Frontiersman.* Palo Alto, California, 1937.

Rhodes, May Davison. *The Hired Man on Horseback: My Story of Eugene Manlove Rhodes.* Boston, 1938.

Stidger, William L. *Edwin Markham.* New York, 1933.

Stone, Irving. *Sailor on Horseback: The Biography of Jack London.* Cambridge, 1938.

LOCAL, STATE, AND REGIONAL STUDIES

Bartlett, Dana W. *The Better City: A Sociological Study of a Modern City* [Los Angeles]. Los Angeles, 1907.

Carr, Harry. *Los Angeles, City of Dreams.* New York, 1935.

Caughey, John W. *California.* New York, 1940.

Cleland, Robert Glass. *California in Our Time (1900-1940).* New York, 1947.

Fergusson, Erna. *Our Southwest.* New York, 1940.

Guinn, James M. *A History of California and an Extended History of Los Angeles and Environs.* 3 vols. Los Angeles, 1915.

Hill, Laurance L. *La Reina: Los Angeles in Three Centuries.* Los Angeles, 1929.

An Illustrated History of Los Angeles County, California. Chicago, 1889.

McGroarty, John Steven. *California: Its History and Romance.* Los Angeles, 1911.

McWilliams, Carey. *Southern California Country.* New York, 1946.

Mayo, Morrow. *Los Angeles.* New York, 1933.

Willard, Charles Dwight. *The Herald's History of Los Angeles City.* Los Angeles, 1901.
_____. *History of the Chamber of Commerce of Los Angeles.* Los Angeles, 1899.

Workman, Boyle. *The City That Grew. . . .* Los Angeles, 1936.

MONOGRAPHS AND SPECIAL STUDIES

Cummins (Mighels), Ella Sterling. *The Story of the Files: A Review of Californian Writers and Literature.* San Francisco, 1893.

Dumke, Glenn S. *The Boom of the Eighties in Southern California.* San Marino, California, 1944.

Hill, Joseph J. *The History of Warner's Ranch and Its Environs.* Los Angeles, 1927.

Luxon, Norval Neil. *Niles' Weekly Register: News Magazine of the Nineteenth Century.* Baton Rouge, 1947.

Malin, James C. *The Grassland of North America: Prolegomena to Its History.* Lawrence, Kansas, 1947.

Markham, Edwin. *Songs and Stories.* Los Angeles, 1931.

Mead, Elwood. *Irrigation Institutions.* New York, 1903.

Mott, Frank Luther. *A History of American Magazines.* 3 vols. Cambridge, 1938-1939.

Powers, Alfred. *History of Oregon Literature.* Portland, 1935.

Rice, William B. *The Los Angeles Star, 1851-1864.* Berkeley and Los Angeles, 1947.

Smythe, William E. *The Conquest of Arid America.* New York, 1907.

Walker, Franklin. *A Literary History of Southern California.* Berkeley and Los Angeles, 1950.

———. *San Francisco's Literary Frontier.* New York, 1939.

Webb, Walter Prescott. *The Great Plains.* New York, 1931.

PERIODICAL MATERIALS

Anderson, Henry S. "The Little Landers' Land Colonies: A Unique Agricultural Experiment in California," *Agricultural History,* V (1931), Oct., 139-50.

Benjamin, Marcus. "David Starr Jordan," *Scientific American,* CII (1910), Jan. 1, 13, 16-17, 19.

"Charlotte Perkins Gilman's Dynamic Social Philosophy," *Current Literature,* LI (1911), July, 67-70.

"Charlotte Perkins Stetson as Social Philosopher and Poet," *Poet Lore,* XI (1899), Mar., 124-28.

Cleaveland, Agnes Morley. "Three Musketeers of Southwestern Fiction," *Overland Monthly,* N. S., LXXXVII (1929), Dec., 385-86.

Connor, Torrey. "A Poet in the Making [Charles A. Keeler]," *Overland Monthly,* N. S., LXXXII (1924), Sept., 431-33.

[De Voto, Bernard]. "Horizon Land," *The Saturday Review of Literature,* XIV (1936), Oct. 17, 8.

Dickie, G. W., Leverett Mills Loomis, and Ransom Pratt. "In Memoriam: Theodore Henry Hittell," *Proceedings of the California Academy of Sciences,* 4th ser., VIII (1918), June 17, 1-25.

Dobie, J. Frank. "Gene Rhodes: Cowboy Novelist," *The Atlantic Monthly,* CLXXXIII (1949), June, 75-77.

Earle, Henry Edmond. "An Old-Time Collector: Reminiscences of Charles F. Lummis," *California Folklore Quarterly,* I (1942), Apr., 179-83.

Espinosa, J. Manuel. "Some Charles F. Lummis Letters, 1897-1903," *The New Mexico Quarterly Review,* XI (1941), May, 147-56.

Ewing, Russell C. "Modern Histories and Historians of the Spanish Southwest," *The Arizona Quarterly*, III (1947), Spring, 71-82.

Far, Sui Sin [Edith M. Eaton]. "Leaves from the Mental Portfolio of an Eurasian," *The Independent*, LXVI (1909), Jan., 125-36.

Field, Ben. "Charles Fletcher Lummis," *Overland Monthly*, N. S., LXXXVII (1929), July, 197-203, 223.

Gale, Zona. "Charlotte Perkins Stetson Gilman," *The Nation*, CXLI (1935), Sept. 25, 350-351.

Gilbert, Hope. "He Discovered the Southwest for Americans," *The Desert Magazine*, VII (1944), Sept., 13-16.

Gordon, Dudley C. "Southwest Crusader," *New Mexico Magazine*, XIX (1941), Oct., 10-11, 31-32.

Green, Charles S. "Magazine Publishing in California," *Publications of the California Library Association*, No. 2 (1898), May, pp. 2-14.

Haverland, Della. "Charles Fletcher Lummis," *Pacific Bindery* (1935), pp. 7-12.

Hess, Pauline. "Interesting Westerners: A Youthful and Useful Octogenarian [Theodore H. Hittell]," *Sunset*, XXXII (1914), Feb., 398-400.

Hewett, Edgar L. "Lummis the Inimitable," *Papers of the School of American Research*, Archaeological Institute of America, Santa Fe, New Mexico (1944), pp. 1-13.

Hopkins, F. M. "American Poets of Today: John Vance Cheney," *Current Literature*, XXIII (1898), Feb., 112-13.

"In Memoriam: Washington Matthews," *American Anthropologist*, VII (1905), Sept., 514-23.

James, George Wharton. "Charles F. Lummis: A Unique Literary Personage of Modern America," *National Magazine*, XXVII (1912), Oct., 129-43.

———. "Charles Keeler: Scientist and Poet," ibid., XXXV (1911), Nov., 35-52.

———. "Founding of the Overland Monthly and History of the Out West Magazine," *Overland Monthly*, N. S., LXXXI (1923), May, 7-11.

Jones, Helen Lukens. "The Home of an Author-Craftsman," *Good Housekeeping*, XL (1905), Jan., 18-24.

Knowland, Joseph R. "Native Sons' Landmarks Work," *The Grizzly Bear*, XX (1917), Jan., 6-9.

Lummis, Charles F. "The Mission Indians," *The Outlook*, LXXIV (1903), July 25, 738-42.

Maclay, Mira Abbott. "Charles Keeler, Poet," *Overland Monthly*, N. S., LXVIII (1916), July, 67-71.

N[ewell], W. W. "In Memoriam: Washington Matthews," *The Journal of American Folk-Lore*, XVIII (1905), Sept., 245-47.

Newmark, Marco R. "Charles Fletcher Lummis," *Historical Society of Southern California Quarterly*, XXXVIII (1950), Mar.

————. "A Short History of the Los Angeles Chamber of Commerce," ibid., XXXIII (1945), Sept.

Orcutt, Eddy. "Passed By Here: A Memorial to Gene Rhodes," *The Saturday Evening Post*, CCXI (1928), Aug. 20, 20-21, 48.

O'Sullivan, Reverend St. John. "Charles F. Lummis: An Appreciation," *The Tidings*, XXVIII (1922), Apr. 21, 9-10.

Parker, Charles Franklin. "Out of the West of Long Ago [Sharlot Hall]," *Arizona Highways*, XIX (1943), Jan., 6-11, 35.

Pearce, T. M. "Mary Austin and the Pattern of New Mexico," *Southwest Review*, XXII (1937), Jan., 140-148.

Pielkovo, Ruth. "Dixon, Painter of the West," *International Studio*, XLVIII (1924), Mar., 468-72.

Russell, Isaac. "David Starr Jordan," *The World's Work*, XXVII (1914), Apr., 649-55.

Salzman, Maurice. "Charles Fletcher Lummis: The Very Last of the Mohicans," *Progressive Arizona and the Great Southwest*, VIII (1929), Jan., 14-18.

Smith, Charles W. "The Periodical Resources of American Libraries," *The Library Journal*, LIV (1929), 532-36.

Steffens, Lincoln. "Mary Austin," *The American Magazine*, LXXII (1911), June, 178-81.

Tolerton, Hill. "The Art of Maynard Dixon," *International Studio*, LV (1913), May, Supplement, xcii-xcv.

Vore, Elizabeth A. "A Successful Pacific Coast Writer: Ella Higginson," *Overland Monthly*, N. S., XXXIII (1899), May, 434-36.

Watkins, Frances E. "Charles F. Lummis and the Sequoya League," *Historical Society of Southern California Quarterly*, XXVI (1939), Sept.

Winther, Oscar Osburn. "The Rise of Metropolitan Los Angeles, 1870-1900," *The Huntington Library Quarterly*, X (1947), Aug., 391-405.

Woehlke, Walter V. "Our Twelve Great Scientists: XI, Dr. David Starr Jordan," *Technical World*, XXIII (1915), Mar., 26-32, 108.

Wynn, Dudley. "Mary Austin, Woman Alone," *The Virginia Quarterly Review*, XIII (1937), Spring, 243-56.

Young, Vernon A. "Paso Por Aqui: Recent Interpretations of the Southwest," *The Arizona Quarterly*, III (1947), Summer, Autumn, 164-78, 269-75.

BIBLIOGRAPHIES AND GUIDES

Cowan, Robert Ernest. *A Bibliography of the History of California and the Pacific West, 1510-1906*. 3 vols. San Francisco, 1933.

Dobie, James F. *Guide to Life and Literature of the Southwest*. Austin, Texas, 1943.

Hinkel, Edgar J. *Bibliography of California Fiction*. Oakland, California, 1938.

Major, Mabel, Rebecca W. Smith, and T. M. Pearce. *Southwest Heritage: A Literary History with Bibliography*. Albuquerque, 1938.

Saunders, Lyle. *A Guide to Materials Bearing on Cultural Relations in New Mexico.* Albuquerque, 1944.

———. "A Guide to the Literature of the Southwest," *New Mexico Quarterly Review*, XII (1942), Summer.

Wagner, Henry Raup. *The Spanish Southwest, 1542-1794: An Annotated Bibliography.* 2 vols. Albuquerque, 1937.

MISCELLANEOUS REFERENCE MATERIALS

Ayer, N. W. and Sons. *American Newspaper Annual.* Philadelphia, 1893.

Bepler, Doris West. "Descriptive Catalogue of Materials for Western History in California Magazines, 1854-1890, with an Introduction on the History and the Character of the Magazines." Master's thesis, University of California, Berkeley, 1920.

Hinkel, Edgar J. and William E. McCann. *Biographies of California Authors and Indexes of California Literature.* 2 vols. Oakland, California, 1942.

Maxwell's Los Angeles City Directory and Gazetteer of Southern California, 1893. Los Angeles, 1893.

The National Cyclopedia of American Biography. 42 vols. New York, 1927-1942.

Rowell, George P. *American Newspaper Directory.* New York, 1895.

Willard, Frances E. and Mary A. Livermore, eds. *American Women.* 2 vols. New York, 1897.

INDEX

Bandelier, Adolph F.: meets Lummis, 13; archaeological work of, 13-14; influence on Lummis' work, 16; figures in Lummis' book, 17; Lummis' son named for, 23; mentioned, 144, 190

Bandelier, Fanny R.: reviews *The Spanish Pioneers*, 17

Banker's Alliance of California, 65

"Bar Cross Liar, The": quoted, 163

Bard, Sen. Thomas R., 116, 124-25

Barnes, Lillian Corbett: short story of, 74

Bartlett, Lanier, 120

Basket Maker, The, 156

Battle of Wounded Knee, 75

Beecher, Henry Ward, 180

Beecher, Lyman, 180

Bell, Maj. Horace: in street names controversy, 20; publisher of *Porcupine*, 36

Benavides, Fray Alonso de, 18, 55

Bennett, Arthur B., 134

Benton, Arthur Burnett, 74

Beveridge, Sen. Albert J., 84-85

Bierce, Ambrose, 36, 73

"Big Bonanza," 168

Bigelow, C. H., 76-77

Birch Bark Verses, 6

Bird-Notes Afield, 176

Bitter Creek (Colorado), 92-93

Blackburn College, 155

Board of Land Commissioners of 1851, 114-15

Boer War: in Rhodes's story, 75; Lummis opposes, 91; in Mary Austin's verse, 157

Bolivia: Lummis' and Bandelier's expedition to (1892), 14

Bonebrake, George H., 64

Borein, Ed: career in brief, 179, 180; drawings of, 179-80; mentioned, 144

Borglum, John Gutzon, 49, 51

Boston *Transcript*, 94

Bostwick, E. E., 65

Boynton, Julia. *See* Green, Julia Boynton

Braun, F. W., 64

Brewster Hotel, 46

Britannica: Lummis contributor to, 27

British imperialism: Rhodes against, 75; Lummis critical of, 91; Mary Austin against, 157

Bronco Pegasus, A., 29, 34

Brook, Harry Ellington: career in brief of, 39; and *Land of Sunshine*, 39-40; mentioned, 65

"Brother Burro," 74

Brown, John, 123

Brown University: dismissal of president of, 99-100

Bryan, William Jennings: endorsed by Lummis, 88-89

Bunnell, Louise Mapes. *See* Keeler, Louise Bunnell

Bureau of Ethnology, 16, 116, 125

Bureau of Indian Affairs: criticized by Lummis, 113; "hair-cut order" of, 129n; appropriation for Indian relief, 126

"Burgher's Wife, The": quoted, 157

Burroughs, John, 21

Burton, Charles E.: Superintendent of Hopis and Navajos, 128; complaint against, 128-29; violates Indian School Service rules, 130; administration evaluated, 130; reprimanded, 131

Business history of Lummis' magazine, 64-69

"Butcher Bird," 176

Butler, George, 124

"By Moonlight," 183

Cactus and Pine, 153

"Cactus Hedge, The," 165

Cadmus: Sequoya, the Indian equivalent of, 116

Cahuilla Indians, 114n

California: folk songs of, 28; early publishing ventures in, 36-37; cultural potential of, 49; predominant theme in Lummis' magazine, 72, 75, 77; effect of climate on Anglo-Saxons in, 74; *Out West* on water problem of, 76; responsible state government for, 78; booster comment in the Lion's Den on, 80-81; climate of, 80-82, 139; importance of, 85; Lummis' history of, 136-41; contributions to nation of, 137-38; reform of water law in, 146-47; compared with Italy, 174-75

California, University of. *See* University of California

California Academy of Sciences, 176

California bear, 79

Hearst, Phoebe A.: helps finance *Out West*, 66-67; contributes to Landmarks Club, 108
Hemingway, Ernest, 17
Herald, Los Angeles. *See* Los Angeles *Herald*
Herald, San Diego. *See* San Diego *Herald*
"Here Was a Woman," 75
Herrick, Bertha F., 75
Hewett, Edgar L., 31
Hewitt, J. C., 52
Hidatsa Indians, 169
Higginson, Ella, 73
Hill, Thomas, 21
Hispanic American Historical Review, 17
Historical Society of Southern California, 104
History of California, 167-68
Hitchcock, Ethan, 117
Hittell, Theodore: career in brief of, 166-67; California history of, 167-68; estimate of, 167-68; on California geography, 168; mentioned, 73, 134, 164
Hodge, Frederick W.: opinion of Lummis' work, 16; and Benavides *Memorial*, 18; climbs Enchanted Mesa, 92; and Sequoya League, 116; mentioned, 73, 144
Hoover, Herbert, 141n
Hopi Indians, 128-32, 133
Hubbard, Elbert, 32
Hunt, Sumner P., 26
Hunter, Mary. *See* Austin, Mary
Huntington, Collis P., 185

Idyls of El Dorado, 176-77
Illustrations: in Lummis' magazine, 53
Immigration: Lummis aims to attract, 40-42; nature of to southern California, 48; Lummis opposes Chinese, 98; Japanese, 171
Imperialism: W. C. Patterson differs with Lummis on, 56; Lummis opposes, 84, 86-90, 91, 103
Indian Affairs. *See* Bureau of
Indian agents: southern California, 114
Indian Industries League (Boston), 125

Indian lands: threatened loss of, 113-14
Indian reform, 111, 112-13, 128-33. *See also* Sequoya League
Indian rights. *See* Sequoya League
Indian Rights Association, 114
Indians, California: crusade on behalf of, 111, 113-28, 133. *See also* Mission Indians; Southern California Indians; Southwest Indians; Warner's Ranch Indians
Indians, Southwest. *See* Southwest Indians
Indian School Service: indicted by Lummis, 112; rules of violated, 128-30
Inscription Rock (New Mexico), 16, 136
Institute of the West, 27
"In the Lion's Den": regular feature of Lummis' magazine, 75; possible source of name, 79; analysis of, 80-102; general character of, 80; slogan of, 80; anti-imperialism dominant theme in, 80; California booster comment in, 80-81; historical comment in, 82-83; topics of locality in, 83-84; crusade to preserve California place names, 83-84; statehood urged for Arizona and New Mexico, 84-86; anti-imperialism, 86-90; Enchanted Mesa controversy in, 92; error combatted in, 92-95; simplified spelling controversy in, 93-95; literary criticism in, 95-96; Lion's social conscience mirrored in, 97-100; as source of biographical material, 97; comment on racial problems, 97-98; comment on religion, 98; comment on labor, 98-99; comment on press, 99; issue of academic freedom, 99-100; Lummis defends use of capital letters, 100; Lummis defends costume, 100-101; Lummis' editorial record appraised, 101-102; limitations in coverage, 102; as reflection of Lummis, 102; issues call to save missions, 104. *See also* Lummis, Charles F.
"In Western Letters," 144
Irrigation: movement for national, 103, 144-47, 149, 151, 180; at Pala, 124. *See also* Smythe, William E.
Isleta, 12, 14, 15

tive numbers described, 74-78; compared to the *Nation*, 102; Landmarks Club department in, 105; role in Landmarks Club work, 103-11, passim; as instrument of Indian reform, 103, 111-15; Major Pratt slurs, 113; major contributors to, 135-63; Lummis as literary critic in, 142-44; Smythe joins staff of, 146; and "20th Century West," 146-51; Sharlot Hall as contributor, 152-55; and Mary Austin, 155-59; and Eugene Manlove Rhodes, 159-63; lesser contributors to, 164-91; as reflection of cultural tastes of readers, 187-89; significance summarized, 187-91; as outlet for western writers, 190; as training ground for western writers, 190; as crusading journal, 190; as reservoir of western lore, 191. *See also* Lummis, Charles F.; *Out West*

Land of Sunshine Company, 65-66

Landmarks Club: founding of, 20, 104; work of, 103-11; department in Lummis' magazine, 105; financing of, 105-108, 111; membership in, 105, 106; constitution of, 105; and Camino Real, 108-10; suspends activity, 107; reorganization of, 111; influence outside of region, 110; summary of services, 110; mentioned, 101, 191

Lane, George W., 12

Lane, Franklin K., 150

Lang, Andrew, 6

La Purísima, 111

Lassell Seminary, 4

Lawrence College, 4

Lawton, Henry, 10, 96

League of Western Writers: origin of, 71; nature of, 71-72; names included within, 73; mentioned, 66, 135

Letterman, Dr. Jona, 169-70

Leupp, Francis P., 126-27

Libbey, William, 92

Lick, James, 140

Life, 12, 48

"Life's Rose," 77

Lincoln, Abraham, 87-88

Lincoln-Roosevelt League, 78, 151

"Lincoln the Man of the People," 143

Lines and Interlines, 183

Linnet, 176

"Lion," name for editor Lummis, 79. *See* Lummis, Charles F.

Lion's Den. *See* "In the Lion's Den"; Lummis, Charles F.

Literary comment: on Lummis, 18-19, 34, 102, 156; on C. D. Willard, 39-40; by Lummis, 95-96, 142-44, 161; on Sharlot Hall, 153-55; on Mary Austin, 156-59; on Eugene Manlove Rhodes, 161, 162-63; on Joaquin Miller, 165; on Jack London, 166; on Sui Sin Far, 172; on Grace Ellery Channing, 173-75; on Elizabeth and Joseph Grinnell, 175-76; on Charles A. Keeler, 177; on Nora May French, 183; on Julia Boynton Green, 184; on John Vance Cheney, 185; on the magazine in general, 187-88, 190

Little Landers movement, 150

Lockett, S. W., 39

Lockwood, John S., 125

Lodge, Henry Cabot, 86

Lohs, C. R. *See* Lummis, Charles F.

Lomalinda: place-name controversy, 83

London, Chatham, and Dover Railway, 46

London, Jack: stories of, 166; mentioned, 73, 187

Los Angeles: conditions in 1880's, 11; early newspapers in, 36; economic development during the 1890's, 38; advertisers in *Land of Sunshine*, 46; pronunciation of, 84; Camino Real convention in, 108-109; national convention of Indian educators in, 112; and Mission Indians, 125, 127; easternness of, 140; compared with San Francisco, 140; and irrigationists, 145; writing group in, 156; compared with Rome, 174; Chinese massacre of 1871 in, 188-89

Los Angeles Business College, 46

Los Angeles Chamber of Commerce: as promoter of southern California, 37; Harry Brook associated with, 39; Frank A. Pattee associated with, 39-41; *Land of Sunshine* connection with, 40-41; and Camino Real plan, 108-109; and Sequoya League, 127

Los Angeles Chinese, 74, 188-89

Los Angeles City Water Company, 64

Los Angeles Commission on Street Names, 20

Rhodes, 161; on Theodore H. Hittell, 167; friendship with David Starr Jordan, 171; befriends Keelers, 176; encourages Maynard Dixon, 178; treatment of Southwest materials, 188-89; independence of, 190; as interpreter and promoter of Southwest, 190-191; primary purpose of magazine, 191
Lummis, Dorothea, 6, 14. *See also* Dorothea Rhodes
Lummis, Eva, 28-29, 156
Lummis, Harriet Waterman Fowler, 3-5
Lummis, Henry, 3-5
Lummis, Jordan, 23, 171
Lummis, Keith, 23
Lummis, Turbesé: quoted, 25; mentioned, 14, 23, 120
Lummis, Rev. William, 3
Lummis Caracol Tower: dedication of, 27, 191

McClure's, 44
McGrew, Clarence Alan, 76
McGroarty, John Steven: on Lummis, 32, 33
McKinley, William: Lummis on, 87-88
McLoughlin, James, 121n
McWilliams, Carey: on Mission Indians, 114n
Madden, Jerome, 37
"Madness of the Rector, The," 174
Magazine publishing: early California, 36-37
Magazines. *See* under specific titles
Maier and Zobelein brewery, 45
Maine: compared with California, 139
Mandan Indians, 169
Man Who Married the Moon, The. See Pueblo Indian Folk Stories
"Man with a Hoe," 96, 143, 185
Markham, Edwin: Lummis critical of, 96, 143; mentioned, 21, 73, 134, 144, 154, 185
Marmion, 79
Martin, Lannie Haynes, 51
Mathis, Juliette Estelle, 134
Matthews, Brander, 93-94, 95
Matthews, Dr. Nicholas Blayney, 169
Matthews, Washington: career in brief of, 168-69; and study of Navajos, 169-70; mentioned, 73, 164

"Maying," 77
Membership: in League of Western Writers, 72-73; in Landmarks Club, 105; in Sequoya League, 117
Memorial of Fray Alonso de Benavides, 1630, The, 18
Memorial to Commissioner of Indian Affairs, 115-16
"Mercy of Nah-Ne," 155
Mesa, Canyon and Pueblo, 16, 28. *See also Some Strange Corners of Our Country*
Miles, Gen. Nelson A., 10
Mill, John Stuart, 180
Miller, Joaquin: and *Overland Monthly*, 36; and *Out West*, 75; verse quoted, 164-65; mentioned, 21, 73, 134, 154
"Mine by Me," epitaph for and by Eugene Manlove Rhodes: quoted, 161
Mission Indians: and Sequoya League, 111, 113-28, 133; relief of, 111, 113-28, 133; defined, 114n; and Helen Hunt Jackson, 114; decision against, 114; investigating commission formed, 117; home sites for examined, 121-22; moved to Pala, 123-24; destitute at Campo, 125-26; mentioned, 76, 77, 189. *See also* Indians, California; Sequoya League; Southern California Indians; Southwest Indians; Warner's Ranch Indians
Missions, California: preservation of, 103-108, 111; and Landmarks Club work, 103-108, 111; mentioned, 74. *See also* Landmarks Club and under individual missions
"Mist," 183
Mitchell, E. Pryce, 65
Modjeska, Helena, 21
Mojave Desert, 75
Mojave Indians, 153-54
Monserrate properties: compared with Pala, 121-22
Moody, Charles Amadon: joint editor, 51, 77; assistant editor, 67, 70-71; worried about magazine, 67; article by, 75; as book reviewer, 76, 142; and Hopi investigation, 129-30; mentioned, 66
Moqui. *See* Hopi Indians
Mormonism, 24
Mott, S. H., 64

ruary, 1903, number, 75-76; description of May, 1907, number, 77-78; espouses national irrigation, 103; for reclamation of western lands, 103; champions western regionalism, 103; demands justice for Indians, 103; for preservation of missions, 103; against imperialism, 103; preserver of historic landmarks, 103-11; instrument of Indian reform, 103, 113-33; official organ for Sequoya League, 116; monthly department of Sequoya League in, 117; staff of, 134; major contributors to, 135-63; Lummis as literary critic, 142-44; and "20th Century West," 146-51; and Sharlot Hall, 152-55; and Mary Austin, 155-59; and Eugene Manlove Rhodes, 159-63; lesser contributors to, 164-91; as reflection of cultural tastes of readers, 187-89; summary of significance, 187-91; promotional purpose of, 187; general nature of offerings, 187-89; as outlet for western writers, 190; as training ground for western writers, 190; as crusading journal, 190; as reservoir of western lore, 191

Out West Company, 62, 66
Out West Magazine Company, 62, 67
Overland Monthly: sales of, 44; recognizes *Land of Sunshine*, 45; absorbs *Out West*, 51; disliked by Lummis, 60-61; mentioned, 36, 134, 156, 178
Overland Monthly and Out West Magazine, 51
Owens River Valley, 156
Oxford Dictionary, 94

"Pacific Monthly": rejected by Lummis as magazine title, 58-59
Paine, G. H., 62
Paiute Indians, 158
Pala: *asistensia* of San Luis Rey, 105, 107, 108
Pala, new home of Warner's Ranch Indians, 120-25
Palace Hotel, 46
Panama: compared with California, 139

Panama canal: Lummis on, 89-90
Partridge, Charles L., 115, 120
Pasadena, 46, 74, 106
Pasadena Art Institute, 179n
Paso por aquí, epitaph for Eugene M. Rhodes, 161
Pattee, C. R.: quoted, 42
Pattee, Frank A.: and magazine, 38, 40, 64, 65, 66, 70; career in brief of, 39
Patterson, W. C., 56, 64
Peet, Jeanie, 74
Penitentes, 12, 16, 136
Penrose, Boies, 6, 117
People of the Abyss, 166
Perkins, Charlotte. *See* Gilman, Charlotte Perkins
Perkins, George C., 117
Perry, J. C., 67
Peru, 14, 17
Petrified forests (Arizona), 74, 136
Philippines: annexation of opposed by Lummis, 88
Photoengraving, 61
Picher, Ana B., 108
Pico, Pio, 110
Pima Indians: record rod of, 77
Pixley, Frank, 97
Place names: Spanish, 83-84, 87, 110
Plaza, Los Angeles, 110
Point Loma colony, 94
Pomona, 38, 46
Porcupine, 36
Post Office Department, 84
Powell, Maj. John W., 116
Pratt, Maj. Richard H., 112-13
Prescott (Arizona), 152, 154
Prescott, William H., 16
Preservation of missions, 103-108, 111. *See also* Landmarks Club; Missions; and under specific missions
Press: Lummis on, 99
Promotional emphasis: in Lummis' magazine, 42, 49, 59, 75, 76-77, 78, 80-81, 83
Promotional literature: in southern California, 37-38
Promotional writing: appraisal of Lummis', 83
Proud Sheriff, The, 161
Puck, 12
Pueblo Indian Folk Stories, 15
Puerto Rico, 88
Purple, May Davison, 160. *See also* Rhodes, May Davison

Wampum League, 116
Wanderer's Songs of the Sea, A, 177
Ward, Eunice, 77
Warner, Charles Dudley, 74, 75
Warner's Hot Springs: description of, 118-19; and Mission Indians, 118-19
Warner's Ranch: home of group of Mission Indians, 22; dispute over title to, 114; value of improvements on, 119
Warner's Ranch Commission: appointed, 117; work of, 120-121; report of, 122
Warner's Ranch Indians, 76, 113, 114-25. *See also* Mission Indians; Sequoya League; Southern California Indians
Water law: reform of in California, 146-47
Wellesley, 139
Wesleyan University, 4
West: Lummis' definition of, 55-56; as theme for magazine, 72-73, 77, 78; climate of, 80-82; Arizona and New Mexico statehood important to, 85; importance of, 85; hope for a literature of, 95-96
Western artists, 21, 73, 135, 141, 144, 154, 164, 178-79, 180. *See also* under individual artists
Western birds, 175-76
Western idiom, 75, 162

Western irrigation, 103, 124, 144-47, 149, 151, 190. *See also* Irrigation
Western lands, 103
Western News Company (Chicago), 62
Western Writers, League of, 66, 71-72, 73, 135. *See also* League of Western Writers
White, Stephen M., 60
White Mountains, 6
Whittier, John Greenleaf, 75
Wildman, Rounsevelle, 60
Willard, C. D.: offers Lummis *Land of Sunshine* editorship, 19; career in brief of, 39-40; and *Land of Sunshine*, 39-41, 45; on Lummis, 47-48; mentioned, 64-65, 71
"Wind Song," 154
Winship, George Parker, 73, 144
Wister, Owen, 75
Wollacott, H. J., 46
Woman and Economics, 180
Wood, J. W., 74
Wood, Leonard, 10n, 89
Woodbury, Charles J., 77
Worden, Perry, 30
World War I, 111
Wright, George S., 75
Wright, L. A., 123

Yale, 166-67
Yavapai Hills (Arizona), 152
Youth's Companion, 15, 69, 173
"Yucca, The": quoted, 184